Grace and Incarnation

Grace and Incarnation

The Oxford Movement's Shaping of the Character of Modern Anglicanism

Bruce D. Griffith
with Jason R. Radcliff

James Clarke & Co

James Clarke & Co
P.O. Box 60
Cambridge
CB1 2NT
United Kingdom

www.jamesclarke.co
publishing@jamesclarke.co

Paperback ISBN: 978 0 227 17788 4
PDF ISBN: 978 0 227 17809 6

British Library Cataloguing in Publication Data
A record is available from the British Library

First published by Pickwick Publications, 2020

This edition published by James Clarke & Co, 2022,
by arrangement with Wipf and Stock Publishers

Copyright © Bruce D. Griffith and Jason R. Radcliff, 2020

All rights reserved. No part of this edition may be reproduced, stored electronically or in any retrieval system, or transmitted in any form or by any means, electronic, mechanical, photocopying, recording, or otherwise, without prior written permission from the Publisher (permissions@jamesclarke.co).

Contents

Prologue: The Oxford Movement's Context in Church History
    | by Jason Radcliff | vii

Introduction | xv

1. Justification, Sanctification, and Regeneration: The Revival of Dispute | 1
2. Edward Bouverie Pusey: The Reality of Sacramental Grace | 32
3. John Henry Newman: The Imparting of Righteousness | 61
4. Robert Isaac Wilberforce: The Incarnational Basis of Grace | 102
5. Critics and Opponents | 133
6. Penitential Ministry: The Tractarian Experiment | 158

Epilogue: The Oxford Movement and the Twenty-First Century
    | by Bruce Griffith | 174

Bibliography | 183

Prologue

Anglicanism: Reformed and Catholic

As the former Orthodox Archbishop of Thyateira and Great Britain, Methodios Fouyas, said: "Anglicanism is not a Protestant Church, but a reformed Catholic Church . . ."[1] Indeed, Anglicanism is hard to place in the world of "denominations." It is neither simply Protestant nor is it simply Catholic. Since its "inception" (if we may use the term) by Henry VIII, the Church of England has embraced *both* the Reformation *and* the medieval tradition, avoiding the Tridentine and Protestant extremes.[2] Anglicanism preserved herself from the extreme Reformational solifidian focus on Galatians and Romans, etc., and the extreme counter-reformational strict doctrinal way of looking at tradition by (unlike many of the Protestant churches)[3] never rejecting the biblical interpretations of the church fathers (Richard Hooker and Lancelot Andrewes come to mind as illustrative examples of an Anglican way of interpreting the Bible in light of the church fathers and medievals and ending up as a *via media*, avoiding Protestant and Roman extremes)[4] and not completely setting aside

---

1. See Fouyas, *Orthodoxy, Roman Catholicism, and Anglicanism*, 88.

2. Although as it developed, Anglicanism also swayed to the extremes of Protestantism and Catholicism. See Hooft, *Anglo-Catholicism and Orthodoxy*, 21: "Protestantism was never more dominant in the Church of England than at the time when the Oxford Movement began" (Canon Lacey). It may be more accurately said that the Anglican *via media* of Hooker, Andrewes, and the later Oxford Movement was forged because of these extreme poles.

3. This is the so-called *via media*.

4. See Diarmaid MacCulloch's phenomenal "Richard Hooker's Reputation" in *All Things Made New*, 279–320 for an account of Hooker as encapsulating the *via media*.

the understandings of the first 500 years of Christianity. In other words, the English Reformation is, rather uniquely for the time, not reactionary, partly attributable to the place of the two great universities of Oxford and Cambridge, which in many ways served as the heart of the English Church until the twentieth century. In short, the English church never forgot that it is in line with the patristic church and medieval church.[5]

The Oxford Movement emerges into the English church in this context. Their recovery of sacramental reality and efficacy, auricular confession, and union with Christ was indeed not anything novel for the English church, although it had indeed been forgotten for a while. Thus, The Oxford Movement recovered something very traditional for English Christianity: a medieval and patristic theology and practice. Yet, in recovering a very patristic and medieval way of being Christian into a church that went through the Reformation, The Oxford Movement, like the English Reformation itself, avoids the extreme solifidian and works-righteousness poles of the Reformation and Trent respectively and in some ways this shows how The Oxford Movement cuts behind the Semi-Pelagian/Augustinian controversy as it reappeared in the Protestant Reformation by arguing that God's grace undergirds justification and good works, rather than distinguishing the two in a polarized fashion.[6] In so doing, The Oxford Movement recovers and, indeed, reconstructs[7] medieval English Christian thought and practice in light of the reformational doctrine of incarnational grace, making it one of *the* great moments in the history of the Christian church and shaping the character and charting the path for modern

---

5. Alister McGrath aptly noted that more generally European Protestant Christians have a sense of their continuity with the medieval church (at least more so than Christians from other parts of the world); with ruins of medieval churches and monasteries all around (not to mention the many parish churches dating from the medieval period), it is not difficult to imagine why. See McGrath, "Trinitarian Theology," 52.

6. See further Michael Ramsey's exceptional chapter "The Gospel and Church Order" in *The Gospel and the Catholic Church*, 47–57. Ramsey's *via media* approach of avoiding these two extremes poles is incredibly indebted to the Oxford Movement and illustrative of the maturation of that approach. Ramsey's statement on the Papacy is representative: "A Papacy that expresses the general mind of the Church in doctrine and that focuses the organic unity of all the Bishops and of the whole Church might well claim to be a legitimate development in and through the Gospel. But a Papacy that claims to be a source of truth over and above the general mind of the Church and that wields an authority such as depresses the due working of the other functions of the One Body fails to fulfil the main tests." See p. 55. See also Yelton's *Anglican Papalism* for a definitive account of an Anglican stream that embraced the Papacy.

7. See Thomas F. Torrance, *Theology in Reconstruction* for a similar argument about Karl Barth and "reconstruction" of theology and practice in light of the Reformation and early church fathers.

Anglicanism as well as providing a template for how to do the Reformation well, namely, working towards ecumenical rapprochement by retrieving and reconstructing the catholic faith.

The Oxford Movement: An Anglican Theology of Retrieval

Another way to think about The Oxford Movement is (to use a more modern definition) as a "theology of retrieval." According to the introduction of the recent collection of essays published as *Theologies of Retrieval*, "theologies of retrieval unsettle present discussions by offering resources from beyond the current horizon with a view toward enriching ongoing theological debates."[8] The Oxford Movement did this precisely: beginning with the issue of church and state and the appointment of bishops during the so-called "National Apostasy," The Oxford Movement quickly moved beyond this to the issue of retrieving the medievals and patristics for application in the Church of England during the nineteenth century in order to understand its catholic nature in such areas as the doctrines of justification and sanctification, the eucharist, baptism, and devotional practices such as liturgy and auricular confession.

As such, The Oxford Movement's retrieval spanned both theological (e.g., the doctrines of justification and sanctification) and practical (e.g., the eucharist and auricular confession) and, as Eamon Duffy was apt to put it in his recent and remarkable book on Newman:

> The Oxford Movement succeeded beyond its wildest expectations. In little over a generation it was to transform the theology, preaching, worship, and even the architectural style of the Anglican Church: over the next century even conventionally middle-of-the-road parish churches were transformed from the preaching boxes of the eighteenth century into numinous settings for the celebration of ceremonial liturgy: village orchestras in the gallery gave way to surpliced choirs in the chancel, coloured stoles replaces black scarves, and Holy communion, once an occasional service happening four or five times a year, became a monthly or weekly event. Tractarianism was to be the single most important influence in shaping the character of the modern Anglican communion.[9]

---

8. Sarinsky (ed.), *Theologies of Retrieval*, 2.
9. Duffy, *John Henry Newman*, 9.

Anglicanism in the later nineteenth and twentieth centuries became marked by weekly celebrations of the eucharist, private confession, anointing for healing, a recovery of episcopal authority, and neo-gothic architecture. The Oxford Movement drove and undergirded all of this, whether acknowledged or not. Indeed, Anglicanism in England and beyond—even of the lowest variety—was forever changed by The Oxford Movement.

The Oxford Movement: One of the Great Movements of the Church

However, the influence and indeed importance of The Oxford Movement's retrieval goes far beyond Anglicanism and deserves to be placed as one of *the* great movements in church history. In her book, *The Great Emergence*, Phyllis Tickle—a key figure in the so-called Emergent Church Movement of the early 2000s—argues that every 500 years or so the church goes through a great upheaval and reformation of sorts out of which a key moment or movement in church history occurs.[10] Tickle's ultimate point is contemporary: she wants to argue that currently (i.e. in the early twenty-first century, with the emergence of The Emergent Church), the church has reached the most recent iteration of these once-every-500-year moments. Working backwards, therefore, she argues that the Reformation was another such moment, as was the rise of the high Middle Ages, and the period of the ecumenical councils in the East, 500 and 1,000 years respectively. Compelling as Tickle's argument is (and this is certainly not to disagree with her), it does reveal a notably Protestant emphasis on the Reformation of the sixteenth century.[11] Whilst, on the one hand, one cannot argue with Tickle about the significance of the Reformation for world history, on the other hand if her clearly Protestant lens is removed and replaced by a more ecumenical one, her 500 year cycle could look a bit different, for example: the fourth century and the First Council of Nicaea follows 500 years later with the eighth and ninth centuries and the iconoclastic controversy which then leads 500 years later

---

10. See the whole book, but Tickle introduces the concept, referring to the Anglican Mark Dryer, in Tickle, *The Great Emergence*, 9.

11. As the Edinburgh theologian Thomas F. Torrance says his *Memorandum A on Orthodox Reformed Relations* (an important document inaugurating The Orthodox-Reformed Theological Dialogue, an ecumenical movement of great importance of the late twentieth century), "The 'Reformed Church' does not set out to be a new or another Church but to be a movement of reform within the One, Holy, Catholic, and Apostolic Church . . ." See Radcliff, *Thomas F. Torrance and the Orthodox-Reformed Theological Dialogue*, 129–43 for the text as well as the book more generally for an account of this ecumenical dialogue. In other words, the Reformation was not meant to be a big deal.

to the fourteenth century and high medieval scholasticism, ultimately fitting The Oxford Movement nicely into the most recent iteration of the 500 year cycle. Of course, one must not make too much of Tickle's 500 year cycle on the basis of chronology alone. Indeed, looking back at the key moments in church history (including Tickle's once-every-500-year-upheavals as well as the modified version discussed above), one could argue that the key moments in church history are the rediscoveries/emphases on God's grace in Jesus Christ, including the ecumenical councils, the Protestant Reformation, the Counter Reformation, as well as The Oxford Movement.

The Oxford Movement's Greatness: A Reconstruction of the Medieval Doctrine of Grace around the Incarnate Person of Jesus Christ

In 1948, Thomas F. Torrance, arguably one of the most important English-speaking theologians of the twentieth century,[12] published his dissertation entitled *The Doctrine of Grace in the Apostolic Fathers* at the suggestion and under the supervision of his beloved mentor Karl Barth, arguably the most important theologian of the twentieth century.[13] Whereas Torrance would eventually depart from his early critique of the early fathers' doctrine of grace substantially,[14] his argument that all the great movements of the church avoided "detach[ing] the thought of grace from the *person* of Christ"[15] was an emphasis of his which he almost certainly learned from Barth. Torrance's forceful argument throughout his book is that for the New Testament authors—especially Paul—grace is "actualised in the person of Jesus Christ, with which grace is inseparably associated."[16] Torrance argues that subse-

---

12. Torrance's importance ranges across the spectrum of theology and religion, ecumenical dialogue, dogmatic theology, Barthian theology, Scottish Theology, and, perhaps most important, the retrieval and reconstruction of the church tradition. See Radcliff, *Thomas F. Torrance and the Church Fathers* as well as Myk Habets' excellent intro to the recent republication of *Trinitarian Faith* and his excellent *Theology in Transposition* for recent appraisals of Torrance's importance in this regard. More generally, see the recently published *T. & T. Handbook of Thomas F. Torrance* edited by Paul Molnar and Myk Habets for an outline of Torrance's theology and relevance.

13. See Hunsinger, *Reading Barth with Charity* and von Balthasar, *Karl Barth* for appraisals from a Reformed and Catholic perspective, respectively. Pope Pius XII said Barth was "the greatest theologian since Thomas Aquinas." No small praise! See, e.g., Gorringe, *Karl Barth*, 316.

14. See, e.g., *Trinitarian Faith*.

15. Torrance, *The Doctrine of Grace in the Apostolic Fathers*, v.

16. See Torrance, *The Doctrine of Grace in the Apostolic Fathers*, 34 for the quote, but more generally 1–35 for this argument and indeed the entire book.

quent church history goes wrong whenever it forgets that grace is inextricably associated with the person of Christ (e.g., Arianism, scholastic theology, and Westminster Calvinism, all of which in Torrance's mind proffer some version of "created grace" or at least grace which is problematically disconnected from the person of Christ).[17] For Torrance, the key movements of the church can be found in connecting the dots between the movements in church history that emphasized God's grace as inherent to the person of Jesus Christ as a sort of "golden thread" of church history.[18]

This is a point with which the best-selling Episcopalian author Robert Farrar Capon and one of the greatest champions of the doctrine of grace would wholeheartedly agree. Capon, in his book *Between Noon and Three*, says:

> The Reformation was a time when men went blind, staggering drunk because they had discovered, in the dusty basement of late medievalism, a whole cellarful of 1500-year-old, 200-proof grace-of bottle after bottle of pure distillate of Scripture, one sip of which would convince anyone that God saves us single-handedly.[19]

For Capon, the rediscovery of grace by the Reformers is what makes the Protestant Reformation so unique and important.

Combining Capon and Torrance and modifying Tickle's chronological schema to a more thematic one, one could argue that the emphasis on unconditional grace inherent to the person of Jesus Christ is the hallmark of the key moments throughout church history. Athanasius and the Council of Nicaea emphasized God's grace as present in Christ himself via their emphasis on the doctrine of *homoousion*,[20] Anselm and later scholasticism applied this to the connection between faith and reason by saying the former undergirds the latter,[21] the Reformation applied this to the grace of God by saying it is God himself who saves not human works or "created

---

17. See Torrance, *The Trinitarian Faith*, "Karl Barth and the Latin Heresy," and *Scottish Theology*, respectively. In short, by calling the Son created, by defining grace as created, and by rooting "election" in God's decrees, Arianism, Scholasticism, and Westminster Calvinism all dualistically separate grace from the person of Christ, according to Torrance.

18. See Radcliff, *Thomas F. Torrance and the Church Fathers*, 115ff.

19. Capon, *Between Noon and Three*, 114.

20. One could argue this point was the crux of all seven of the great ecumenical councils of the church, held in the east from the fourth through eighth centuries, especially the doctrine of the *hypostatic union*.

21. See e.g. Eugene Fairweather's introduction to *A Scholastic Miscellany*, 17–32, especially 31–32. Anselm's *Fides Quarens Intellectum* could certainly be read this way.

grace,"[22] Karl Barth applied this to God's Word and the doctrine of election in the mid-twentieth century with his multi-volume *Church Dogmatics*,[23] and Vatican II and such luminaries as von Balthasar, Ratzinger, and Rahner applied this to the life of the Roman Catholic Church, especially the doctrine of the Trinity and the departure from neo-scholasticism in the Roman Catholic seminaries in the 1960s.[24]

To this list of movements centered on the doctrine of grace as inherent to the person of Jesus Christ, the authors of this book would add The Oxford Movement. In exploring Pusey, Newman, Wilberforce, and their doctrines of justification and sanctification and their application in church life, this book illustrates why The Oxford Movement deserves to be placed in this grace-based line as one of *the* key movements in church history, not least Anglicanism. *Grace and Incarnation* tells the story of Pusey, Newman, Wilberforce (and others) and their rediscovery of a doctrine of grace inherent to the incarnate person of Jesus Christ, a doctrine of grace that articulates grace as divine and personal rather than created and static, a doctrine of grace that says it is God alone who saves, God alone who justifies, and God alone who communicates God's very self through the sacraments because it is Christ himself acting and communicating himself by the Holy Spirit in salvation and sanctification, and offering himself to us through the sacraments.

Grace and Incarnation

Grace and Incarnation explores the theological debates of this period in Anglican and wider church history as well as the practical applications in church ministry they undergirded, arguing that The Oxford Movement, particularly the doctrine of grace as inherent to the person of Christ they rediscovered and the medieval and patristic figures and ideas they retrieved on this basis, is among the great movements of church history, furthermore placing Anglicanism itself from early figures such as Hooker and Laud through to The Oxford Movement and beyond as an essential piece and moment in the story of the church and of Christianity.

---

22. As Torrance states: "the divine Giver and the divine Gift are one and the same. At the Reformation that Nicene principle was applied not only to the Word of God and to the Spirit of God but also to the grace of God." See Torrance, *Preaching Christ Today*, 20. Calvin's *Institutes* could be read as making this point above all else.

23. Barth's *The Word of God and the Word of Man* as well as his very early *The Epistle to the Romans* also make this point.

24. See the *Documents of Vatican II* as well as Karl Rahner's *The Trinity*. See also Fergus Kerr's *Twentieth-Century Catholic Theologians*.

Ultimately, the book therefore points to The Oxford Movement as an embodiment of ecumenical renewal: the Reformation's end was not to create a new church but rather a movement of reform by grace. The English Reformation has, at its best, embodied this impetus. This book shows how Pusey, Newman, Wilberforce, and The Oxford Movement embodied this impulse and therefore the best of the English Reformation in their applying the doctrine of grace and Christology to patristic and medieval doctrines of justification and sanctification, reforming them by the grace of God. The Oxford Movement's rediscovery of Anglicanism's catholic nature serves as an example to all churches stemming from the Protestant Reformation and indeed an encouragement for all churches to rediscover and retrieve their own catholic roots with an eye towards ecumenical renewal and reunion.

Introduction

Anglican theology credits itself with two features that most of the Western theological tradition might as easily term defects. First, it possesses no tradition of defined, conciliar dogmatic formulations against which the writings of any individual or school may be judged. Second, it possesses no individual who is regarded as the founder of a unique Christian theological tradition held in common by all members of the community. It does not have Trent or Vatican I, nor does it have Calvin or Luther.

Anglicanism has as its common heritage two distinctive documents, the *Book of Common Prayer* and the *Thirty-nine Articles of Religion*. Both were originally open to alteration, though only the *Prayer Book* can rightly be said to have developed. The *Thirty-nine Articles* never developed much, but they ground Anglican doctrinal developments in the specific heritage of the English Reformation. On the whole, it is possible to argue that the *Thirty-nine Articles* are decidedly Protestant, while it is equally possible to argue that the *Prayer Book* is rather Catholic; but what is of much greater importance than that age-old debate is that until at least the end of the nineteenth century every English Anglican theologian was bound to take those two documents into account, and to defend his theology in terms of its acceptability within their framework. Since the *Prayer Book* and the *Thirty-nine Articles* are, in many ways, opposed documents, the task of doing Anglican theology was never uncontroversial.

It is superficial to argue that Anglicanism has always contained just two parties, one Catholic, the other Protestant. The history of Anglicanism will not bear such an interpretation. From the beginning of the English Reformation every strain of Christian theology has been present. The English Reformation was built upon the Lutheran and Calvinist traditions (though there was some early Zwinglian influence); and the reforming party itself was split from the beginning. Both factions were solifidian, both believed in the unique primacy of scripture, but on the questions of individual predestination and the efficacy of sacraments there was little unanimity.

Within a generation the Catholic influence reappeared in the person of Richard Hooker. Hooker was deeply sensible of the medieval tradition, as well as the traditions of the patristic age and the Reformers. Hooker's *Of the Laws of Ecclesiastical Polity*, Anglicanism's first great theological work, brought all three traditions to bear on the emerging Anglican theology. The Catholic mindedness apparent in Hooker came to the fore in the episcopate of William Laud. Laudian High Churchmen revived interest in Anglicanism's Catholic heritage and were, in many ways, the founders of the High Church party.

The seventeenth century produced not only Laudian churchmanship and the Caroline divines, but the English Puritans, the Cambridge Platonists, the Latitudinarians, and the Non-Jurors. By the end of that century English churchmen were bitterly divided. The accession of William and Mary brought the Latitudinarians to power in the person of John Tillotson, but the Catholic tradition did not completely disappear.

William and Mary brought not only greater political stability, but greater latitude and stability in religion. The Church, so often in conflict with the crown, became more of an arm of government. The result, in terms of Church life, was that peculiar eighteenth-century settlement that few find interesting and even fewer find laudable. Doctrinal disputes gave way to settled, refined living. Richard Church provided a picture of that period which was hardly enthusiastic:

> The idea of clerical life had certainly sunk, both in fact and in the popular estimate of it. The disproportion between the purposes for which the Church with its ministry was founded and the actual tone of feeling among those responsible for its service had become too great. Men were afraid of principles; the one thing they most shrank from was the suspicion of enthusiasm. Bishop Lavington wrote a book to hold up to scorn the enthusiasm of Methodists and Papists; and what would have seemed reasonable and natural in matters of religion and worship in the age of Cranmer, in the age of Hooker, in the age of Andrews, or in the age of Ken, seemed extravagant in the age which reflected the spirit of Tillotson and Secker, and even Porteus ... But the fortunes of the Church are not safe in the hands of a clergy, of which a great part take their obligations easily. It was

slumbering and sleeping when the visitation of days of change and trouble came upon it.[1]

Out of that context came the fiery zeal of Evangelicalism, first in the Methodists, then in those who became the Evangelical party in the Church of England. Selena, Countess of Huntingdon, gathered around her salon the likes of Watts, Doddridge, Whitefield, Newton,[2] and the Venns. As this

---

1. Church, *The Oxford Movement*, 10f. Cf. J. C. D. Clark's compelling chapter "Church, Parties, and Politics." Clark gives a more nuanced perspective on the rationalism of the eighteenth century than Church offers here, suggesting Church's account may contain some of the classic trope's and assumptions the Tractarians held about the eighteenth-century Church. As we introduce R. W. Church into this narrative, we should pause to note that Church remained a devoted friend of Newman's (and vice versa) until death, and their deaths came within months of one another in 1890. Church therefore serves as more of a primary text eyewitness to movement than a secondary historical analysis of it. Indeed, Church did not seem to intend to write a history of the Oxford Movement so much as a memoir of what he and many saw as the most significant constitutive time in what was a history that began at least ten years before 1833. Peter Nockles would, we think, argue for a much earlier date (see Nockles masterful introduction to the historiographical issues in his *The Oxford Movement in Context*), as the authors here have done by going back at least half the way to 1760 and carrying the line until at least the 1880s. It is fair to say that Church kept Newman at the very center of the narrative and, of course, figured heavily in Newman's censure being suppressed. Church was on his way out of Oxford just after R. I. Wilberforce delivered his work on the incarnation and preached his university sermon "The Sacramental System" [published in *Sermons on the New Birth of Man's Nature*], all this a few years after 1845. He would not set to work on assembling his Oxford Movement papers until the 1880s, while in Oxford Gore was looking forward to a new birth of modern scholarship. All this is to say that in our work we have chosen not to dig deeply into the historiographical questions and scholarship surrounding Church's memory of the sequence and importance of people and events, let alone institutions and cultures; rather we accept Church for who and what he was, a man of his time for whom the later questions might not have been so pressing. True, he would always choose for friend and moment. These qualities, we think, along with his undoubted abilities, was what led Gladstone to hold him in Whatley until St. Paul's Deanery was vacant. Church was not only a part of the Oxford Movement, and even though he wrote no tracts or serious studies during that time (save for his translation of Cyril of Jerusalem's *Catechetical Lectures* in the Library of the Fathers), he held to its principles and beliefs, remained in contact with its core leaders, and lived its piety. His daughter Mary edited a volume of his *Life and Letters* which provides an admittedly affectionate view of the course of his life and the depth of his integrity. The importance of this volume lies not only in its record of events, but also in its preservation of his correspondence which is the proof of the consistency of his faith, friendship, and devotion to the principles and players in the movement of 1833.

2. Present-day sensitivities require noting that John Newton, best remembered as the writer of the text "Amazing Grace," as a result of his conversion gave up the slave trade and took up the ministry (thus his association with Wilberforce). However, Adam Hochchild reminds us in *Bury the Chains* that Newton continued to own the ship that he had previously captained. We have avoided Simeon because he is rather *sui generis*. Yes, he is influenced by and associated with the elder Venn of Yelling, but he remains a

Evangelical Party splintered, the Clapham Sect emerged as the dominant force in religio-political terms, including as it did the great statesman, William Wilberforce, Henry and John Venn, and abolitionist Henry Thornton. Best remembered for the abolition of the slave trade, the religious outlook of the "sect" reached great numbers of the clergy. Its main theological opposition came from the lesser known Hackney Phalanx, which did include a significant number of the orthodox Anglican establishment and holders of important ecclesiastical appointments. Joshua and John Watson. H. H. Norris and others made an important contribution to the Tractarians of the next generation by founding the *British Critic,* which would become a major organ of the Oxford Movement.

Party designations in the Church of England present an ongoing problem for any reader of Anglican theology. Low Church, High Church, Evangelical, Broad Church, and Liberal are among the designations commonly applied to the various parties. Such labels are as dangerous as they are helpful. They aid the reader in determining some broad categories in which various writers may be placed, but they are dangerous in that from one period to the next certain doctrinal opinions may shift from one party to another. For instance, the Latitudinarians of the late seventeenth century were undoubtedly Low Churchmen regarding the doctrines of the church and sacraments. By the early nineteenth century, the Latitudinarian doctrine of the church would be categorized as Liberal, while their doctrine of the sacraments (such as it was) would be thought more Evangelical than Low. Likewise, as will be seen in the body of this volume, both Bishop Bull and Archbishop Laurence were considered High Churchmen of their respective times, but their opinions on justification and sanctification were hardly similar.

In the last and current centuries it has been common to speak of Low, Middle, and High, or Evangelical, Broad, and Anglo-Catholic, but in the era with which this work is concerned Low does not equal Evangelical, there is no Middle in the sense of Broad (Liberal is not the equivalent of Broad), and High is certainly a more comprehensive designation than Anglo-Catholic. Indeed, the period from 1800 to 1885 is the time in which many of the old designations found new definitions. Dean Church preferred the two-fold distinction of "orthodox Churchmen" and the "religious party"—everyone else and the Evangelicals. He then divided the "orthodox Churchmen" into High Churchmen and everyone else (presumably Low Churchmen and the few Liberals). This last group of everyone else was commonly thought of as the Calvinists, though they held only a very mild doctrine of individual predestination, if

---

rather interior character and he is more difficult to categorize. He was quite persecuted in his College at Cambridge.

they held that doctrine at all. The use of "Calvinist" as a designation presents another problem, however, since the High Churchmen often referred to everyone other than themselves as Calvinists.

Some effort is required, therefore, to make a little sense out of the parties which existed in the Church of England at about 1800 lest what follows be incomprehensible. The Evangelicals—Church's "religious party"—placed their greatest emphasis on the doctrine of conversion, which yielded a sense of being justified. The first Anglican Evangelicals were Calvinists. They held strong doctrines of election and reprobation. Later Evangelicals, however, were almost uniformly anti-Calvinist. The Evangelicals were constantly accused of antinomianism, and were derided as zealots.

The "orthodox Churchmen" who were not High Churchmen held that the church was a body composed of believers in Christ, governed in a number of possible ways, one of which was through the ministry of bishops. They tended to place their greatest emphasis on the instrumentality of faith in justification and sanctification. They did not demean the sacraments, but they were generally sacramentally unconcerned. They held that baptismal regeneration required accompanying faith and was therefore almost never possible in infants. Though often called Calvinists, they were mostly opponents of any notion of predestined eternal damnation, though most held some mild doctrine of individual election.

High Churchmen viewed the church as the divinely constituted body of Christ, the mystical body over which God had set bishops as the visible embodiment of the ministry of Christ and his apostles. Some, like Laurence, held to justification by faith alone, while others, like Alexander Knox, held to a doctrine of infused righteousness. Most held that infant baptism was regenerating in every case.

Throughout these brief descriptions of the parties of the Church of England many qualifications have been introduced. At times it appears that theology in the Church of England can be reduced to a series of cases of one. This is not true, but neither is it true that all members of a given party agreed on even fairly fundamental theological points. All this will become obvious in the first chapter, which deals with the doctrines of grace and its means in the period just prior to The Oxford Movement. Historically this period runs from about 1775 to 1832.[3]

---

3. A great advance in our appreciation and understanding of this era was made by Peter Nockles in his deep study *The Oxford Movement in Context: Anglican High Churchmanship 1760-1857*. His masterful historiography is complemented by the breadth of Lawrence Crumb's 936-page *The Oxford Movement and Its Leaders: A Bibliography of Secondary and Lesser Primary Sources*.

The heart of this volume is in chapters 2, 3, and 4. These deal with E. B. Pusey, J. H. Newman, and R. I. Wilberforce. They represent the development of the Anglican theology of grace, its means, and its basis in the incarnation. It has been commonly held that Tractarian theology was a function of its piety, that the deep religiosity of the Tractarians led them to investigate the grounds of the religion that they practiced; nothing was further from the truth. The long noticed and often admired piety of the Tractarians came from their *theology*, as will become evident in the heart of this volume.

Chapter 5 deals with the critics and opponents of The Oxford Movement. Not all High Churchmen were enamored of the Tractarians. Others— Evangelicals, Liberals, Low Churchmen—became the active opponents of The Oxford Movement, seeing in it dangers both to theology and piety. Chapter 6 employs two related examples to demonstrate that The Oxford Movement expressed its theology in founding a new style of church life in England, which was much more than ritualistic; indeed, which helped to blaze the trail of concerned Christian social action.

Finally, before moving on to the substance of this work, three other points will aid the reader in understanding what follows. First, there are three terms that will be used to designate the main characters and the opinions that they expressed—Tractarian, Oxford Movement, and Anglo-Catholic. It would be tempting to restrict the use of Tractarian to those few who actually wrote the *Tracts for the Times*, but that sense would be too narrow.

Tractarian is employed here to designate those individuals who were a part of the early days of The Oxford Movement, and who tended to remain within the company of one another until at least the mid-1840s. The Oxford Movement is used to describe the slightly larger company of those who gathered around the Tractarians and supported them within the University. The Oxford Movement also denotes that body of ideas and actions that gave rise to the new style of church life emerging in the 1830s and '40s. Anglo-Catholic, on the other hand, is used to describe the movement as it left the precincts of the University and became a part of the wider life of the Church of England. Anglo-Catholics, as a group, are the second and succeeding generations who inherited the theology and piety of the Tractarians.

Secondly, so many histories of the events of The Oxford Movement exist that little material relating to the events themselves has been included in the text; however, a note of caution is in order. Until well into the last century it was a common opinion that The Oxford Movement ceased on that day in 1845 when Newman met Father Dominic, the Passionist, at Littlemore. Dean Church advanced this opinion so eloquently and forcefully that it found widespread acceptance. Among the effects of this was the almost total neglect of the importance of R. I. Wilberforce, and the mistaken impression that many Tractarians went with Newman.

Another Tractarian, Isaac Williams, dealt with the issue of Newman's secession in this way:

> It seems to be a popular notion that the original writers of the Tracts have generally joined the Church of Rome, and that therefore that movement of itself has been so far a failure; but this is very far from being the case, for it is a very remarkable circumstance, and one which I find very much strikes everyone to whom I have mentioned it, that out of all the writers in the "Tracts for the Times," one only has joined the Church of Rome.[4]

If we are to believe Williams, then Newman's real influence was with those who surrounded the Tractarians, those associated with the wider aspects of The Oxford Movement, and not with the original Tractarians themselves:

> But what is most striking, there does not appear to have been any who associated with Newman on terms of equality, either from age, or position, or daily habitual intercourse, or the like, in unrestrained familiar knowledge, who have followed his example in seceding to the Roman Church, such I mean, as Fellows of Oriel, who lived with him (and some of them friends in the same staircase), as Rogers, Marriott, Church, the two Mozleys (his brothers-in-law), John Bowden, Copeland, J. F. Christie, Pusey, the Kebles.[5]

Williams' corrective is important, for it shows that The Oxford Movement did not end with Newman's departure, though it did change. Williams' point also leads to the final point of this introduction.

Newman looms so large in the history of English-speaking theological thought in the nineteenth century that his shadow has tended to obscure others and lead to the impression that he was the fulcrum of The Oxford Movement (again, the influence of Dean Church). The work before you strives to correct this impression by drawing attention to the ongoing importance of E. B. Pusey. The shy Regius Professor of Hebrew affected the religious consciences and lives of Oxford students and scholars for more than fifty years. Pusey endured great personal loss and persecution, but he continued to fight for the Tractarian cause with dogged determination.

---

4. Williams, *The Autobiography of Isaac Williams, B.D.*, 119f.
5. Williams, *The Autobiography of Isaac Williams, B.D.*, 121f.

His devotion to parochial and conventual life imbued his allies with the courage to practice Catholic piety amid scorn and derision. Pusey's personal piety framed the ideals of Anglo-Catholic church life, as his writings had suggested the topics for his colleagues to pursue. Pusey was The Oxford Movement's steady rock, Newman was its adventurer, Wilberforce was its philosopher. The three together brought a new life to Anglican theology.

1

Justification, Sanctification, and Regeneration

The Revival of Dispute

Two controversies are generally acknowledged as being at the center of Anglican theology in the late eighteenth and early nineteenth centuries, the Calvinist controversy and the baptismal regeneration controversy. They were not new controversies in the history of Anglican doctrine; both had been issues since the English Reformation. The names of most Churchmen associated with the revival of these disputes have slipped into obscurity. A few are recognized today, but usually for contributions to the social order rather than for their theological positions. William Wilberforce, the great reformer, Charles Simeon, the supporter of the missions to India, John Newton, the hymn writer; all were active Churchmen who contributed to the rise of the Evangelical party in the Church of England. L. E. Binns once wrote of the Evangelical movement that it was "one of the offshoots of the great Methodist revival of the eighteenth century."[1] Binns correctly perceived that the Evangelicals drew their great enthusiasm from the Methodists, but he missed another equally important point: the early Anglican Evangelicals were not Methodist in their theology, they were convinced Calvinists.

The source of the early Evangelicals' Calvinism remains somewhat mysterious. While there were conforming Calvinists among the clergy of the English Church in the eighteenth century, there are no names that leap to mind as Calvinists of high repute. From the Restoration to the mid-eighteenth century Calvinist theology was hardly evident in Anglicanism. Then, hand in hand

---

1. Binns, *The Evangelical Movement in the Church of England*, 3.

with the Methodist movement, Calvinism re-enters the life of the Church of England as the theological stance of the early Evangelicals.

One of the earliest Evangelicals, William Romaine, provides a good example of the style and content of early Evangelical preaching. In a sermon on justification, while attempting to convince his hearers of the depravity of their nature and condition, he wrote:

> ... the greatest part of mankind are not sensible of their guilt, nor apprehensive of their danger. Sin has nothing in it terrible to them. They love it, ... they see not their want of, and therefore, have no desire for, the gospel salvation. But when one of these persons awakes and opens his eyes, he is then terrified at the sight of his present state. Sin appears to him in a new light: he finds it to be exceedingly sinful, and the wrath of God revealed from heaven against it to be beyond measure dreadful.[2]

Mankind, asserts Romaine, deserves no justification, nor is there any inherent principle within it that would make it seek God. Only an awakening to a sense of sin, a sense of utter, total depravity, can make man desire God; a desire about which man can do nothing. One must simply cast himself on Christ's merits. But how, then, is a man to be righteous? Romaine answers:

> God imputes righteousness to them who believe, not for a righteousness which is in them, but for a righteousness which he imputes to them. As their iniquities were laid upon Christ, and satisfaction for them required of him, as a debt is of a bondsman, although he had none of the money, so is the righteousness of Christ laid upon them. In like manner, as their sins were made his, so is his righteousness made theirs. He is sin for them, not inherently, but by imputation; they are righteousness through him, not inherently, but by imputation.[3]

Romaine was one of the first to reintroduce a strong doctrine of forensic justification. Forensic justification, the notion that we are justified through an external imputation of the merits of Christ (an imputation that seems to be best defined as an exchange), had a long history in Anglican theology. It was an obvious feature of the doctrine of justification held by the Reformers. It obviously was the dominant opinion of the *Thirty-nine Articles*. Yet, it was the early Evangelicals who reintroduced the English Church to the doctrine of forensic justification. Romaine was not alone in this; indeed, the more famous John Newton of Olney was equally insistent on the point.

2. Romaine, *Works Volume 3*, 171f.
3. Romaine, *Works Volume 3*, 171.

Little difference in theology can be found between Newton and Romaine, but Newton's second interest, hymn writing, provides another insight into the early Evangelicals. Second only to preaching Newton viewed hymn singing as a powerful new instrument of evangelization. His greatest production in this area was the "Olney Hymns." None are now in use, and only a few of his later hymns have survived and are in common use. "Glorious things of thee are spoken" is not a typical Newton hymn, but "Amazing grace" and "How sweet the name of Jesus sounds" are both typical and popular. Newton's hymns were always theologically explicit, and in one from the "Olney Hymns" we gain a sense of the supreme role of preaching in the Evangelical tradition:

> O Thou, at whose almighty word,
> The glorious light from darkness sprung,
> Thy quick'ning influence afford,
> And clothe with power the preacher's tongue.
> Thus we would in the means be found,
> And thus on thee alone depend,
> To make the gospel's joyful sound
> Effectual to the promis'd end.[4]

It is the spoken word that maintains the contact between man and God. The grace of perseverance is bound to hearing that spoken word.

Perhaps Newton's greatest contribution to the Evangelical Movement was his careful and patient conversion of Thomas Scott. Scott finally succeeded Newton at Olney, and after an unproductive decade moved to London to become one of the key figures of the Evangelical Movement. The range of his influence is evidenced by the fact that Newman cites Scott as one of the writers who most influenced his early years.[5] Scott served as the first secretary of the infant Church Missionary Society, founded a college for missionaries to India at Bedlow, and wrote powerfully in the Evangelical tradition.

Unlike Romaine and Newton, Scott felt that the doctrine of predestination was not central in the exposition of Christian doctrine, but he clung tenaciously to solifidian teaching. In an essay on justification he defended the forensic interpretation of the terms "to justify" and "justification" in St. Paul, but sought to broaden the scope of justification. While there is no reason to believe that Newman was influenced by this tendency in Scott, it is interesting to note that Newman, too, wished to broaden the interpretation of justification.

4. Newton, "Olney Hymns" Book 2, no. 18 in *The Works of the Rev. John Newton*, II.
5. Newman, *Apologia pro Vita Sua*, 18.

Scott adroitly separates the term justification from forgiveness of sins (the latter being too restrictive), and then writes:

> The *justification* therefore *of a sinner* must imply something distinct from a total and final remission of the deserved punishment; namely, a renewed title to the reward of righteousness, as complete and effective as he would have had if he had never sinned, but had perfectly performed, during the term of his probation, all the demands of the divine law ... the *justification* of the pardoned sinner gives him a *present* title to the reward of righteousness, independent of his *future* conduct, as well as without respect to his past actions. This is evidently the scriptural idea of justification ... This does not prove, that "not imputing sin," and "imputing righteousness," are synonymous terms: but merely, that where God *does not impute sin he does not impute righteousness*; and that he confers the title to eternal life, on all those whom he rescues from eternal punishment. Indeed, *exemption from eternal punishment*, and *a right to an actual and vast reward*, are such distinct things, that one cannot but wonder they should be so generally confounded as they are, in theological discussions.[6]

Removal of sin produces, at best, a neutral state; whereas justification produces the positive state of election whereby men become true inheritors of the kingdom of God. The differentiation is important: it allows Scott to separate the means of grace from the effect of grace. Justification need not be the immediate effect of baptism even though baptism can be said to remove the taint of original sin. Justification is linked to the faith of the individual, a personal, conscious faith. Faith, in turn, is an independent gift from God which can be given at any time. In almost all cases it precedes justification.

Scott does not argue that the divine acceptance wrought in justification is built upon man's previous faith; rather, he separates faith into justifying faith and true faith. True faith is a result of justification, not a cause. The faith called "justifying" is actually "*a disposition readily to receive the testimony, and to rely on the promises, of God.*" This disposition causes us to become interested in, and attached to, that righteousness which God will impute to us, and through which we will become acceptable in his sight.

Scott's position on predestination was confusing. While he held a doctrine of double predestination, he was not willing to preach it. By his own admission the doctrine of eternal decrees was one of the last he embraced

---

6. Scott, "Essays," in *Theological Works*, V, 242f.

after his conversion.⁷ Scott preferred to characterize himself as a Methodist in his enthusiasm, and a Calvinist in his adherence to the English Reformation tradition.⁸ Writing on predestination, however, he sounded a good deal more Calvinist than Methodist: "If *sinners* deserve the punishment inflicted upon them, it cannot be *unjust* in the great Governor of the world to predetermine their condemnation to it."⁹

While the early Evangelicals were mostly Calvinists, their influence diminished as the movement approached its zenith. Among the more famous Evangelicals, the Venns, Wilberforce, the Milners, and Simeon, none were inclined to the Geneva tradition (though they were called Calvinists by some High Churchmen who tended to lump together all their adversaries under that name). The early Evangelicals had been ignored by the scholarly world, but in Cambridge the Evangelicals gained a foothold in the person of John Milner, the Evangelical historian, who published a highly influential history of the church.

The plan of Milner's *History of the Church of Christ* reveals the subjective nature of Evangelical doctrine. Milner's history is conceived around an interesting plan: only those who held the doctrine of justification by faith alone can be counted as part of the true church of Christ. Not surprisingly Augustine and Luther dominate the study. The entire medieval tradition is viciously attacked as an eleven-hundred-year hiatus in Christian history. So convinced was Milner of the truth of his proposition that he could write of Augustine:

> From the review of the Pelagian controversy, the attentive reader will see, that the article on justification must be involved in Augustine's divinity; and doubtless it savingly flourished in his heart, and in the hearts of many of his followers; yet the precise and accurate nature of the doctrine itself seems not to have been understood by this holy man. He perpetually understands St. Paul's terms to justify, of inherent righteousness, as if it meant sanctification; still he knew what faith in the Redeemer means; and those parts of Scripture, which speak of forgiveness of sins, he understands, he feels, he loves; but St. Paul's writings concerning justification he understands not sufficiently, because the precise idea of that doctrine entered not formally into his divinity.¹⁰

---

7. Scott, *Works*, I, 6.

8. It should be noted that Scott, by his own admission, was in no sense a Methodist in his feelings about the National Church.

9. Scott, *Works*, I, 80.

10. Milner, *The History of the Church of Christ*, Volume 1, 449.

John Milner died before completing his massive project, and the task was completed by his brother, Isaac. The second volume, which Isaac wrote from an outline prepared by John, gave Luther a position second only to that of St. Paul. Luther, it turned out, was to be trusted more than Calvin and even Augustine, for both Calvin and Augustine held too radical views on predestination.

Milner's work may have been somewhat eccentric, but it was widely read and highly influential. It was from Milner that Newman first learned of St. Augustine,[11] and it was to refute Milner that Alexander Knox wrote on justification. Knox's ideas will occupy us later, but his criticism of Milner's historical view is mildly amusing:

> It was not peculiar to the Roman Catholic divines of that day [the period of the English Reformation], to represent justification as a moral, and not merely a relative change. Mr. Milner, the author of the Church History, is, on this point, a most decisive witness; being himself as much devoted to the forensic notion of justification, as any Roman Catholic could be to the moral idea. And yet, from the end of the first century, to the Reformation, he is, with hardly an exception, lamenting over the obscurity and confusion (as he deems it) of the fathers of the church.[12]

While Evangelical theology found a home, though not a particularly happy one, at Cambridge, its piety was centered in the little village of Yelling. The Vicar of Yelling was Henry Venn, a Cambridge man, father of the Vicar of Clapham, and spiritual leader of the Evangelicals. Venn's Evangelical piety and theology are evident in his *Complete Duty of Man*:

> But it is of the highest importance, that you examine, yourself, where the stress of your dependence for the welfare of your soul rests? Where are you looking for pardon, strength, comfort, and sanctification? Is it to your own repentance, endeavours, prayers, and good qualities, or, through them all, to the exhaustless treasury God has provided poor, guilty, helpless men, in the person of the saviour? Blessed are you, if you have a testimony in your conscience; that, lamenting your natural ignorance and blindness, you call upon the Lord to enlighten your mind, and to give you a distinct, effectual perception of the great things which concern your everlasting peace. Blessed are you, if, feeling your utter inability to stand acquitted before God, by your

---

11. Newman, *Apologia*, 18.
12. Knox, *Remains*, Volume 1, 282.

reformation, duties, and prayers, you have no hope but in what Christ has done and suffered.[13]

Yelling is only a few miles from Cambridge, and young men serious about the Christian faith were often found making journeys to the vicarage. One such serious undergraduate was Charles Simeon.

Whereas Newman was under a strongly Evangelical influence during part of his youth, finally abandoning that influence in favor of the High Churchmen, Simeon had been steeped in the writings of the older High Churchmen before encountering the Evangelicals. While he abandoned most High Church theology, he never lost his deep sense of the church as a divine body. Often he was accused by his fellow Evangelicals of being too much of a "Churchman." This love for the Church of England led to his strong encouragement of the early Evangelical foreign missions.

Simeon sought a balance between the doctrinal and pastoral interpretation of scripture. In the preface to his *Horae Homileticae* he was critical of those of his own Evangelical persuasion who dwelt only on doctrine. Writing in the third person Simeon notes: "He regrets to observe, in some individuals, what he knows not how to designate by any more appropriate term than that . . . of an *ultra-Evangelical* taste; which overlooks in many passages the *practical* lesson they were intended to convey, and detects in them only the leading *doctrines* of the Gospel."[14] In the two thousand sermon outlines of the *Horae* Simeon never fails to draw out the practical applications of the texts.

Simeon, who died in 1836, can be taken as representative of the best of the Evangelical tradition in its most vigorous years. Like all Evangelicals he placed the doctrine of justification by faith alone at the very heart of the gospel. The volume of the *Horae* that deals with Romans reads like an extended commentary on that doctrine. Writing on Romans 4:1–8 Simeon makes this key point about St. Paul: "We must bear in mind what the point is which he is endeavoring to maintain: it is, that the justification of the soul before God is not by works of any kind, but simply, and solely, by faith in Christ."[15] If justification is sought in any other way, or on any other terms, then it becomes an exchange of one good for another. This would make justification something which man could claim as a right. But no claim to righteousness is allowable. Righteousness can only be a free gift of grace imputed to the believer: "Let us bear in mind what the Apostle's statement is: it is this, that if, in any part of our salvation from first to last,

---

13. Venn, *The Complete Duty of Man*, 132f.
14. Carus, *Life of Simeon*, 311.
15. Simeon, "Horae Homileticae" in *Works*, Volume XV, 93.

our works form the meritorious ground of our acceptance with God, our salvation is not of grace, but of works."[16]

Such a low estimation of works did not, in Simeon, carry any sense of antinomianism, yet the charge was continually leveled against the Evangelicals. Theologically, the problem of the role of works raised the issue of sanctification. Simeon replied that too little emphasis had been placed on Christ as the author of sanctification as well as of justification, righteousness, and wisdom. The death of Christ is not only the cause of our justification, but of our sanctification as well. How? "In that it displays the evil and malignity of sin," "obtains for us power to subdue sin," and "suggests motives sufficient to call forth our utmost exertions."[17] Simeon's call to sanctity lacked an appeal to moral law, preferring to rely on the force of the example of Christ and our gratitude for justification. These are the sources of good works.

Showing the strong side of his Evangelical faith Simeon insisted that the event of justification consists primarily in the experience of conversion. Conversion regenerates men, resulting in a change whereby "God instructs them in the 'form of sound doctrine.'"[18] Men are then able to "obey from the heart", and this obedience yields thankfulness for the moral change which has taken place in their orientation and action.[19]

To those who have experienced conversion, Simeon offered this advice, showing how fully he saw the moral effects of regeneration:

> Such persons will do well to reflect on the mercy they have received: the recollection of their past guilt will serve to keep them *humble*. A consciousness of their remaining infirmities will make them watchful: a view of the change wrought in them will make thankful . . . let them press forward for higher degrees of holiness and glory.[20]

The emphasis on conversion certainly distinguished the Evangelicals from all other Anglicans; but Simeon was also wont to point out his differences with the Calvinists. His commentary on Romans 8:29, 30 is among the longest in the "Horae." Simeon saw the doctrine of predestination as wholesome, but difficult. It could lead to antinomianism. Thus, it demanded careful treatment. As he said, "The subject of predestination is confessedly very deep and mysterious; nor should it be entered upon

---

16. Simeon, "Horae Homileticae" in *Works*, Volume XV, 409.
17. Simeon, "Horae Homileticae" in *Works*, Volume XV, 193f.
18. Simeon, "Horae Homileticae" in *Works*, Volume XV, 153f.
19. Simeon, "Horae Homileticae" in *Works*, Volume XV, 153f.
20. Simeon, "Horae Homileticae" in *Works*, Volume XV, 153f.

without extreme caution, both as to the mode of stating it, and to the persons before whom it is stated."[21]

The substance of the doctrine of predestination, Simeon agrees, concerns those whom God has eternally decreed to be saved. This is God's purpose, and it will be worked out infallibly. God does this for his own glory. In a more general sense, predestination applies to two ends, that of mankind and that of Christ: Ours is an immediate end, predestining us to three things, holiness, suffering with Christ, and glorification. Christ's is an ultimate end, for he was predestined to be the head of the church. The foreordaining of Christ is absolutely necessary, otherwise man's freewill might have made the death of Christ to be of no account in the world. This point Simeon contends in a question: "But can we conceive that God would have given his Son to bear the iniquities of a ruined world, and have left it to mere chance, whether any single individual should ever obtain mercy through him, or become a jewel in his crown?"[22] It would seem that Christ was in need of an assured congregation of faithful adherents, rather than himself constituting that body through his Spirit.

While Simeon appears open to a doctrine of predestination of individuals, he takes great exception to any doctrine of double predestination. He writes:

> ... as long as God declares with an oath that "he has no pleasure in the death of a sinner, but rather that he turn from his wickedness and live," so long we may rest assured, that, notwithstanding he has predestined many to life, he has not predestined one single soul to death; nor is the doctrine of absolute reprobation a just and necessary consequence of predestination.[23]

Pressed to the limit, Simeon might well have agreed that there is indefectible grace whereby some are eternally included in the company of the saved; yet the real emphasis in Simeon is on the process whereby most sinful men are brought to salvation. God foreknows men in love; in this life God calls men, and their response of conversion and faith brings on God's activity of justification, imputing righteousness to them. In turn, men do the will of God, not by virtue of any inherent moral law or principle, but by virtue of their thankfulness for justification. Man's subsequent sanctification is a process whereby God's desire bears fruit in men's lives until God finally glorifies them.

21. Simeon, "Horae Homileticae" in *Works*, Volume XV, 313.
22. Simeon, "Horae Homileticae" in *Works*, Volume XV, 316.
23. Simeon, "Horae Homileticae" in *Works*, Volume XV, 316.

This brief introduction to the Evangelical contribution to the revival of the dispute over justification spans more than a fifty year period.[24] The Evangelicals were not as interested in theology as they were in the practice of religion. Their contributions to the development of Anglicanism were great, but in the area of doctrine they served only to rekindle the flames of certain smoldering issues. In their way they helped to set the stage for The Oxford Movement, but they were not truly worthy intellectual adversaries. In their own time the Evangelicals were met head-on by weightier minds, whose opinions ranged over a large area, but who are generally regarded as High Churchmen.

Precursors

Undoubtedly The Oxford Movement owed a great deal to the vigorous theology of the seventeenth century, but at times acknowledgement of this debt has obscured the links with the High Churchmen of the early nineteenth century. The most prominent group of High Churchmen in the first third of the nineteenth century was the Hackney Phalanx. This group, like the Clapham Sect, had as its titular head a layman, Joshua Watson. The members of the Hackney Phalanx were of the "high and dry" persuasion; but on the issues of the doctrine of the Church and Church-State relations they could be anything but "dry." They founded the *British Critic* (later edited by Newman) which was to become the organ of The Oxford Movement; they fought the encroachments of emerging Liberal politics; and, like their Tractarian successors, they labored to place the doctrine of the church before the many factions of the Church of England.

Among the High Churchmen of the next generation it was Pusey who felt the relationship with the Hackney Phalanx most deeply. He held great admiration for Thomas Sikes of Guilsborough. Sikes died in 1834, but eight years later Pusey recounted (second-hand) a conversation in which Sikes had commented on what we now know was the strongest bond between the two generations:

> Wherever I go all about the country I see amongst the clergy a number of very amiable and estimable men, many of them much in earnest, and wishing to do good. But I have observed one universal want in their teaching: the uniform suppression of one great truth. There is no account given anywhere, so far as I see, of the one Holy Catholic Church . . . Now this great truth is an article of the Creed and if so, to teach the rest of

---

24. For more see Nockles, *Oxford Movement in Context*, 256–69.

JUSTIFICATION, SANCTIFICATION, AND REGENERATION

the Creed to its exclusion must be to destroy "the analogy or proportion of the faith."[25]

Sikes saw the lack of a strong doctrine of the church as the chief defect of the Church of England in the early nineteenth century. The Tractarians began their pamphleteering with the intention of drawing attention to this defect, but the chief controversy of Sikes' time was not over the doctrine of the church, it was over justification and sanctification. At times this battle, known now as the Calvinist controversy, seemed more than a bit quixotic. Canon Overton made that point when he wrote:

> This controversy, an unhappy legacy from the eighteenth century, produced a certain amount of *soi-disant* theological literature . . . Oddly enough, it is almost all on one side . . . the so-called Calvinists expressly deprecate any controversy on the subject, and explain away the part of their teaching which raised the most opposition [predestination and election].[26]

Overton's point is well taken: there was very little theological production among the Evangelicals (or the few conforming Calvinists, for that matter). The issue, however, is a bit more intricate than Overton indicated. The High Churchmen, be they members of the Hackney Phalanx or others, considered the Evangelicals to be Calvinists even though that description was often highly inaccurate. This impression of Calvinism may well have been drawn more from the popular preaching of the lesser Evangelical clergy than from the leaders of the movement. Overton did assemble some evidence that indicated that many followers of the Claphamites were quite convinced Calvinists, and that this Calvinism led many of them to preach an explicit antinomianism. It was this disregard for the moral law that led many nineteenth century High Churchmen to attack the Evangelicals as radical Calvinists. Thus, what may at first have appeared to be a joust with a windmill, now appears to be a response to a small but popular movement within the Church of England.

The reply to the Calvinists took many forms, but it was concentrated on two issues, justification and baptismal regeneration. On both sides the arguments were still restricted by the desire to find the true English Reformation tradition. The fact that these positions seem so narrow to a modern reader is further evidence of the broad influence of The Oxford Movement which, as it developed, managed to transcend the isolation of

---

25. Liddon, *Life of Edward Bouverie Pusey*, I, 257f.
26. Overton, *The English Church in the Nineteenth Century*, 185.

earlier Anglican theology, stretching out to embrace a wider portion of the Christian tradition.

Chief among those who took an interest in the Lutheranism of the Reformers was Professor (later Archbishop) Laurence. Laurence was a very moderate High Churchman of a Lutheran persuasion. He was also a convinced anti-Calvinist. His Bampton Lectures of 1804 draw together the writings of English and German Reformers in such a way as to preclude any Genevan interpretation of the *Thirty-nine Articles*. In the sixth of his "divinity lecture sermons" he was at his most combative. In discussing the sense of 'justification' in the *Articles* he argued for what he felt was the larger and more Lutheran sense of the term:

> ... it has not unfrequently been overlooked or disregarded; and the word Justification been contemplated only in the sense, in which it is applied by the followers of Calvin. But our Reformers entertained no such idea of its application. They believed it not to be a blessing, which we may in vain sigh to behold above our reach, granted to certain individuals alone, and always irrespectively, by a divine decree, fixed and immutable; but one, which we all possess in infancy, and of which nothing but our own folly can afterwards deprive us. They never asserted the total inability of a Christian to perform a good action, or even to think a good thought, until the arrival of some destined moment, when it shall please God, without his own endeavors, to illuminate his understanding, and renovate his affections. The gift of grace, not to be purchased by human merit, but always bestowed gratuitously, they confined not to a selected few, the predestined favorites of Heaven; but extended to all, who neither by willful perversity oppose its reception, nor when received, by actual crime discard it.[27]

God's grace is freely given and open to all. No one can be ruled out of the possibility of salvation. Justification, whenever and wherever it may occur (and for Laurence it occurs most commonly in baptism), is a possibility for all men. Laurence's moderate High Church position, based on the Lutheranism of the Reformers, caused him to see the true debate of the Reformation as centered on the meritorious cause of justification. Everyone was willing to affirm that justification meant remission of sins, but the doctrine of justification by faith alone was really directed against the notion that a change occurs in man that merits justification, i.e., that sanctification precedes justification, and that this infusion of virtue merits justification. For Laurence the true

27. Laurence, *An Attempt to Illustrate Those Articles of the Church of England which the Calvinists Improperly Consider as Calvinistical*, 110.

JUSTIFICATION, SANCTIFICATION, AND REGENERATION

position of the Anglican Reformers was this: it is Christ's merits alone that count us righteous, and not on account of our faith in those merits, but on account of the object of our faith. The gift of grace in justification does not change our sinful nature: we remain sinners, but the gift of grace does change our condition; our sinfulness no longer bars us from salvation. Laurence, a most moderate High Churchman, remained an advocate of the extrinsic application of Christ's merits by imputation.

Laurence's work was widely read among the educated members of the Church. He sought to defeat any Calvinist interpretations of justification or baptismal regeneration. The real issue, however, has always been predestination. Laurence would never admit of a Calvinist interpretation of predestination, but his influence on the matter was restricted to those who could read his work with considerable theological acumen. On the other hand, William Jones of Nayland, a member of the Hackney Phalanx, was widely read by Churchmen throughout England. He took on the battle with the Calvinists on very specific terms when he wrote with that Hackney view of the centrality of the church in all things: "Election therefore, as it is spoken of in the Scripture, hath been grossly misunderstood: for there is no such thing as any election of individuals to final salvation, independent of the ordinances of the Church."[28] The little "Essay on the Church," from which this quotation comes, was one of the most popular religious works of its time, but Jones's battle with the Calvinists found its highest expression in his two "Letters to a Predestinarian."

Jones contended that there were three fallacies in Calvinist predestinarian doctrine: 1) that if one admits a doctrine of eternal individual election, then it makes God a respecter of persons, taking away the efficacy of the ordinances of the church, and placing one member in higher esteem than another; as he put it, "You will be saved in preference to others: I humbly hoped to be saved even as others";[29] 2) the assurance of this predestination to eternal life is based only on one's feeling that it is so, and if this is the only witness to its truth it cannot be very true; 3) if those who are to be saved are already predestined to it, how will God judge the world? It is an affront to the wisdom of God and the natural order of things to admit any doctrine that assures salvation to a few individuals. The extent to which Jones saw the doctrine of the church being overthrown by the doctrine of individual election can be seen in this statement from a sermon preface: "By means of predestination falsely stated, the rights of God

---

28. Jones, "An Essay on the Church," 45.
29. Jones, "An Essay on the Church," 260.

and his ministry are so far forgotten, that we are getting every day nearer to Babel, and further from Jerusalem."[30]

Echoing Jones's sentiment on predestination and election another prominent High Churchman, George Tomline, Bishop of Lincoln and then Winchester, agreed that predestination and election are corporate terms. They denote all who do (or will) accept the mercy of the gospel and persevere in it. As for Jones, so for Tomline, there are no eternal individual decrees, there is no indefectible grace.[31] Yet even as devoted a High Churchman as Tomline retained a forensic notion of justification. "Justification," he wrote, "in the language of Scripture, signifies the being accounted just or righteous in the sight of God; or the being placed in the state of salvation."[32] Man is not *made* righteous, he is *counted as being* righteous.

Incorporating the seventeenth-century tradition of Bishop Bull, Tomline sees the relationship between Paul and James as wholly consistent. Paul is speaking of being justified, James as persevering in justification. "Faith," he writes, "is not opposed to Works, but the merit of Christ is opposed to the merit of our Works."[33] Works, though insufficient, are not unimportant; they are the living witness and fruit of a lively faith.

> "Faith," say he [James] repeatedly in the same chapter, "without works is dead"; that is, although a man believes in the divine mission of Christ, and in consequence of that belief has been admitted into the Gospel Covenant, yet if he does not afterwards obey its precepts, his faith is ineffectual; he will not continue justified; and if he perseveres in his disobedience, he will not inherit eternal life.[34]

The Irish Layman

Sikes, Jones, Tomline, and Laurence were among the most prominent High Churchmen of their times. Their writings were widely distributed and carefully read. Alexander Knox, on the other hand, was read by fewer people and enjoyed only a limited, scholarly reputation.[35] He represented a quite distinct High Church strain, one which many (most notably G. S. Faber)

---

30. Jones, "Preface to the Sermon 'Calling and Election,'" IV, 31.
31. Tomline, *Elements of Christian Theology*, II. 270.
32. Tomline, *Elements of Christian Theology*, II. 256.
33. Tomline, *Elements of Christian Theology*, II. 257.
34. Tomline, *Elements of Christian Theology*, II. 261f.

35 For a recent and notable engagement with Knox, see McCready, *The Life and Theology of Alexander Knox*.

found too accommodating to the Roman Catholic doctrine of grace. Faber's later criticism was somewhat correct; Knox, with his insistence on infused virtue, strikes one as more Tridentine than the Tractarians. Beyond insisting on the priority of sanctification in the theology of grace, Knox sought a larger context for the discussion of grace and its means. He disliked the current Anglican preoccupation with the Reformation heritage.

In 1807 Knox's long-time correspondent, John Jebb (later Anglican Bishop of Limerick), wrote to him concerning Laurence's Bampton lectures: "Laurence has, to my conviction, satisfactorily proved, that our church is rather lutheran, than calvinistic; but I should be glad . . . to prove, that we are melancthonian, rather than lutheran."[36] Knox's reply to Jebb is not known, but it is probable that he would have pointed out to Jebb that a Melancthonian church was hardly different than a Lutheran church. Knox's influence on Jebb can be seen in Jebb's next letter in which he shows an awareness of the larger Christian tradition. Using the example of forensic justification while discussing the comprehensive historical and doctrinal basis of the *Book of Common Prayer*, Jebb wrote of a third alternative in the theology of grace. This third alternative, communicated righteousness, seems to contain the seed of the later Tractarian doctrine of imparted righteousness:

> And I think it may be proved, that, at the era of the reformation, there was, in the protestant church, a spring-tide, in favour of forensic justification; which, perhaps, was the only counteractive then attainable, to the popish exaggerations of human merits but which, it must be admitted, threatened to overwhelm the pure, and holy principles, of communicated righteousness, and spiritual regeneration.[37]

Jebb's comments are significant because they show the beginnings of the search for the larger Catholic tradition, a search to which Alexander Knox was to contribute much.[38]

Knox's life (which was reclusive both from choice and almost constant physical indisposition) spans the whole of our introductory period. He was a friend and correspondent of John Wesley's. His admiration for the Methodist founder, though tempered by Wesley's break with Anglicanism, was life-long. In a letter to the great Evangelical Mrs. Hannah More, Knox wrote in criticism of Southey's Life of Wesley:

36. *Thirty Years Correspondence Between Bishop Jebb and Alexander Knox*, I, 55.
37. *Thirty Years Correspondence Between Bishop Jebb and Alexander Knox*, I, 376.
38. A fine and much broader description of this background than we have room for here is to be found in chapter 5 of Nockles, *Oxford Movement in Context*. His descriptions of the eighteenth-century background are very valuable.

> I deny not, that, on a superficial view, many parts of John Wesley's conduct might seem to evince a strongly ambitious mind; but Mr. Southey, as a philosopher, ought to have reflected, that, according to the laws of human nature, the vice [gross ambition] which he imputed was inconsistent with the virtues which he acknowledged.[39]

Though Knox came to disagree at almost every theological point with Wesley, he may have gained from Wesley a single feature which was to characterize all his writings, i.e., a genuine sense of God's loving concern for mankind, a warmth in the relationship between God and man that was not characteristic of the period .

As his correspondence with Mrs. More indicates, Alexander Knox was well-known and respected by those whose views he could hardly have been said to share. His measured appreciation of the Evangelicals makes him one of the most valuable contributors to the controversies of the times. He knew and appreciated the Evangelical point of view, even though he disagreed with it, and he never reduced himself to mere name-calling. Throughout his long career, Knox was captivated by the doctrines of grace and its means. Almost all of his literary remains are devoted to those topics. In another letter to Mrs. More he shows this concern in a particularly revealing way, by contrasting the practical effects of the Protestant-Catholic controversy: "In my judgement there is, at this day, one great controversy, which calls for all our mental strength and wisdom; that is, whether Christianity be a sickly and painful struggle at best (for there are many who place it much lower still), or a healthful and happy principle?"[40] In the last year of his life, Alexander Knox was still writing on this controversy.[41]

The "healthful and happy principle" to which Knox refers is to be found in a doctrine of grace which brings out a sense of God's loving concern for man as well as a sense of man's gratitude to God. This mutual affection elicits from man a desire to obey God's law. Knox found in Wesley a true understanding of the loving divine-human relationship:

> ... he hit astonishingly, or rather he was wonderfully led to, the union of grace with holiness of which I speak[;] ... in my opinion, it is there, in a more complete form than I have ever met it elsewhere; and, therefore, I have been always as desirous to take

---

39. Knox, *Remains*, III, 460f.
40. Knox, *Remains*, III, 460f. The letter is dated 1807.
41. Knox, *Remains*, III, 592f.

from John Wesley lessons for myself, as I have been cautious of leading others to an indiscriminate perusal of his writing.[42]

Knox's appreciation of the depth of the controversy over justification was acute. In replying to the substance of his differences with Mrs. More he wrote, "certainly I do consider the too common method of stating justification to depend so wholly on our blessed Saviour's merits, as to rest in no respect on moral qualities in us, to be the grand error of the present religious world."[43] Knox feared that forensic justification, strictly applied, mitigated the notion of holiness. Not only did the Calvinists believe that high degrees of holiness were unobtainable, they were driven by the logic of their system to deem them less than desirable.

In the same letter to Mrs. More (which was over one hundred pages in length), Knox went on to demonstrate his point by refuting the Evangelical notion of Romans 4:16ff. He argued that Abraham's faith was a moral quality, the "essence of all genuine righteousness," and because of this moral quality, Abraham was counted righteous. Knox never denied that imputation of Christ's merits is a part of justification, but he vigorously denied that justification is possible where this moral quality is absent in the justified person or in the change that is brought about. Pusey later accused Knox of losing sight of this point, but Pusey's charge now seems unfounded;[44] what is clear is that Knox placed righteousness before justification.

What then of Abraham's faith, justifying faith? Faith is necessary not only so that we may know that we are justified, but for our being justified or accepted by God. Faith is not a work of man, but a gift of God. The result being, "to say, then, that our acceptance depends upon our faith, is only to affirm that God makes us what He would have us to be before He takes any pleasure in us," or put in biblical imagery, "God first brings light out of darkness, and order out confusion in the human heart, and then blesses his own work, as in creation."[45] Thus, justifying faith is the fruit of a radical change in man brought about by God's sanctifying activity. God's activity results in a moral excellence that leads man to desire holiness and to pray that God will grant the ability to be holy. There is no human merit involved in works of holiness; they are the fruit of the divine activity in man which undergirds his perseverance.

Knox understood that on the issue of human merit he could agree with the Calvinists. "There is, really," he wrote, "no more of man's righteousness,

---

42. Knox, *Remains*, III, 78f.
43. Knox, *Remains*, III, 81.
44. Pusey, "Tract Sixty-Seven: Scriptural Views of Holy Baptism," 19f.
45. Knox, *Remains*, III, 85.

in this view of our acceptance with God, than in that of the Calvinists; the only difference is, that God is regarded as actually giving, in the one case, what he is supposed only to impute, in the other."[46] Here Knox reveals the crux of his disagreement with the Calvinists. If one speaks of the objective reality of God's salvific activity, forensic justification cannot do justice to that activity. The love of God for mankind brings forth a real gift, actually given and received; the forensic notion of an exchange in which no radical change takes place in man demeans the reality of the gift. Imputation changes a man's condition, but more is necessary; there must be an actual change in man, a gift received, whereby the recipient can be counted righteous. With this groundwork laid, Knox now presses home to Mrs. More a definition of justification that was greatly different from that which she would have heard so often from John Venn at Clapham. Justification, Knox argues, is a privilege of God's children. And we are God's children by adoption and grace; but we become God's children through regeneration. While there may be some difference in the two terms, justification and regeneration, Knox maintains that justification is subsumed under the larger heading of regeneration. Thus, justification is a blessing which is inherent in regeneration. His logic is simple:

> Thus, he who regains perfect health, ie thereby necessarily freed from sickness; and he who rises to opulence, is, by inevitable consequence, no longer poor. Precisely, in like manner, he who is regenerated, and made a child of God by a communication of the Divine nature, is of course, and *a fortiori*, no longer under guilt and condemnation... and, consequently, to attain regeneration is to possess justification, whether we do or do not advert to this distinction of terms.[47]

In another published letter, this time to D. Parken, editor of the *Eclectic Review*, Knox made his major statement on justification. Arguing for a broad doctrine of justification which does not limit it to the removal of sin, he states:

> This, I humbly conceive, is the main point on which the Church of England itself, and many of those who deem themselves its only true members, look absolutely different ways. The question discussed in the homily [on salvation] is, clearly and simply, How is a man to obtain the blessing of justification, when he seeks it at first; or when, through his frailty, or unfaithfulness, he needs a revival of it? The answer is, He is to seek it with sole

---

46. Knox, *Remains*, III, 92.
47. Knox, *Remains*, III, 95f.

recourse to God in Christ; and to look wholly off himself to the Fountain of Grace and Mercy. But he is to come, that he may be quickened; and, when so quickened, he will be another man in God's reckoning, and in his own conscious feelings God will admit him into spiritual life wholly for Christ's sake; but he will esteem him spiritually alive only in consequence of his own gift of living faith; and he will make this living faith the exclusive test, because this alone is the vitalizing tie: every thing else lives by this; but this lives through God alone—Father, Son, and Spirit. That, in the judgement of the Church of England, justification by faith embraces the whole of this, might be proved from the whole tenor of the *First Book of Homilies*; and may be seen at once, on carefully considering the import of the 16th article.[48]

Knox desired a doctrine in which justification could be both reputative and efficient, a doctrine which embraced both forgiveness of sins and a positive change in man. The Evangelicals had argued that giving justification a sense that was more than reputative was to confuse it with sanctification. Knox, in turn, argued that in the Evangelical doctrine man remained essentially unchanged, only his apprehension of his condition was changed. Moreover, Knox argued, the Evangelicals had confused sanctification with "all inherent goodness." For Knox, sanctification was a distinctive term for "goodness grown into maturity," the actual state of complete holiness. Justification is the first, necessary preparation for sanctification, indeed, it is its efficient cause; but, the goodness of justification is, in degree, less than that of sanctification. This, alone, would have made Knox the object of criticism among some Anglicans, but his statements on the basis of justification would open him to much greater criticism.

We have already seen Knox argue for a principle upon which justification must be based. Now, he draws this out more specifically:

> But what I am impressed with is that our being reckoned righteous coram Deo (before God), always, and essentially, implies a substance of δικαιοσύνη (righteousness), previously implanted in us; and that our reputative justification is the strict and inseparable result of this previous efficient moral justification. I mean, that the reckoning us righteous, indispensably presupposes an inward reality of righteousness, on which that reckoning is founded.[49]

---

48. Knox, *Remains*, III, 295f.

49. Knox, *Remains*, I, 306. Scripturally, Knox based this assertion on an analysis of 1 Corinthians 4:4 and Titus 3:5–7.

Here, Knox believes he has found the essential Pauline doctrine of justification. In his analysis of Romans he put the question to which Newman would address himself twenty years later:

> It seems, however, a question yet unsettled, whether, in this elaborate discourse, the Apostle means to represent the leading design of the Christian dispensation, as a mysterious provision for the acquittal of believers in Christ from legal condemnation, or for their deliverance from oral thraldom, and their purification from moral pollution.[50]

Knox proceeds to answer his own question in the following manner: if St. Paul had said that the sin of Adam was merely imputed to every person, then a simple, external imputation of the merits of Christ would suffice. However, this is not what St. Paul intended. The sin of Adam, far from being merely imputed, becomes a part of every man. When Adam sinned an actual change took place in his moral disposition; man inherits this changed disposition. Thus, the only possible cure must be an act on God's part which effects an actual change within man. To be regenerate, born again, is not simply the cancelling of a debt, it is a rebirth through the grace of Christ. One is not simply counted righteous or just, one is made righteous and just "I think," wrote Knox, "with St. Augustin, that, in St. Paul's sense, to be justified, is not simply to be accounted righteous, but also, and in the first instance, *to be made righteous by the implantation of a radical principle of righteousness*."[51]

The "radical principle of righteousness" is both general and specific. Generally, moral righteousness enters the world after the salvific events of Christ's ministry. Until the coming of Christ sin reigned in the world. The death of Christ, however, ushers in the new condition of righteousness. From Christ's death flows the grace to rectify the whole order and its representation in each person. Christ's propitiation is general; it must still be applied to each individual through the appointed sacramental means.[52] For Knox the death of Christ was a communication of the energy of divine love. The death of Christ opens the possibility of salvation to humanity: it removes from man's corporate condition the otherwise unreachable bar of immorality. The atonement is an act of reconciliation in which man is reconciled to God. It was Knox's opinion that the forensic notion of justification, which seemed to him a mere exchange, destroyed the essentially

---

50. Knox, *Remains*, II, 13.

51. Knox, *Remains*, II, 60.

52. See A. Knox to J. Jebb, February 25, 1818, in *Thirty Years Correspondence Between Bishop Jebb and Alexander Knox*, II, 49–55.

personal nature implied by reconciliation. His principle of personal and corporate reconciliation through the death of Christ and regeneration was his highest argument against the Calvinists.

Once implanted and bestowed, the "radical principle of righteousness" does not exist as an idle gift or assure salvation. It is a gift which must be nurtured through obedience. Faithful obedience will cause righteousness to grow towards its end, holiness. Thus, in Knox, the process of salvation moves from regenerating righteousness to justification, to holiness. The key to the process is obedience to the moral character established in the implantation of the "radical principle." Again, he based his analysis of obedience on his interpretation of Romans:

> This sense of the term, obedience, comes distinctly before us in the next verse (vi. 17th), in which St. Paul thanks God, that the Christians at Rome, the once servants of sin, on being made acquainted with the Gospel, had so obeyed it from the heart, that its doctrine was a mould to form them into a new character. 'ye have obeyed from the heart,' says the original, "that type (or model) of doctrine into which we were delivered." . . . We have here, then, beyond controversy, the true nature of justifying faith. It is such obedience, from the heart, to the objective faith of the Gospel—in other words, such an affectionate reception of the divine facts and principles which the Gospel propounds,—as alters the course, changes the character, and morally renovates the man: that is, evidently, obedience unto righteousness; or, as it is afterwards described in this epistle, believing with the heart unto righteousness. And need I add, that we have here a fresh and most conclusive elucidation of the righteousness to which the whole discourse refers? For, as obedience unto righteousness can be neither more, nor less, than believing with the heart unto righteousness, through faith in the operation of God; so the righteousness thus attained, must, like its root and principle, be a disposition of the heart, a divinely established rectitude, which gives a pure and happy direction to desire and temper, to thought, word, and conduct. Thus, the question of justification by faith receives a fresh solution. All agree, that to be justified is to attain to righteousness.[53]

The centrality of obedience points to another issue over which Knox was at odds with the Calvinists, predestination.

In an early letter to Jebb, Knox argued that a rigid doctrine of individual predestination was not only unbiblical (being a one-sided perversion

---

53. Knox, *Remains*, II, 74f.

of St. Paul), but dependent on one of God's attributes to the exclusion of another:

> But, I think, of few things I can be more sure, than that calvinistical predestination is not in the Bible: providential predestination runs all through it; and a warm imagination, when the idea was taken up, made it easy to transmute the one into the other. The predestination which St. Paul dwells upon, I think is that, which brought those whom he addressed, providentially within the influences of the Gospel . . . That this, and this only, is the predestination St. Paul speaks of (I mean including all which this includes), appears from this obvious fact, that, after St. Paul has described the whole nation as cut off, he still expostulates, in order that, by any means, he might save some. This, consequently, was not calvinian cutting off; for, after that, there is no place for repentance . . . There is one thing which these theologians do not, I think, enough consider. If absolute, unconditional, indefeasible, election be that, which makes a man holy here, and happy here after and, if this election, and its results, be, as calvinists say, a mere matter of will, . . . where is the room for divine wisdom? And why so extended and concatenated an intervention of second causes, if their operation was thus infallibly anticipated? Wisdom acts by instruments a will fiats the thing.[54]

In a later letter to Jebb, Knox had much the same to say, except that he gives credit for consistency to the Calvinists, a consistency he did not find in the watered-down predestinarianism of the Evangelicals:

> Redemption is resolved into an arbitrarious electing decree, which supercedes conditions, and supposes the event inevitable. This is the only rationale of the systems of doctrinal faith. In all, therefore, who do not hold irreversible decrees . . . it involves absurdity; for, absolute election apart, doctrinal faith can contemplate only that salvability (in itself, and its supposed grounds) which is common to all men; the equal privilege, of the penitent, and the profligate.[55]

Knox, like all the High Churchmen, believed election was a corporate gift, and that obedience, a sense of God's wisdom, and sacramental sustenance belonged to salvation. In Knox we have seen the most severe High Church reaction to the Calvinists. In many ways Knox anticipated The Oxford Movement, especially in his emphasis on obedience, and on the gift of

---

54. *Thirty Years Correspondence Between Bishop Jebb and Alexander Knox*, I, 185f.
55. *Thirty Years Correspondence Between Bishop Jebb and Alexander Knox*, II, 51.

righteousness as a preparation for justification. This will become apparent in the chapters which follow, but now we must turn to the other controversy which set the stage for the Tractarians.

Evangelical Response

The Calvinist controversy was essentially a controversy over the doctrine of grace. It produced a second controversy, this time centered on the means of grace, specifically on baptism. The baptismal controversy, which was at least as heated as the Calvinist controversy, focused on the interpretation of the meaning of regeneration as it is employed in the baptismal service in the *Book of Common Prayer*; but it, too, had a wider context, and was to be of great importance in the life of the Church in the first half of the nineteenth century. This wider context was nicely set by Jones, again writing to a predestinarian:

> I have heard you talk much about doctrines of grace; as if our doctrines were not of grace; but if we enquire what your doctrines of grace are, we shall find they are doctrines, to which none of the means of grace are necessary: and the promises of God follow the means he has appointed, which means of his cannot be had without his church . . . You say the grace of God is free; understanding that it can act *with* the instituted means, or *without* them. So it can; for God is not bound by the laws by which he binds us. Grace, with respect to him, the Giver, is free; but if we, therefore, think it is free to us, the receivers, we shall introduce that confusion under which grace itself will soon be lost.[56]

God may freely grant the gifts of grace, but we are bound to receive them in the appointed way, and we must accept that they carry with them the obligations of moral law. Failure to carry out those obligations can mean the loss of the gift itself.

If there are divinely constituted means of grace, what is the way whereby we enter the life that makes them effective in and for us? What constitutes the new birth whereby we become inheritors of the kingdom of God? For the High Churchmen the answer was undoubtedly baptism; for the Evangelicals the answer was somewhat more varied, but was centered on conversion.

Two Evangelicals who represented the opinions of their brothers on this matter were Scott and Simeon. For Scott regeneration was a gift

---

56. Jones, *Works*, VI, 265.

that came after the gift of faith. Scott defines regeneration as being "this gracious operation of a divine power in changing . . . the heart."[57] Regeneration becomes a process somewhat akin to sanctification, a process whereby men come to love God more and sin less. Regeneration affects the understanding, renews men's minds, and operates primarily on the heart (will) of the individual.

If this is the core of regeneration, then what can be said of infant baptism? Scott says that it is primarily the outward sign of Christian initiation. The inward grace of baptism is regeneration, but it comes later as a child grows in understanding. Baptism effects no change in character, confers no new creation; instead, it marks a beginning and testifies to the faith of the parents and sponsors.

Adult baptism, however, marks a conversion from the old life to the new. One statement from Scott may be seen as typical of the Evangelical position:

> . . . the administration of infant-baptism has great influence, in giving vast multitudes some ideas of the gospel, especially of original sin, regeneration, and the doctrine of the Trinity: and whilst all who act profanely, deceitfully, or formally, in this matter, must answer for their own crimes; if good be done either to parents, children, or others, and if the name of God be in any measure glorified, the end of the institution is so far answered, even though no special benefit should be thought to accrue to the baptized person . . . If the child live, the transaction may be useful by way of subsequent improvement: we must allow, that the Holy Spirit may in some cases regenerate the infant, in answer to the prayers of believing friends, even at the time of baptism; and yet not confound the outward sign with the thing signified, or suppose the sacrament to produce the effect by its own inherent energy.[58]

Scott and Simeon shared the Evangelical suspicion of any notion of the efficacy of sacraments that was not tied to the faith of the recipient. Infant baptism presented that interesting case in which something was supposed to take place before conscious faith. Therefore, the only thing which could happen was a sort of witnessing to the power of God.

In Simeon it is interesting to note that where he could quite logically have spoken of baptism he did not. Examining Romans 6:1–4 Simeon chose to speak of the practice of holiness, and relegated the baptismal questions to

---

57. Scott, *Works*, V, 264.
58. Scott, *Works*, V, 525.

the realm of a profession of faith. Baptismal vows are the items of importance. The seriousness of these vows is found in their application to life after conversion.[59] Simeon, however, was interested in the baptismal regeneration question. His position is best seen in a short excerpt from the work which he considered his best endeavor, the "Appeal to Men of Wisdom and Candor":[60]

> But the chief source of the fore-mentioned error [that baptism always confers a change of nature] is, that men do not distinguish between a change of *state* and a change of *nature*. Baptism is, as we have shown, a change of state; for by it we become entitled to all the blessings of the new covenant; but it is not a change of nature. A change of nature may be communicated at the time that the ordinance is administered but the ordinance itself does not communicate it now, any more than in the apostolic age. Simon Magnus was baptized, and yet remained in the gall of bitterness and the bond of iniquity, as much after his baptism as he was before. And so it may be with us; and this is an infallible proof, that the change, which the Scriptures call new birth, does not always and of necessity accompany this sacred ordinance ... and if only our opponents will distinguish the sign from the thing signified, and assign to each its proper place and office, there will be an immediate end of this controversy.[61]

The Evangelicals were never prepared to say that regeneration could not accompany baptism; that would have been to limit God's sovereign activity. They sought to separate, as Simeon says, the "sign from the thing signified." Baptism stood for regeneration, but did not necessarily bring the gift of new birth. Only faith could be the instrument of new birth itself. Some High Churchmen would have agreed with a portion of the Evangelical position. Richard Laurence, Archbishop of Cashel, stating an opinion that would find an echo in J. B. Mozley a generation later, affirmed that regeneration accompanies baptism in most instances. The exceptions to this rule were adults whose baptisms were not accompanied by a repentant faith;[62] in infants, however, regeneration always accompanies baptism.[63]

The critical point between the Evangelicals and the High Churchmen was infant regeneration. The High Churchmen were uniformly believers

---

59. Simeon, *Works*, XV, 141f.
60. See letter to Bishop Burgess, October 24, 1820, in Carus, *Life of Simeon*, 316f.
61. See letter to Bishop Burgess, October 24, 1820, in Carus, *Life of Simeon*, 319f.
62. See Laurence, *The Doctrine of the Church of England upon the Efficacy of Baptism*.
63. Laurence, *The Doctrine of the Church of England upon the Efficacy of Baptism*, 83–95.

in the regeneration of all baptized infants (though they disagreed on exactly what that meant). There was a third opinion weighed in by an early Liberal, Reginald Heber, which deserves brief notice before passing on to the High Churchmen.

Heber, in his Bampton Lectures for 1815, attempted to develop a theory based on the rational and reasonable quality of the sacraments. Heber maintained that no mysterious connection need be affirmed between the sign and the thing signified, the act and the grace:

> The sacraments, accordingly, are styled the means whereby we receive grace; not as if they were vehicles through which the Spirit of grace thinks exclusively to convey his gifts to the hearts of men, but because they are the appointed medium of our devout and acceptable aspirations to his throne. They are not the means whereby God gives us grace, but they are the means whereby we ask and obtain grace from God.[64]

Heber's opinions hardly found wide acceptance, but they were noted in Oxford where the liberalism of the Oriel common rooms was coming into its own; but four years before Heber's Bamptons' an Oriel Fellow who could hardly be described as a Liberal, Richard Mant, later Bishop of Down and Conner, ascended the pulpit of the University Church to deliver a series of Bamptons' which still ranks among the most outspoken. The issue he faced is best described in the title of the lectures, "An Appeal to the Gospel, or an Inquiry into the Justice of the Charge, Alleged by Methodists and Other Objectors, that the Gospel is not Preached by the National Clergy." Lectures six and seven, on baptismal regeneration and conversion, were later republished by the SPCK and excited such indignation (from Daniel Wilson among others) that Mant was forced to temper his language lest the SPCK be dissolved.

Mant's stated objective was to refute the Methodists, especially Whitefield and his followers, but his arguments cut across denominational lines and deeply offended the Evangelicals. Mant's analyses of the Prayer Book formularies and scriptural evidence linking baptism and regeneration were typically comprehensive. Having demonstrated the agreement of scripture, the church fathers, the *Book of Common Prayer*, and Anglican divines on the

---

64. Heber, *The Personality and Office of the Christian Comforter*, 356. Heber's position relies on the moral causality of our acceptable attitude. The integrity of our aspirations makes the sacraments effective means for our salvation. Heber, in this, represents the development of the Low Church position inherited from the Latitudinarians of the seventeenth and eighteenth centuries.

reality of baptismal regeneration as the only type of regeneration known to the gospel tradition, Mant threw down the gauntlet:

> And if the new birth be not conveyed by baptism, rightly administered; or if, when once regenerated, it be (I will not say necessary, but) possible for any one to be born again, doubtless there is scriptural authority to that purpose. Let the authority then be adduced. Let it be shown from holy writ, that any person to whom baptism was rightly administered, was not regenerated; let it be shown, that any person, having been once baptised, is described under any circumstances whatever of repentance, reformation, renovation, or conversion, to have been again regenerated.[65]

Baptism is the only way of rebirth, the only instrumental cause of regeneration. Any emotional sense of sin and sudden forgiveness is not only false when viewed by gospel standards, but is actually harmful to the individual. It perverts his faith. Conversion is not regeneration.

What then is conversion? It is a "rational conviction of sin, and a sense of its wretchedness and danger."[66] The sense here communicated of separating the sin and the sinner, of speaking of sins as somehow distinct from him who commits them, gives us a good picture of the difference of positions. In the Evangelical position one is encouraged to think of the wretchedness of the sinner himself who has no justification in the sight of God, no previous principle of righteousness wrought by rebirth. Mant's High Church position makes the distinction: the sins are wretched, and the sinner must repent; but the sinner is already a new creature through baptism. The condition of his life is that of the new man, the reborn man, rather than that of the old man. Mant's position is that of the old High Churchmen: the new birth achieved in baptism tends to mitigate the seriousness of subsequent, post-baptismal sin. Our personal sinfulness becomes less frightening.

Mant's doctrine of baptismal regeneration remains within the Anglican reformed position which made justification and sanctification sequential portions of the Christian life. Interestingly, Mant's doctrine of sanctification surfaces in terms of conversion; in this he made somewhat the same error as Simeon, who had made regeneration into sanctification. Conversion is a slow, dispassionate process leaving in its wake a sense of security rather than violently felt emotions. "The triumph of such conversion as this," he writes, "is not attended by alterations of extreme joy and despondency; of the most ecstatic rapture, and the most gloomy despair; sometimes by heavenly

---

65. Mant, *An Appeal to the Gospel*, 71.
66. Mant, *An Appeal to the Gospel*, 591.

exultation, and sometimes by the agonies of hell."[67] True conversion is essentially repentance; it may begin at some identifiable moment, but it is not the *sine qua non* of a true churchman.[68] Mant's ministry lasted another forty years. The stability of his theological position is attested to in some of his later poetry. Two examples from his "Musings on the Church and Her Services" are typical of the continuing old High Church tradition. First:

> Preaching Evangelical:
> Say, what is Gospel-Preaching? 'Tis to show,
> How from his Father's love by wilful deed
> Man fell; and how, for ransom'd man to bleed,
> The Son of God took in this world of woe
> Our flesh, and quell's by death our mortal foe:
> And what his Spirit's aid; and whither lead
> His laws; his means of grace; and what the meed
> Of faith, matured by love; and what we owe
> The Three in One! This knowledge, passing reach
> Of man's device or angel's, broad and deep,
> God by His Son delivers; this to teach Mankind,
> He charged the shepherds of his sheep:
> If man or angel other Gospel preach,
> He "sows the wind, and shall the whirlwind reap."

Second:

> Holy Baptism:
> To the enlivening font the sponsors came,
> Bearing their infant charge; the white-robed priest
> Stood there beside Then with meek pray'r addrest
> To the Great Sire the promised boon to claim,
> The babe, unconscious yet of sin or shame,
> With greeting kind the holy man embraced,
> And on his brow the cleansing water cast,
> And spake the mystick words, the Triune Name.
> The sight was common: but withal a sight,
> So sweet, so lovely, to behold a Son

---

67. Mant, *An Appeal to the Gospel*, 71.

68. Mant is taking to task an obscure pamphlet entitled "The True Churchman Ascertained."

Of God adopted by his own blast rite
Methought that seraphs round about the throne might gaze thereon o'erjoy'd and with delight
Hail the newborn a brother of their own.

Some of the strongest language concerning baptism to come from the Episcopal bench during this period was used by Bishop Tomline. On the one hand, as we noted in the section on justification, Tomline held a forensic notion of justification; on the other hand, in baptismal theology he seemed to desire a movement towards a position which allowed for a doctrine of sanctification at baptism. Writing on the twenty-seventh *Article of Religion* he says of St. Paul's baptismal texts:

> Baptism, therefore, is not a mere external badge or token of our being Christians; it is a new birth from the death of sin, and a regeneration to a new life in Christ; it is a change and a renovation of nature by the spirit and grace of God; it is an infusion of spiritual life into the soul, by which it is made capable of performing spiritual actions, and of living unto God.[69]

The above needs the corrective of another short statement from Tomline. Left alone it could appear that Tomline was struggling to regain the principle of infused righteousness which was so strongly stated by Alexander Knox; but Tomline could not escape the juridical language which we saw in his theology of justification. In a passage made remarkable by one of the few High Church uses of the term "federal" Tomline concludes on baptism:

> Baptism therefore is a federal admission into Christianity; it is a seal of a contract in which all the privileges and blessings of the Gospel are on God's part conditionally promised to the persons baptized; and they on the other hand engage by solemn profession and vow to maintain the doctrines, and observe the precepts, of the Christian Religion.[70]

In 1820 Alexander Knox published an essay entitled "The Doctrine respecting Baptism held by the Church of England." It is among the more dispassionate and reasonable presentations produced during the controversy. Knox notes that the crucial issue remains baptismal regeneration in infants. He concedes that it is possible to say that regeneration does not always accompany baptism simply because it is possible to show that an adult can

---

69. Tomline, *Elements*, II, 465.
70. Tomline, *Elements*, II, 467.

receive baptism without the necessary repentance; this, in turn, would cause an obstruction or bar to the necessary operation of the Spirit in regenerating the adult. But what of infants who are without any sin which would bar the operation of the Spirit? Are they always regenerated in baptism? Knox argues that to deny this is to deny the obvious sense of the liturgy:

> On this sole ground, could "hearty thanks" be given to the Father of mercies, for having regenerated the baptised infant with his Holy Spirit, and for having received him for his own child by adoption . . . These words have been already quoted against those who, by asserting that baptism is regeneration, would resolve the inward and spiritual grace into the mere reception of the outward sign; and if they are conclusive on this point, they equally establish the spiritual regeneration of every duly baptised infant; because to every such child, they unequivocally and solemnly ascribe that inward and spiritual blessing.[71]

Inward and spiritual blessings can be lost and regained. Baptismal regeneration does not assure eternal life; rather it assures the possibility of eternal life. It assures that the grace necessary for subsequent repentance and restoration can and will be freely communicated to those who truly and earnestly repent. Baptismal regeneration makes the whole man new (again, Knox's preference for submitting justification under regeneration), makes him righteous, makes him what God would have him be, an inheritor of eternal life.

Alexander Knox represents the most advanced High Church opinion of his day. He, alone, held forth the notion of infused righteousness, and he, in concert with some other High Churchmen, was a devoted advocate of baptismal regeneration in all but the most extreme cases of unrepentant adult baptism. The debate and controversy raged on, but it was soon to change character.

The Stage Is Set

The theological spectrum of the early nineteenth-century Church of England was narrow. It was a spectrum of such subtle shadings that many of its writers seem, in retrospect, not to fall into any definable category. The issues which so inflamed the hearts and pens of the writers were important issues, but they were restricted by an all too often obsessive insularity. All sides lacked a sense of the wider world of Christian theology.

---

71. Knox, *Remains*, I, 503.

JUSTIFICATION, SANCTIFICATION, AND REGENERATION

This chapter has sought to establish the state of the questions concerning grace and its means in the period immediately before The Oxford Movement. With the exception of Alexander Knox forensic justification was present in some form in all the writers. On baptism the rift was clearer between those who held for baptismal regeneration and those who did not.

It is now clear that the issues which were to be at the heart of The Oxford Movement did not arise from a void;[72] they were issues which had occupied the best minds of the previous generation. The Tractarians inherited the ferment of this earlier period, and added the breadth of knowledge and appreciation for the wider theological tradition which was to give their writings not only greater influence, but greater weight.

The Tractarians were also deeply personally involved in the issues of the day. They knew the good and the bad that the previous era had wrought. They admired the sincerity of the Evangelicals but could not tolerate their reliance on human emotions. Among the Tractarians Pusey had the greatest personal stake in the controversy with the Evangelicals. His fiancée, Miss Barker, was living in the delightful Georgian town of Cheltenham. Francis Close, a deeply Evangelical clergyman whom we shall meet in a later chapter, was the incumbent of Cheltenham. Miss Barker had written often to Pusey about Close's theological opinions, and was troubled over Close's insistence on a painful sense of repentance. Pusey, in a statement typical of the emerging High Churchmen, wrote back to her:

> I have taken the opportunity of talking over with my friend Luxmoore, who is a thoroughly practical and excellent Christian, without prejudice, several of the subjects of Mr. Close's sermons, which we together discussed . . . He thoroughly agrees with me, that the employing the feelings as a criterion of religion is mischievous, because delusive . . . that a *deep* repentance is perfectly distinct from a *painful* or distressing one; that the only repentance which one has a right to preach or induce others to look for is that which is defined by our Church with a beautiful moderation, "a repentance whereby we forsake sin."[73]

---

72. For a full-blown treatment see Nockles, *The Oxford Movement in Context*, passim.

73. Liddon, *Life of Pusey*, I. 124.

2

Edward Bouverie Pusey

The Reality of Sacramental Grace

Recalling the early days of The Oxford Movement, John Henry Newman reflected on the importance of Pusey:

> I had known him well since 1827–8, and had felt for him an enthusiastic admiration. I used to call him ὁ μέγας. His great learning, his immense diligence, his scholar-like mind, his simple devotion to the cause of religion, overcame me; and great of course was my joy, when in the last days of 1833 he showed a disposition to make common cause with us ... There was henceforth a man who could be the head and centre of the zealous people in every part of the country, who were adopting the new opinions; and not only so, but there was one who furnished the Movement with a front to the world, and gained for it a recognition from other parties in the University.[1]

Newman's estimation of Pusey should not stand as the only testimonial to Pusey's importance to The Oxford Movement. R. W. Church, the great Dean of St. Paul's, London, in his history of The Oxford Movement, wrote of Pusey's entrance into the movement: "It gave the movement a second head, in close sympathy with its original leader, but in many ways very different from him. Dr. Pusey became, as it were, a guarantee for its stability and steadiness: a guarantee that its chiefs knew what they were about, and meant nothing, but what was for the benefit of the English Church."[2]

---

1. Newman, *Apologia Pro Vita Sua*, 59f.
2. Church, *The Oxford Movement, Twelve Years, 1833–1845*, 95.

The depth of change wrought by Pusey is best described by another statement from Dean Church. Remembering the effect of *Tract Sixty-seven*, Church notes, "The Tract on Baptism was like the advance of a battery of heavy artillery on a field where the battle has been hitherto carried on by skirmishing and musketry. It altered the look of things and the condition of the fighting. After No. 67 the earlier form of the Tracts appeared no more."[3]

Pusey's first written contribution to The Oxford Movement was a short tract on fasting (number eighteen). This modest effort was followed by a short appendix (number sixty-six) which appeared a few months later. *Tract Eighteen* was unremarkable, but Pusey had fixed his initials to it, a sure sign that the Tractarians had gained a very powerful ally.

Pusey felt that the tracts lacked depth. He wanted them to be not only provocative but scholarly. Leading the way in this change, Pusey published *Tract Sixty-seven: Scriptural Views of Holy Baptism*.[4] His reasons for writing on baptism were many, but four stand out quite clearly. First, Pusey had an immediate and personal concern with the issue of baptismal regeneration fueled by his wife's earlier contact with Francis Close.[5] Second, one of his students was close to leaving the Church of England because of its apparent stand for baptismal regeneration. Liddon reports Pusey as remembering:

> A pupil of mine was on the verge of leaving the Church for Dissent, and on the ground that the Church taught Baptismal Regeneration in the Prayer-book. So I set myself to show what the teaching of Scripture about Holy Baptism was. My tract was called "Scriptural Views of Holy Baptism." By Views I did not mean doctrines, but only such aspects as Baptism would present to any one who looks at Holy Scripture.[6]

Third, Pusey possessed a strong sense of the life of the church. This sense of the church's life spilled over into a concern for a right understanding of the way in which a person becomes a member of the church, i.e., what is meant by baptism. Pusey knew the baptismal regeneration controversy. He had seen the divisions it had caused, and desired to look to the biblical roots for a solution. Fourth, there was the issue of scriptural interpretation and

---

3. Church, *The Oxford Movement, Twelve Years, 1833–1845*, 67.

4. *Tract Sixty-seven* is used throughout to designate what first appeared as three tracts, number sixty-seven, sixty-eight, and sixty-nine. Pusey's revision of *Tract Sixty-seven* incorporates virtually all the material in the original three tracts plus enough new material to more than double the length of the original three. *Tract Seventy* was a catena of Anglican divines on baptismal regeneration. Quotations in this chapter are all from the revised *Tract Sixty-seven*.

5. Liddon, *Life of Pusey*, I, 124.

6. Lidon, *Life of Pusey*, I, 345.

the authority of the ancient church in the life and teachings of the modern church. To deny baptismal regeneration, in Pusey's mind, was to deny a broad interpretation of scripture. This was usually done by concentrating on a few specific baptismal texts and ignoring both the wider biblical baptismal tradition and the interpretations of the church fathers.

In *Tract Sixty-seven* Pusey brought the full weight of his scholarship to bear on the issue of baptism and its effects. It was the first serious study attempted by the Tractarians. It suffered from the lack of a serious study of grace upon which it might build; but it contributed the sense of the necessity for a study of grace. *Tract Sixty-seven* became a vehicle for exposing a serious deficiency. Newman, who would soon make up that deficiency, seemed to sense the need for a study of grace when he wrote, in the preface to volume two of the *Tracts for the Times:*

> Indeed, this may even be set down as the essence of Sectarian doctrine . . . to consider faith, and not the Sacraments, as the proper instrument of justification and the other gospel gifts; instead of holding, that the grace of Christ comes to us altogether from without, (as from Him, so through externals of His ordaining,) faith being but the *sine qua non*, the necessary condition on our parts for duly receiving it.

By writing on the means of grace Pusey set the stage for Newman. *Tract Sixty-seven* was not an introduction to Newman's *Lectures on the Doctrine of Justification*, but it did establish an argument for sacraments as the proper instruments of God's salvific activity. By accomplishing this, the questions concerning the nature of justification could be asked. Pusey's lifelong concern with the means of grace would prompt scores of works on sacramental theology, but none of them would be the equal of Newman's *Lectures on the Doctrine of Justification*.

Pusey never developed a theology of grace to undergird his sacramental theology. He preferred to rely on Newman. During the worst part of the controversy over the "Romish tendencies" of The Oxford Movement, Pusey wrote to the Bishop of Oxford, "'Justification' having been lately the subject of a very elaborate and meditative work by one (Newman) accused of departing from the Articles, it is less necessary to trouble your Lordship with any lengthened detail upon it. Had they, who bring charges, studied and mastered it, they might have been benefited by it, and these charges been spared."[7] Twenty pages of this letter are devoted to the

---

7. Pusey, *A Letter to the Right Rev. Father in God, Richard Lord Bishop of Oxford, on the Tendency to Romanism Imputed to Doctrines Held of Old as Now in the English Church*, 62.

eleventh Article of Religion, and a full thirteen of those pages are direct quotations from Newman.

The similarity between Pusey and Newman will become apparent in the next chapter, but two passages from the latter to the Bishop of Oxford are worth quoting here to show how completely Pusey and Newman agreed on the issue of justification. Writing on the article on justification, Pusey says:

> The Article (XI) opposes "Faith" as the origin of our justification, to works: it excludes works from being any meritorious cause of justification; "faith only" means in its language "faith, not works." A modern school has very strangely extended the reference of the Article, and opposed man's faith to the Sacrament of His Lord. They say, "faith only" means, that Faith,—as opposed to everything else, not works only, but Baptism,—is the channel whereby the merits of Christ are conveyed to the soul to its justification.[8]

Pusey's criticism of the Evangelicals was not his only interest in the interpretation of Article Eleven. He felt that Articles Nine through Seventeen were not intended to apply to the question of baptism, but only to apply to the relationship of faith and works to justification. Thus, he goes on:

> Whether He be pleased to convey justification directly to the believer's soul, or through His own ordinance of Baptism, is wholly foreign to their subject . . . Neither again does the Article say anything about the means whereby man is retained in a justified state, nor wherein our justification consists; so that it may be perfectly true, that we are "justified by faith" only, as the means whereby *we* receive it, and yet through Baptism as the means or channel, through which God conveys it; or "by the Spirit" as the sanctifying Presence which makes us acceptable in God's sight; or "by works" as St. James says, as that by which the Justification is continued on in us; or, as it has lately been very concisely and clearly expressed, "Justification comes *through* the Sacraments; is received *by* faith, *consists* in God's inward presence, and *lives* in obedience."[9]

This closing definition, as we shall see in the next chapter, belonged to Newman, and is another instance of Pusey's reliance on him. Years after

---

8. Pusey, *A Letter to the Right Rev. Father in God, Richard Lord Bishop of Oxford*, 32.

9. The quotation with which Pusey ends is from J. H. Newman, *Lectures on the Doctrine of Justification*, 312. It may be that this is one of the more important sentences Newman ever wrote.

Newman had become a Roman Catholic, Pusey continued to employ Newman's analysis (and often Newman's own words). In 1853 Pusey preached a University sermon on justification. Naively he asserted, "all agree that God, in justifying us, not only *declares* us, but *makes* us, righteous."[10] All, certainly, did not agree, and Pusey seems to sense this when he goes on to hammer home his point in words that are pure Newman:

> He does not declare us to be that which he does not make us. He makes us that which we were not, but which now, if we are in Him, (whatever there still remain of inward corruption), we by His gift are, holy. He does not give us an untrue, unreal, nominal, shadowy righteousness; or He does not impute to us *only* a real outward righteousness, "the righteousness of God in Christ;" for which, being unrighteous still, we are to be accounted righteous. But what He imputes, that He also imparts. He creates in us an inchoate and imperfect, yet still a real and true righteousness; inchoate and imperfect, because "we all," while in the flesh, "in many things offend;" yet real and true, because it is the gift of God, and the first fruits of His Holy Spirit.[11]

Pusey's interest in the debate over justification was limited to its applicability to the sacramental controversies. Throughout his long life he concentrated on the theology of the means of grace. As we have just seen, when called upon to comment on grace, he continually relied on Newman.

Early Incarnationalism

Almost one hundred years ago Yngve Brilioth argued that justification and sanctification are the doctrines over which Protestantism and Catholicism part company. No doubt this was, and to some degree still is, true; but an equally valid case can be made for the parting of ways being the result of radically opposed ideas of the genesis of spiritual life. "The spirituality of the early Tractarians had its roots in the doctrine of the indwelling Christ. They looked primarily to the Incarnation. It was this that separated them sharply from their Evangelical brethren."[12]

---

10. Pusey, "Justification, a Sermon preached before the University at St. Mary's, on the 24th Sunday after Trinity, 1853," 7.

11. Pusey, "Justification, a Sermon," 7f. The extent of mutual indebtedness that existed between Pusey and Newman can be seen by comparing these statements of Pusey's with those of Newman in 1838 found in the next chapter.

12. Brilioth, *The Anglican Revival*, 274f. Brilioth (d. 1959), as a Swedish Lutheran theologian and Bishop (he became Archbishop of Uppsala and Primate of the Church

Father Northcott rightly pointed out that the Tractarians were trying to recapture the spirit of the early church. They looked to a theology of baptism, based on the incarnation, as one way of accomplishing this. They may have been naive, but they managed to place the incarnation not only in the center of theology, but at the center of Christian living as well.

Pusey was the first of the Tractarians to give incarnational themes a prominent position. Early in *Tract Sixty-seven* he points out that an integrated theology of the incarnation and baptism is fundamental to the spiritual life:

> Baptismal regeneration, as connected with the Incarnation of our blessed Lord, gives a path to our Christian existence, an actualness to our union with Christ, a reality to our sonship to God, an interest in the presence of our Lord's glorified Body at God's right hand, a joyousness amid the subduing of the flesh, an overwhelmingness to the dignity conferred on human nature, a solemnity the communion of saints, who are the fulness of Him, Who filleth all in all, a substantiality to the indwelling of Christ, that to those who retain this truth, the school which abandoned it must needs appear to have sold its birthright.[13]

Here is the core of the Tractarian piety. Many have referred to the mysticism of the Tractarians. While they were undoubtedly mystics, their mysticism was not an abandonment of self in order to be caught up in the oneness of God; rather, it was an incarnational mysticism, steeped in the belief that in baptism Christ comes to dwell in the believer. Christ's humanity, dignifying our humanity, effects the union between man and God.

Pusey develops his incarnational principle in an analysis of John 1:1–14. First he makes a distinction between the conditions of regeneration, and the gift of regeneration itself. Faith and repentance are the conditions, but the gift of regeneration is a free, independent gift; fulfilling the conditions does not cause the gift to be given. Regeneration is an incomprehensible gift. It flows

---

of Sweden in 1950 serving until 1958) would naturally tend to discussions of justification; however, Brilioth's importance lies also in his "Swedish" Lutheranism which gave him a strong interest in topics such as church, sacraments, and worship. He made at least three visits to England in the 1920s and came to understand the wider importance of the Oxford Movement as creating a "Neo-Anglicanism" (see *The Anglican Revival*, 6, note 1). He came to be close to many in Oxford and beyond, and it was the Bishop of Gloucester, A. C, Headlam, a known advocate for church unity (see, for instance, "No Church Perfect, Lord Bishop says", *NY Times*, Oct 27, 1924), who authored the preface to *The Anglican Revival*. This sense of re-creation as a product of the Movement doubtless gave Brilioth comfort in his attempts to strengthen liturgy and worship in his own church.

13. Pusey, *Tract Sixty-seven: Scriptural Views of Holy Baptism*, 12f.

from the greater gift of the incarnation. For the connection between incarnation and regeneration to exist there must be a point of contact that is readily discernible. The agency of the Holy Spirit is that point of contact.

The supernatural agency of the Spirit and the natural agency of Mary yields the mystery of the incarnation. In the mystery of the incarnation all those gifts which are bound to the Pauline theology of the Spirit are to be found. All the gifts which Paul ascribes to the agency of the Spirit are subordinate gifts. There is only one supreme gift, from which all others flow, the incarnation. Christ, himself, is the gift. In Christ's incarnation everything is given. Pusey connects these gifts with the incarnation in a sermon, "Christ Risen for our Justification":

> ... but the One Gift in all is our Incarnate Lord, Who is Himself "Made unto us Wisdom, and Righteousness, and Sanctification, and Redemption:" "the Way, the Truth, and the Life." He doth not give merely these gifts as gifts, precious indeed, yet still outward to and without Himself. He is Himself them and all to us. He doth not *shew* us the Way, nor *give* us Wisdom only, nor *cause* us to be sanctified. He Himself, by the Condescension of His Living Presence in us, *is* our Way to the Father, our Righteousness, and Wisdom, and Acceptableness in Him.[14]

In baptism the supernatural agency of the Spirit of Christ and the natural agency of water yields the mystery of our new birth, our regeneration. It is through the power of supernatural and natural agencies acting together that we receive the birth from above and become sons of God. Pusey insisted on this point, and further insisted that it was fundamental in understanding other scriptural texts on baptism:

> The words of our Lord, then "birth *from above* of water and the Spirit," are a key to other Scripture; they are in themselves a high revelation, not to be closed up when we come to read other Scripture ... flowing over into other parts, and imparting to them the light which they contain concentrated within them. Thus when we read the words "to them that received Him gave He power to become the sons of God, to them that believe in His name, who were born not of blood, nor of the will of the flesh, nor of the will of man, but of God," we are not to take this as a figurative way, as if it were a distinct statement, that through faith we are *accounted* as it were sons of God, but, as it stands, in connexion with the Incarnation; as it there follows,

---

14. Pusey, "Christ Risen for our Justification" in *Sermons from Advent to Whitsuntide*, 219.

"and the Word was made flesh, and dwelt among us;" and both, in union with that mystery, whereby we are made partakers of the Incarnation, being "baptized into one Body," the body of our Incarnate Lord, being actually "born from above of water and the Spirit of God."[15]

The incarnation is the principle of new life, the truth of which was borne out in the resurrection. At baptism this principle is implanted in us, doing away with the old principle of death which we all assumed at the fall of Adam. Pusey saw this linking of incarnation, resurrection, and baptism as the truest interpretation of Romans. Commenting on Romans 8:34, he wrote:

> Our incarnate Lord imparted to our decayed nature, by His indwelling in it, that principle of life, which through Adam's fall it had lost: and when "by the Spirit of Holiness," which resided in Christ, He raised it from the dead, He made it not only "the first fruits," but the source of our resurrection, by communicating to our nature His own inherent Life . . . He took our flesh, that He might vivify it; He dwelt in it, and obeyed in it, that He might sanctify it . . .[16]

Christ's incarnation becomes the earnest by which we know that the power of the resurrection dwells in us through baptism. Pusey, like Newman, gave the resurrection a central place in the scheme of salvation. Too often the Tractarians have been read as having an incarnational doctrine of sacramental efficacy, an atonement centered doctrine of eucharistic presence, and little or no theology of the resurrection. Yet, the evidence is on the other side. Listen to Pusey preaching on the Christian life, "The Resurrection then of our Lord is not only a pledge of our own; it is our own, if we be His. His Body is a pattern of what is in store for us, since we, if His, are a part of It."[17]

Further evidence of the resurrection theology of Pusey can be found in his Easter sermons. In one from which we have already quoted another portion, Pusey writes on the resurrection as our justification. It is our justification because it ushers in a whole new order. It is the beginning of our salvation. The whole Christ-event is taken up in the resurrection:

---

15. Pusey, Pusey, *Tract Sixty-seven*, 48f.
16. Pusey, *Tract Sixty-seven*, 101.
17. Pusey, "The Christian Life in Christ" in *Sermons from Advent to Whitsuntide*, 249.

> With the Resurrection, began, (if one may reverently so speak,) this new order of events in Glory. The Birth was for Suffering, and Atonement, and Death. The Resurrection was for Life, spreading and expanding Itself on every side; Life first in His Body, now wholly spiritualised and made Life-giving, and then descending upon His Body, the Church, at Pentecost; . . . His Death atoned for us; His Resurrection justifies us . . . This declares His Resurrection to have been the immediate cause of our very acceptableness in the sight of God. As truly then as the Death of Christ was the True Remission of our sins, though not yet imparted to us, so truly was His Resurrection our True Justification, imparting to us the efficacy of His Death, and justifying us, or making us righteous in the Sight of God.[18]

Christological themes are always close to the surface of Pusey's theology. He was intensely critical of the Evangelical tendency to separate the incarnation from the gifts of grace, making the incarnation simply a means for the atonement. This separation makes it impossible to understand the relationship between Christ's perfect manhood and our regeneration in baptism:

> Moderns, however, have habitually separated these; the Incarnation is now very commonly looked upon in reference only to the Passion of our Lord, and as a means of His Vicarious Suffering; not as if it had any reference to us, to the sanctification of our nature, because He had "taken the manhood into God." And so they take what is said of baptism, as teaching only, as if it inculcated the same as Circumcision, and imparted a lesson rather than a grace.[19]

Pusey's incarnationalism is interestingly seen in a manuscript fragment on St. John's Gospel. Two points which he makes in the analysis of the prologue support the incarnational base of his sacramental theology. First, Pusey contends that the divine self-disclosure in the Old Testament was primarily prophetic. God could not be fully known under the old law. However, in the *Logos* the "imparting of the fulness of divine grace became historical."[20] That the *Logos* was "full of grace and truth", therefore, means that the whole revelation is now known in Jesus Christ. Second, "Not only is God now known, but he is known in a twofold manner: objectively, i.e. as he is in himself; and

---

18. Pusey, "Christ Risen for Our Justification," 215; 216; 218.
19. Pusey, *Tract Sixty-seven: Scriptural Views of Holy Baptism*, 126.
20. Pusey, Unpublished Manuscript Fragments on St. John's Gospel. Pusey House Library.

subjectively, through the fulfillment of his promises."[21] God fulfils his promises in us. By God's regenerating activity we are made capable of knowing that which is objectively, historically given. Grace and truth are intimately connected not only in Christ, but in regenerated humanity as well. This division into objective and subjective categories of gracious activity is common to the three major writers we will examine.

Just as the incarnation provides our way of understanding baptismal regeneration, it also is the key to understanding the eucharist. The presence of Christ in us through baptism, and that same presence continued in us through the eucharist, are extensions of the incarnation:

> And of this we have the germs and first beginnings now. This is (if we may reverently so speak) the order of the mystery of the Incarnation, that the Eternal Word so took our flesh into Himself, as to impart to it His own inherent life; so then we, partaking of It, that life is transmitted on to us also, and not to our souls only, but our bodies also, since we become flesh of His flesh, bone of Hisbone, and He Who is wholly life is imparted to us wholly.[22]

Pusey's whole-hearted insistence on the centrality of the incarnation in sacramental theology places him in the tradition of Hooker[23] and the High Churchmen of the seventeenth century. Pusey, however, would have preferred the connexion being made to the ancient church, for he always hearkened to voices from what he often described as "a holier age."

The Primacy of Baptism

Owen Chadwick, commenting on Pusey's *Tract Sixty-seven*, writes:

> He was not subtle, he had no intention of being subtle. His famous *Tract upon Baptism*, with its massed information, whatever its temporary success by way of confirming high churchmen in their belief that the ancient Church taught baptismal regeneration, succeeded only in clouding the issue for his successors; for amid all the texts and quotations about regeneration, he

---

21. Pusey, Unpublished Manuscript Fragments on St. John's Gospel.

22. Pusey, *The Holy Eucharist a Comfort to the Penitent*, 11. It should be noted that there is certain precedent for this in the Scottish church as well. For this, see Robert Bruce's powerful *Sermons on the Sacraments Preached in the Kirk of Edinburgh in A.D. 1589* published in *The Mystery of the Lord's Supper*, translated and edited by Thomas F. Torrance.

23. See Hooker, *Of the Laws of Ecclesiastical Polity*, 3–5; 50.

nowhere considered the meaning of the word regeneration itself, or defined carefully enough the sense in which he was using it, and thereby removed almost all value from the volume, apart from its use as a work of reference.[24]

It is difficult to understand how fine a scholar as Chadwick could have missed such a key point in *Tract Sixty-seven*. Pusey, anticipating just such criticism, meets it head on when he makes this primary introductory distinction:

> ... some may wish to know the meaning here attached to the Scripture words "regeneration," or "new birth," and "birth from above." This were easy for practical purposes, by way of description, so as to set before ourselves the greatness of the gift of Baptism bestowed on us; but it is not so easy by way of a technical definition. This arises from the very nature of the subject; for we can only accurately define that which we understand, not in its effects only, but its cause. Things divine, even by describing, we are apt to circumscribe; much more, if we attempt strictly to define them: the depth of things divine cannot be contained within the shallowness of human words. The more carefully we express ourselves in one way, the more escapes us in the other.[25]

Pusey's reluctance to offer a technical distinction was grounded in his fear of narrowness. He avoided dogmatic definitions because he saw the fruits of such activity in the battle over the meaning of justification. The Reformation notion of forensic justification had been purchased at too great a price, the loss of a comprehensive notion of God's salvific activity and the blessings of being in a redeemed state. The controversy over whether man is made righteous or accounted righteous had become a paramount issue. Pusey believed that this should not have happened. Both notions have a place in a proper theology of justification.[26] It was not for want of ability in producing definitions that Pusey drew back; it was to avoid a fruitless controversy, and to affirm that there are things which we cannot know about divine activity.

This latter point is brought out in his criticism of those who seek the kind of definition that Chadwick seems to think Pusey should have offered. Writing on baptismal regeneration, Pusey says:

> We know it in its author, God; in its instrument, Baptism; in its end, salvation, union with Christ, sonship to God,

---

24. Chadwick, *The Mind of The Oxford Movement*, 47; *Spirit of the Oxford Movement*, 38.

25. Pusey, *Tract Sixty-seven*, 19.

26. It was on this point that Pusey attacked Alexander Knox for forgetting that a person must be counted righteous as well as made righteous.

> "resurrection from the dead, and the life of the world to come." We only know it not, where it does not concern us to know it, in the mode of its operation. But this is just what man would know, and so he passes over all those glorious privileges, and stops at the threshold to ask how it can be? He would fain know how an unconscious infant can be born of God? how it can spiritually live? wherein this spiritual life consists? *how* Baptism can be the same to the infant and to the adult convert? and if it be not in its visible, and immediate and tangible effects, how, it can be the same at all?[27]

Such questions demean both baptism and scripture. Scripture does not speak of the mode of operation of baptism, and baptism admits of description much more than of definition, at least concerning its mode of operation. Pusey would extend definitions only as far as what he believed was the legitimate confines of scripture. If we desire to carry definitions further, then, Pusey states, there are two great barriers. First, and foremost, baptismal regeneration is a mystery, and we cannot know the mode of operation of a mysterious, divine act. Second, and related, any attempt to define a mystery only achieves a lowering of the mystery.

Pusey's intention in *Tract Sixty-seven* is to examine not only the scriptural views of holy baptism, but baptism's place in the scheme of salvation. By so doing he hoped to overcome two major faults of his time, a lack of agreement with the doctrines of the ancient church, and the want of a true basis for spirituality. These two are intimately connected in Pusey's mind: "it is in part owing to the absence of this doctrine of Baptismal regeneration, that while a foundation is often laid, the edifice of Christian piety among us still bears such low and meagre proportions, and still further, that there is not more of early Christianity among us."[28]

In looking back to the ancient church Pusey was not ignorant of the divisions that existed. He knew the problems of East and West, and the different emphases of Augustine and the Greek fathers; but he did not see the differences as irreconcilable. Pusey felt that a larger doctrine inhabited the minds of the fathers and Augustine:

> The two views . . . do in fact coincide, and are only the same great truth looked upon on different sides; for neither did St. Augustine regard the remission of original or actual sin as taking place in any other way than through the union with Christ, nor doubted he that this union infused actual righteousness and

---

27. Pusey, *Tract Sixty-seven*, 23.
28. Pusey, *Tract Sixty-seven*, 12.

holiness, the seed of immortality, the gifts in Christ far more than had been lost in Adam. On the other hand, the Greek Churches, though chiefly dwelling upon the blessings acquired, yet acknowledged Baptism to be for the remission of original, as well as actual sin.[29]

Pusey not only looked back in *Tract Sixty-seven*, he also assessed the current situation. The Evangelical notion that holiness of life began with conversion deeply distressed Pusey. He, like Wilberforce, believed that a turning was necessary in adult life, but that this conversion was not the beginning of the life of holiness. Holiness begins in baptism. It may have to be recaptured through conversion; but conversion is not a beginning so much as *a redirecting back to what was given in baptism*. In a remarkably pastoral comment. Pusey says, "A happier time, we trust, is dawning, when with the energy for conversion which now exists, shall be combined care for the young, such as the belief in God's gift through Baptism brings with it, and the holy calmness of a complete faith."[30]

Fenced 'round by the Trinity

Technical definitions of baptismal regeneration are subversive of the biblical and patristic tradition. This we have already heard Pusey say. Then, how does he describe baptismal regeneration? Through its effects. First, it is an act of incorporation, the means whereby we are incorporated into the church and become inheritors or the kingdom of God. This incorporation takes place through a new birth conferred in baptism. Pusey sees no biblical evidence for severing baptism from regeneration (as the Evangelicals had done); indeed, baptism is spoken of in scripture as the source of rebirth "as is no other cause, save God."[31]

Scripture affirms that baptism is the source of a literal new birth; it is God's instrument for our regeneration. Only God and baptism cause regeneration:

> Holy Scripture, indeed, *connects* other causes besides Baptism with the new birth, or rather that one comprehensive cause, the whole dispensation of mercy in the Gospel, (for this, not the written or spoken word, is meant by the "word," the "word of truth"): but it at once marks, by the very difference of language,

---

29. Pusey, *Tract Sixty-seven*, 22.
30. Pusey, *Tract Sixty-seven*, 16.
31. Pusey, *Tract Sixty-seven*, 25.

that these are only more remote instruments: we are not said to be born *of* them as *of* parents, but *by* or *through* them. They have their appointed place, and order, and instrumentality, *towards* our new birth, but we are not said to be born *of* them.[32]

Because this rebirth is literal, we receive total righteousness through it:

> This is our new birth, an actual birth of God, of water, and the Spirit, as we were actually born of our natural parents; herein then also we are justified, or both accounted and made righteous, since we are made members of Him who is Alone Righteous; freed from past sin, whether original or actual have a new principle of life imparted to us . . .[33]

The dominical words "of water and the Spirit" are the foundation of Pusey's theology of baptismal regeneration. Christ, in linking the two, linked natural and supernatural agencies. Water and the Spirit are the only direct causes of new birth. Regeneration is accomplished only in baptism. The fundamental error of the Reformation was to question this doctrine: he challenges his readers:

> Let a person, then, consider what the evidence is. Every vestige of Christian writing which God has preserved to us from the ancient Church, that explains the words, "Except a man be born of water and the Spirit," assumes, that they declare that in Baptism we are born from above; through our Saviour's gift . . . their whole system of theology presupposes it[;] . . . heretics, whose interest it was aforetime to deny it, retained, in their own sense, their belief in this [the reference here seems to be to the Novatians and Pelagians] until at last, after the Church had borne witness to it for fifteen centuries, one man arose and denied it.[34]

Pusey next extends his analysis of John 3 to the seventh verse. The reading of *anothen* becomes critical. If *anothen* is translated simply in the temporal mode (as the RSV does by translating it "anew"), the sense of the divine origin is lost and the nature of the gift is diminished. *Anothen*, Pusey argues, must be both spatial and temporal in meaning. We are not only born anew, but *from above*. Affirming God as the source of new birth is the only safeguard for a radical sense of the change which takes place. "From above" retains the sense of mystery vital to a notion of literal

---

32. Pusey, *Tract Sixty-seven*, 25f.
33. Pusey, *Tract Sixty-seven*, 23f.
34. Pusey, *Tract Sixty-seven*, 40f.

rebirth. To lose this spatial dimension of *anothen* is to open the door to a notion of figurative rebirth.

Pusey can now press home the necessity of baptism in the name of the Trinity. Through Trinitarian baptism a person is brought into a particular faith and a particular relationship with God. Showing his strong Old Testament background, Pusey asserts that baptism in the triune name conveys the divine power of life, for God is "in some way in His Name."[35] He goes on to describe the force of this patristic teaching:

> It was not then mere glowing language, when the fathers spoke of the baptized as being "fenced round by the Trinity" or the life; they would hereby only express the literal truth; and surely, in that they press the force of "being baptized *into* the Name of the Father, Son, and Holy Ghost," as something real, something efficient, an actual communion with the Blessed Trinity, they adhere more to the analogy of the faith, and the usage of other scripture, and the literal meaning of the text . . .[36]

The force of this patristic interpretation was never lost on Pusey. It was a living symbol for him. Forty years later, in a sermon preached on Trinity Sunday, 1875, he employed the same quotation from Gregory of Nazianzus: Into the name of this our God we were baptized, this confession of the Father the Son and the Holy Ghost we then received. "This was given us as the partner and presider over our whole life, the One Godhead and Power, existing in Unity in the Three and comprehending the Three severally." Hereby we came to dwell "with the Trinity," hereby, as an impregnable wall, we were, if we willed, "fenced round by the Trinity" . . .[37]

In baptism we are incorporated into the Trinitarian faith. In adults faith prior to baptism is only a desire to be healed, a desire to be born again. Faith can long for rebirth, but only baptism can convey it. At baptism faith becomes true faith; this is one of the gifts of baptism. True faith communicates the power to live in obedience to God's will. Put differently, in faith before baptism we choose to be that which we cannot, by our own power, be; in baptism, God chooses us to be, what he would have us be, his children and heirs, thus, one can say that there is a justifying office to faith, but that office

---

35. Pusey, *Tract Sixty-seven*, 71.

36 Pusey, *Tract Sixty-seven*, 73f. Pusey is quoting Gregory of Nazianzus, *Oration 40: Of Baptism*, 10.

37. Pusey, *Parochial and Cathedral Sermons*, 489. The quotations Pusey employs are all from Gregory Nazianzus, *Oration 40: Of Baptism*, 10; 16; 41.

is not exclusive: "Justification *by* faith does not exclude justification *through*, or by *baptism*, any more than salvation *by* grace excludes salvation through faith." Faith and repentance are necessary preludes to adult baptism, but they do not convey regeneration . Baptism is the instrument of regeneration . God acts in baptism in a way which imparts salvation. Pusey says all this in an analysis of John 3, the text which he believes provides the benchmark for all other baptismal texts. In his analysis he provides not only the evidence for baptismal regeneration as the only scriptural doctrine of baptism, but the foundation of Newman's theology of justification.

The relationship formed between God and man in baptism is reciprocal. God comes to dwell in man, and man is taken up into the life of God. This is the fullest meaning of being "in Christ". To get at this point Pusey chooses one of the most controversial Pauline texts, Romans 6:3–6. He recognizes that everyone interprets this text to mean that the baptized ought to lead a new life. The question is, "whether this be all?" whether St. Paul speaks only of duties entailed upon, and not also of strength imparted to, us?[38] Obviously Pusey believes the latter.

Pusey argues that a correct interpretation of this passage must take into account not only what Christ accomplished for us, but our participation in those events through baptism. The true sense of the passage is not so much that as Christ died, so we die in baptism; rather, that by and through baptism we die with Christ. Christ comes to live in us at baptism; henceforth our lives are in Christ. Thus the events of salvation are parts of our new life. They are both objective and subjective, historical and personal. Supremely they are events of the union of God and man:

> It were much, to be buried, to be crucified, with Him, like Him; but it is much more to become partakers of His Burial and Crucifixion; to be (so to speak)co-interred, co-crucified; to be included in, wrapt around, as it were, in His Burial and Crucifixion, and gathered into His very tomb; and this, he [St. Paul] says, we were by Baptism.[39]

Pusey expands the theme of our union with Christ through an examination of Galatians 3:27, 28. As we have put on Christ in baptism, we are sons of God. Thus, when God looks upon us, he does not see us as we were, but as we now are, incorporated into his son's body. God can look upon redeemed humanity with pleasure, since what he sees is his son present in it. Christian duty and obligation result from this incorporation, but the actual grace of regeneration is the important factor. Pusey sees this reality best

38. Pusey, *Tract Sixty-seven*, 93.
39. Pusey, *Tract Sixty-seven*, 95.

expressed in the simple formula, being "in Christ." This is a literal formula, and anything but a literal interpretation of it does violence to the scriptural evidence. As Pusey puts it:

> ... there is a reality in this Scripture language, which is not to be exchanged away for any ... substitutions. As we are *in* Adam, not merely by the imputation of Adam's sin, but by an actual community of a corrupt nature ... so that we have a sad share in him, as having been in him, as being from him, and of him ... so, on the other hand, are we *in* Christ, not merely by the imputation of His righteousness, but by an actual, real, spiritual origin from Him, not physical, but still as real as our descent from Adam.[40]

As Christ came into the world in the incarnation, he comes into the believer at baptism. He takes up residence in the individual. We are in Christ because he condescends to be in us. Christ's dwelling in man is regeneration, the implanting of the principle of new life. It can happen only at baptism, and only once. It is a past fact for those baptized in infancy.

Evangelicals had adopted the notion that regeneration occurred at conversion, and that it could occur often. Pusey argued that the individual was called, chosen, regenerated, justified, sanctified, sealed, given true faith, and saved at baptism. This, he maintains, is the Catholic interpretation of baptismal gifts:

> ... for since Baptism is the instrument whereby God communicated to us the remission of sins, justification, holiness, life, communion with the Son and with the Father through the Spirit, the earnest of the Spirit, adoption as sons, inheritance of Heaven, all which our Lord obtained for us through His Incarnation and precious Blood-shedding, it is obvious that all these gifts, and whatever else is included in the gift of being made a "member of Christ," must be spoken of as having been bestowed upon Christians, once for all, in *past* time at their Baptism. It remains for those, who have ceased to regard Baptism as the instrument of conferring these blessings, to account for the Apostle's language upon *their* views.[41]

Baptismal gifts are permanent gifts. They can only be lost through wilful sin. So long as the individual lives a life of obedience to holiness the gifts of baptism remain. The pure baptismal life is the earnest of the

---

40. Pusey, *Tract Sixty-seven*, 117.
41. Pusey, *Tract Sixty-seven*, 172.

kingdom of God, not simply a figure of it. So long as holiness is preserved we need not aspire to be saved, we are saved. The goal is present through the indwelling of Christ. Both justification and sanctification are present in baptism. On this point Pusey anticipates Newman who, a few years later, would attempt to transcend the notion that sanctification is a slow process built upon justification.

How deeply Pusey felt the power of baptism, the reality of our incorporation into Christ, and the centrality of these themes, can be seen in the following quotation. The whole panorama of Christ's historical existence is made real in and for each believer in the acts of sacramental worship. Again, he hearkened to the "holier age":

> Such was the teaching of the ancient Church; so did everything bind them on to their Lord; the hours of their daily solemn worship spoke to them, and filled them with thoughts, of His being contented to receive the bitter sentence of death for them; of His being nailed to the Cross, of His nailing our sins with His own Body there; of His tasting death for our sins, and commanding His Blessed Spirit into the hands of His heavenly Father: their going to rest, of His being laid in the grave for them; their awakening, of His Resurrection; and so each weekly fast bound them more closely to their Saviour's Cross, that they should not start from it; each Lord's Day they rose with Him; and thus "day unto day uttered speech, and night unto night showed knowledge;" and as the year flowed on, the Festivals of our Lord did not simply commemorate (in modern phrase) "events which took place 1800 years ago," but showed Him to their purified hearts, as *even then* coming into the world, born, suffering, dying, rising, ascending: they longed for His coming; they suffered in His Passion; they rose with Him from the tomb; they followed His Ascension; they awaited His return to judge the quick and the dead, and to receive them to His kingdom. And so in His Sacraments also, He was with them; He fed them in the Eucharist; He washed away their sins in Baptism: and Baptism was to them Salvation, and the Cross, and the Resurrection, because He opened their eyes to see not only the visible minister, but Himself working invisibly; not only the water, but the Blood; and the Holy Spirit, the third witness, applying the Blood, through the water, to the cleansing of the soul.[42]

"Baptism was to them Salvation, and the Cross, and the Resurrection" demonstrates the extensive nature of Pusey's baptismal theology.

42. Pusey, *Tract Sixty-seven*, 171–75.

Everything is communicated in baptism. *It is the whole of God's salvific activity brought to bear on the life of the individual:* to be "in Christ" is to possess everything. This deeply pious character in Pusey's writing was consistent with his life.[43] *Tract Sixty-seven* is the reflection not only of Pusey's mind, but of his heart and will. It is both scholarly and humble. *Tract Sixty-seven* changed not only the course of the *Tracts for the Times,* but their tenor as well. After *Tract Sixty-seven* the piety of Tractarian writing became much more sensible of the mysteries it addressed.

Applying Grace

Tract Sixty-seven established Pusey as a formidable exponent of Tractarian theology; moreover, it was the first work in what proved to be a life-long concern for the theology of the means of grace. Pusey's insistence on the imparted holiness of baptism raised serious questions concerning the gravity of post-baptismal sins. His teachings were regarded as extremely severe. Many felt they could never recapture the holiness of life which had been theirs at baptism. Many became morose over the wretchedness of their condition, the depth of their offenses.

Hoping to correct this view Pusey chose to preach a University sermon on the "Holy Eucharist a Comfort to the Penitent." His choice of topics was intended to introduce the subject of forgiveness in a way hopefully less controversial than a discussion of absolution. As Pusey later recalled:

> When people said that I had scared them about post baptismal sin, I was led to preach a course of sermons on Comforts to the Penitent. Of these the sermon on the Holy Eucharist was one. It was a singular case of mistaking what people's feelings would be. For I chose the Holy Eucharist as the subject at which they would be less likely to take offence than at Absolution. But we know what happened.[44]

What happened was this: Pusey was condemned by the "Six Doctors" and barred from preaching any University sermons for a period of two years. It was not Pusey's stance on the reality of forgiveness communicated in the eucharist that led to his censure; but a rather ambiguous statement on eucharistic presence to which the authorities objected. In a way, Pusey's

---

43. Brilioth, *The Anglican Revival,* 313–14.

44. Liddon, *Life of Pusey,* II, 307. For a fuller statement see Pusey, "Preface" to *The Holy Eucharist a Comfort to the Penitent.*

sermon on forgiveness began the controversy on the nature of Christ's presence in the eucharist.

"The Holy Eucharist a Comfort" was designed to make two points: first, that the eucharist strengthens our life in Christ; second, that the eucharist contains within itself the power of forgiveness. The former is the primary grace of the eucharist, and it acts within us:

> It is not, then, life only as an outward gift, to be possessed by us, as His gift; it is no mere strengthening and refreshing of our souls, by the renewal and confirming of our wills, and invigorating of our moral nature, giving us more fixedness of purpose, or implanting in us Christian graces; it is no gift, such as we might imagine given to the most perfect of God's created beings in himself.[45]

The primary grace of the eucharist goes far beyond that. In the eucharist we receive Christ himself, and by receiving him we receive all of the benefits of his life. The grace of the eucharist is the continuity of our presence in Christ and his presence in us. In the following statement (a portion of which was quoted earlier) Pusey draws together the incarnation and the eucharist with the resulting union of man and God in Christ:

> This is (if we may reverently so speak) the order of the mystery of the Incarnation, that the Eternal Word so took our flesh into Himself, as to impart to it His own inherent life; so then we, partaking of It, that life is transmitted on to us also, and not to our souls only, but our bodies also, since we become flesh of His flesh, and bone of His bone, and He Who is wholly life is imparted to us wholly. The Life which He is, spreads around, first giving Its own vitality to that sinless Flesh which He united indissolubly with Himself and in It encircling and vivifying our whole nature, and then, through that bread which is His Flesh, finding an entrance to us individually, penetrating us, soul and body, and spirit, and irradiating and transforming us into His own light and life.[46]

Again, the manuscript on St. John's Gospel helps to clarify this progression of ideas (and to confirm Pusey's notion of the real presence). The Jews, Pusey argues, already possessed a symbolic understanding of the manna in the wilderness as the food of life. Christ inherits this tradition, but goes on to declare that in receiving his bread one "receives him fully

---

45. Pusey, *The Holy Eucharist a Comfort to the Penitent*.
46. Pusey, *The Holy Eucharist a Comfort to the Penitent*, 11f.

and completely." Christ enters into the individual "really", though in a spiritual manner.[47]

For the grace of the eucharist to be effective presupposes the penitence of the worshipper. The reality of personal sin must be known to the communicant. The "comfort" of the eucharist begins with an approach to the sacrament which acknowledges unworthiness. The unworthy communicant, knowing his sinfulness, can then approach the body and blood which was shed for his sins. Hence, the forgiving power of the cross is the same forgiving power present in the eucharist. Coming to the heart of the matter, Pusey writes:

> . . . the penitent's comfort is, that, as, in St. Basil's words on frequent communion, "continual participation of life is nothing else than manifold life," so, often communion of that Body which was broken and that Blood which was shed for the remission of sins over which he mourns, that as the loving-kindness of God admits him again and again to that Body and that Blood, the stains which his soul has contracted are more and more effaced, the guilt more and more purged, the wounds more and more healed, that atoning Blood more and more interposed between him and his sins, himself more united with his Lord, Who Alone is Righteousness and Sanctification and Redemption.[48]

Pusey's tone was practical. Our life in Christ is secured by frequent eucharistic worship and communion. The eucharist will convey forgiveness to a penitent, and in so doing it will strengthen him in the holy life.

With his theology of the two-fold grace of the eucharist in view. Pusey knew that he could not avoid the topic of absolution. The primary grace of the eucharist was elevation, not cleansing; therefore, there must be a sacramental means of grace in which forgiveness is the primary effect. To meet the need of a complete theology of forgiveness, Pusey, upon regaining the University pulpit, preached two sermons on "The Entire Absolution of the Penitent."

Baptism is for incorporation, the eucharist is for perseverance, but sin is an awful reality. Man remains tainted by his original corruption, he remains prone to continuing disobedience. Hence, absolution exists for the purpose of restoration, freeing man from a life of actual sin and restoring him to a life of holiness. Our willful sin has obscured our baptismal life. The newness of life achieved in baptism can be lost. Through absolution God restores persons to the state of the newly baptized:

47. Pusey, *Manuscript on St. John's Gospel*, On John 6:35.
48. Pusey, *The Holy Eucharist a Comfort to the Penitent*, 27.

> . . . sins before Baptism come not into judgement at all; they belong to one who is not; in Baptism he was buried and died, and a new man, with a new life and a new principle of life, was raised through the Resurrection of Christ. Grievous sins after Baptism are remitted by Absolution; and the judgement, if the penitent be sincere, is an earnest of the Judgement of Christ, and is confirmed by Him. Yet the same penitent has yet to appear before the Judgement-seat of Christ, that, according to his sincerity, the Lord may ratify or annul the judgement of His servants. Yet with these limitations, the pardon upon penitence is as absolute as in Baptism itself. Indeed, the commission to set free from sins, has by ancient fathers been thought, in a secondary way, to include the power of Baptism; it is one power, and one pardon, and One Blood diversely applied.[49]

Absolution does not make one new; the forgiven person and the sinner before absolution are the same person. Absolution restores the baptismal state, a state that cannot be totally lost during earthly life. Once made new by baptism, newness can be restored (except in cases of blasphemy of the Spirit). The pain of sin remains, absolution cannot do away with it, but even that pain may be an aid in deepening sorrow and the sense of the majesty of God's grace.

Hence, the spiritual reality of absolution is great. It helps to deepen the spiritual life. It makes us see sin for what it is, an offense to God. Knowing this awful reality we can have greater contrition. Contrition is the foundation of sincerity, and sincerity is our path to true penitence. Truly penitent, we approach confession, and because of our sincere penitence we are assured of absolution. We know that there is a greater judgement than that of the confessor. The future judgement of God produces a holy fear that is the truest form of sincerity.

Pusey's theology of the Christian life was austere. It is hard to imagine just how much "comfort" was realized by listening to his sermons on absolution. Still, he did offer to those who would follow a larger devotional life than was common in the Church of England in the 1840s. Pusey's theology of the sacramental grace of forgiveness was to have far-reaching effects in the Tractarian parishes which were being founded. So, too, his theology of absolution was to excite a controversy that lasted for forty years.[50] Owen Chadwick has commented on the severity of Pusey's theology:

---

49. Pusey, *The Entire Absolution of the Penitent*, 26f.
50. See Chapter Six of this book.

If Newman at times pressed the immediate claims of holiness too earnestly, this was still truer of Pusey. It was not that he failed to recognize the workings of grace, or man's incapacity, or justification by faith, but he was zealous to remind the soul of its awful responsibility as it stands under judgement before God, and he could perhaps create a sense of strain... This concern for responsibility, this devotional (not theological) undervaluing of grace, this reluctance to recognize naturalness and "the seed growing secretly," that sanctification was not only a supernatural life but a supernatural consecration of natural life, affected the young Liddon, Pusey's more intimate friend and follower.[51]

Chadwick is certainly correct in believing that Pusey could produce a sense of strain, and that he did press home the requirements of holiness. Both of these can be attributed to Pusey's reaction to the conditions of the Church in his time. The deterioration of church fabric, the want of regular communicants, the general laxity in the conduct of public worship; all these and more disturbed Pusey deeply. Chadwick's comments, however, are also misleading. His criticism of Pusey's theology of nature and supernature lacks historical perspective. The theology of grace of Pusey's time was the necessary preparation for that of the Liberal Catholics of the late nineteenth century. Chadwick would have us believe that Pusey was a proto-Liberal Catholic. He was nothing of the sort; rather, he helped to introduce some sense of supernature back into a theological climate that swung between the two poles of human worthlessness and natural perfectibility. Furthermore, Pusey could never have spoken of growth in the sense which Chadwick would like. Pusey's theology, as we have seen, was not based on a process of growth towards sanctification; it was based on a notion of the possession of sanctification and justification in baptism. Obedience to the dictates of imparted holiness (rather than growth in holiness *per se*) is a distinguishing characteristic of the Tractarians. Holiness is a gift given, a fruit of baptism. If it is lost it must be restored through absolution. If holiness is to continue in us it must be continually fed in the eucharist. The Tractarians brought supernaturalism to the fore in Anglican theology by their insistence on the centrality of baptismal regeneration. They sought some acceptance of any notion of supernature; they hardly admit of being criticized for missing a later distinction.

Pusey, like most of the Tractarians, found the balance between the natural and supernatural best exemplified in the incarnation. The proper

---

51. Chadwick, *The Mind of The Oxford Movement*, 50; *Spirit of the Oxford Movement*, 41.

role of humanity in the dispensation of grace is understandable only in the hypostatic union:

> "That man from the earth," says St. Gregory the Great, "might have so great power, the Creator of heaven and earth came to earth from heaven, and that the flesh might judge spirits, the Lord, made Flesh for man, vouchsafed to bestow this upon him, because thereby did human weakness rise beyond itself, that Divine Might was made weak below Itself." It may be one of the fruits of the Incarnation, and a part of the dignity thereby conferred upon our nature, that God would rather work His miracles of grace through man, than immediately by Himself. It may be a part of the Mystery of the Passion, that God would rather bestow Its fruits, through those who can suffer with us, through toil and suffering, than without them. It may be part of the purpose of His Love, that love should increase while one member suffers with another, and relieves another.[52]

Real forgiveness—whereby through sorrowful penitence we come to the grace of absolution mediated by the church—is at the heart of Christian obedience. The true comfort of the penitent is found in the life of sacramental grace, not in a mere recollection of one's baptism nor in an act of will and intellect which creates a sense of forgiveness. True forgiveness is an objective reality brought to the penitent by those who hold the apostolic commission to do so. The grace of absolution is defectible, but only at the final judgement which will yield the absolute knowledge of whose penitence was sincere.

While the primary grace of absolution is the restoration of the holiness created in us at baptism, its secondary effect on the heart and mind was also important to Pusey. Through confession and absolution the awful burden of post-baptismal sin is set aside, and the conscience is quieted. This effect is heightened since confession is not a required part of Christian discipline. People must be moved to see their sinfulness, but the movement must originate with God. Recognizing their sinfulness, they can then be moved to confession, not as a matter of discipline, but as a matter of seeking God's grace.

Pusey never advocated confession to those who sought his advice. He wanted to leave advocacy to the Holy Spirit:

> My own private conviction was, that if men would review their lives as a whole, bring before themselves all their past sins, the result would be too long to hear our Lord's absolving voice. But

---

52. Pusey, *The Entire Absolution of the Penitent*, 45f.

> this, as all besides, I left to the teaching of God the Holy Ghost in their hearts. I did not interpose my own. Nothing was said at the time about the *necessity* of confession. Those who feel a disease do not want to be taught about the *necessity* of a cure. They went to the Great Physician and to those whom He had constituted, under Himself, as physicians of souls. They spake *His* word, and *He* healed them.[53]

While Pusey may have been content to leave the initial sense of need for absolution to God's grace, he did not hesitate to aid the process. His preaching could cause the sensitive listener to feel the full weight of sin. As we noted earlier, sorrow was, for Pusey, the sincerest form of penitence. In the second University sermon on Absolution Pusey went to great lengths to excite a sense of sorrow in his listeners. He exhorts his hearers to judge themselves now, so that at the last day they will not be beyond God's righteous mercy:

> Set before you that dread Judgement-seat, where they who have not before sued for mercy, shall find none; imagine every thought, word, deed of shame, all which thou now wouldest hide from thyself, brought to light ... so, while there is yet time, say with that same pious penitent, "I repent, O Lord, I repent; help Thou my unrepentance, and more and yet more, pierce, rend, bruise my heart.[54]

Being in Christ

"That he [Pusey] is properly the *doctor mysticus* in earlier Neo-Anglicanism, has scarcely received sufficient notice from its historians."[55] Throughout this chapter we have noted that to be "in Christ" was the predominant theme of Pusey's theology of the sacraments. It is from this theme in Pusey that Brilioth gained the sense of Pusey being the "*doctor mysticus*" of The Oxford Movement. In the next chapter we shall see that Brilioth's analysis erred in one crucial point—the ascribing to Newman and the other Tractarians of a "substantial" notion of grace—and earlier in this chapter, we noted that if one applies the idea of mysticism to Pusey it must be seen as a Christological mysticism. Nowhere is this more evident than in Pusey's notion of the

---

53. Pusey, "Advice for those who Exercise the Ministry of Reconciliation through Confession and Absolution" in *Gaume's Manual for Confessors*, ix.

54. Pusey, *The Entire Absolution of the Penitent II*, 38.

55. Brilioth, *The Anglican Revival*, 296.

role of works in the scheme of salvation. Our union with Christ in baptism is so complete that our subsequent works of faith can be called good. Pusey defines the manner in which this is the case in the preface to the first volume of his Parochial Sermons:

> Yet it is chiefly in the doctrine of "good works" that the full belief that the Christian is "in Christ" might remove our misunderstandings. There is a morbid fear, lest any mention of "good works" should introduce something of our own, as though men claimed Salvation in part through their own deserts, in part through the Merits of Christ . . . The very reverse is the case as to the Scriptural Doctrine, to be "in Christ. ' With this truth imprinted on the soul, "good works" may be the more fearlessly spoken of, because they are not our own.[56]

There are no good works that belong to humanity. All good works stem from Christ's indwelling through baptism. To claim good works, and to boast of them, is not to glorify the self, but to glorify God. It is Christ, present in the individual, who originates, sustains, and perfects all our works. Christ does this by perfecting our wills. We have the good will to do good works by virtue of being in Christ. Christ's work in us is the creation and preservation of just such a will. It is a work which Christ does *in* us, in the very arena that will be affected by his work. Therefore, it is quite normal to speak of good works as part of the scheme of salvation, because they are Christ's works accomplished by us, his instruments. Good works, like the grace to perform them, begin with Christ. Thus, "Christians may fearlessly confess that 'good works' are the dowry, wherewith Christ adorns the soul which he hath purchased with His Blood, and called, and sanctified by His Spirit; it were ungrateful not to own it."[57]

The person made new in Christ, united to Christ through baptism and sustained in Christ through the eucharist, cooperates in his or her own salvation. Because Christ lives in that person, she or he can cooperate. Personal salvation is not of that person, but of Christ in whom the person dwells and who dwells in him or her personally. In a letter of about 1850 Pusey confirmed this interpretation of the doctrine of good works:

> It is by the grace of God that we have the wish to do anything which pleases God. It is by the grace of God enabling us, that we do it, if we do it. It is by the grace of God that any persevere to the end. And in the end, those who are placed at the Right Hand shall be accepted only for the merits of Jesus, and (as St.

56. Pusey, *Parochial Sermons*, xi.
57. Pusey, *Parochial Sermons*, xif.

Augustine says) "God will crown His own gifts in us." (*Deus in nobis dona coronat sua*).[58]

In one of the strongest and most moving statements Pusey wrote on this subject, he expresses the doctrine of good works and being in Christ in terms of the whole economy of salvation:

> All is of Christ. He is the grace, which brought us out of the mass of our natural corruption in Adam. His was the new principle of life, which in Baptism he imparted to us. His the grace which cherished, nurtured, enlarged that first gift, or if unhappily we wasted it, through repentance, brought us back, converted, renewed, restored us. His, each gift of superadded grace, whereby He rewards the use which, through His grace, we make of each former grace, bestowing grace for grace. And life eternal, too will be from Him, grace for grace.[59]

So thoroughly are we in Christ, that our works are his. The basis of our good works lies in obedience of will, an obedience which stems from our will being conformed to Christ's. The chief characteristic of Christ's human will was that it was obedient to the will of the Father. This, Pusey sees, is confirmed especially in the incarnation and atonement. Since Christ is in us, our wills can be obedient to the Father as was the human will of Jesus Christ. Christ's perfect human will produces actions which merit salvation. If we merit salvation through our good works, it is because the perfect will of Christ dwells in us.

In all this Pusey felt that he had defeated one of the prime tenets of English Calvinism, i.e., that no work of man could be good or righteous in any sense. To believe as Pusey felt the Calvinists believed, was to diminish Christ's indwelling. Our works are good and acceptable, because Christ makes them so. Though Christ's indwelling is extensive, we remain free. We can still commit grievous sins and lose the presence of Christ which makes us capable of good works. Our conversion, our return to Christ, is possible through penitence, absolution, and the gracious life of the eucharist. Being restored to newness of life, we can again act in concert with the will of Christ and perform good works. By continuing in good works we are, more and more, brought into conformity with the life of Christ.

It is not without value to note that when Pusey felt it necessary to point out the differences between his position and that of the Calvinists

---

58. Johnston and Newbolt, eds., *Spiritual Letters of Edward Bouverie Pusey*, 250.
59. Pusey, "Justification" in *Nine Sermons*, 43.

by writing *What is Puseyism?*, he outlined two of the seven points in terms of good works:

> (4) The intrinsic acceptableness of good works, especially of deeds of charity (sprinkled with the Blood of Christ), as acceptable through Him for the effacing of past sins. (5) The means whereby man, having been justified, remains so. The one would say (the Calvinists), by renouncing his own works and trusting to Christ's alone; the other, by striving to keep God's commandments through the grace of Christ, trusting to Him for strength to do what is pleasing to God, and for pardon for what is displeasing, and these bestowed especially through the Holy Eucharist as that which chiefly unites them with their Lord.[60]

Not only did Pusey promulgate a theology of good works, he lived doing deeds of charity. The practical side of Pusey's cooperation with Christ will be seen in chapter 6. For now it is enough to note it.

Groundwork for Newman

Tract Sixty-Seven appeared four years before Newman's *Lectures on the Doctrine of Justification*. The issues left unresolved by Pusey called forth the more facile pen of Newman. Pusey attempted no systematic statements concerning the doctrine of grace. He contented himself with studying and describing the means of grace, most often in the language of the fathers. His insistence on patristic interpretation makes him a key figure in the revival of patristic studies which has marked Anglicanism in the last two hundred years.

In the church fathers Pusey found the language of incorporation into Christ and the church. He appropriated that language, and it permeates his writings. He never spoke of divinization, but in his theology of being in Christ the marks of elevating grace are clear. Everything in Pusey revolves around baptismal regeneration. The grace of other sacraments relates, in every instance, to the new life brought through baptism.

To John Henry Newman fell the task of asking the questions that Pusey did not ask: how does God justify persons? What is the relationship between justification and sanctification? If sacraments are truly means of grace, what is the role of faith in salvation? And, what causes God to save us? Histories of The Oxford Movement have tended to stress the importance of Pusey mainly in terms of his position in the University, a position that gave the Tractarians a status in the larger Church of England.

60. Liddon, *Life of Pusey*, II, 140.

Hopefully this chapter has helped to correct the notion that is implied by those histories, that E. B. Pusey's writings were of a secondary importance in The Oxford Movement. As important as Pusey was in giving status to the Tractarians, his writings, not his position, were his main contribution. In the next chapter it should be evident that Pusey, in many ways, anticipated the issues that would become critical for Newman.

3

John Henry Newman

The Imparting of Righteousness

Nearly one hundred years ago, Yngve Brilioth wrote in *The Anglican Revival*: "Newman's 'lectures on Justification' of 1838, though they have not generally tempted his biographers to close study, form perhaps the chief theological document of The Oxford Movement, the most important attempt to find the theological expression of its piety."[1] Writing from his Lutheran background it is not surprising that Brilioth singled out this theme as among the most important; but Brilioth's point relates to more than a later ecumenical interest in one area of Anglican doctrine. Newman's *Lectures on the Doctrine of Justification* is one of the most important theological documents to come out of the Church of England in the nineteenth century. Writing in 2019, almost one hundred years after Brilioth, Eamon Duffy echoes something of the same sentiment when he writes, "Whatever the inadequacies of Newman's account of Luther's teaching, . . . the *Lectures on Justification* struck out in a new direction by placing the indwelling presence of Christ through the Spirit as the agent and meaning of Justification . . . Newman's introduction of a Trinitarian and Christological dimension to the talk about Justification was a theological insight which would bear ecu-

---

1. Brilioth, *The Anglican Revival,* 282. Since Brilioth's apt insight, more recent scholars have thankfully considered Newman's *Lectures on Justification* in more important light. Charles Hefling, for example, in "Justification: The Doctrine, the Lectures, and Tract 90," argues for the centrality of the *Lectures* and, notably, his conclusions are similar to ours, namely, that Newman's understanding of justification was deeply Christological. For the most recent work on Newman, see Benjamin King's incredible corpus: *Newman and the Alexandrian Fathers, Receptions of Newman,* and *The Oxford Handbook of John Henry Newman.*

menical fruit."[2] It cut away centuries of ever-narrowing debate, and opened a new vista to Catholic-minded Anglicans. Brilioth was enamored of the notion that theology followed piety among the Tractarians; nowhere was this less true than when Newman considered the doctrine of justification. Newman blazed a new trail, a trail that later found expression in the piety of The Oxford Movement, and especially in its baptismal and confessional practice, later in Swedish Lutheranism, and even later in contemporary ecumenism. David Newsome, in his wonderful final book, *The Victorian World Picture*, would go so far as ranking Newman along with Coleridge and very few others, as a true polymath.[3] Yet, in its own time, his *Lectures on Justification* went partially unnoticed. Later, Newman himself almost ignored them when he wrote in the *Apologia*:

> I wrote my Essay on Justification in 1837; it was aimed at the Lutheran dictum that justification by faith only was the cardinal doctrine of Christianity. I considered that this doctrine was either a paradox or a truism,—a paradox in Luther's mouth, a truism in Melanchthon's. I thought that the Anglican Church followed Melanchthon, and that in consequence between Rome and Anglicanism, between high Church and low Church, there was no real intellectual difference on the point. I wished to fill up a ditch, the work of man. In this Volume again, I express my desire to build up a system of theology out of the Anglican divines, and imply that my dissertation was a tentative Inquiry.[4]

This was all that Newman recalled in his *Apologia*; but years before, while preparing the manuscript for publication, he wrote to his sister, Mrs. John Mozley:

> My book on Justification has taken incredible time. I am quite worn out with correcting . . . I write, I write again: I write a third time in the course of six months. Then I take the third: I literally fill the paper with corrections, so that another person could not read it . . . I cannot count how many times this process is repeated.[5]

Two months later, in March of 1838, he wrote to his other sister, Harriett, "The great difficulty was to avoid being difficult, which on the subject of

---

2. Duffy, *John Henry Newman*, 116.
3. Newsome, *The Victorian World Picture*, 259.
4. Newman, *Apologia Pro Vita Sua*, 67.
5. Mozley, *Letters and Correspondence of John Henry Newman*, II, 250.

Justification is not a slight one. It is so entangled and mystified by irrelevant and refined questions."[6]

The *Lectures on the Doctrine of Justification*, while they received some attention when published, slipped from the limelight in a hurry. How this happened is a matter of purest conjecture; yet, it would not be unreasonable to assume that Oxford's rapidly changing circumstances offer some explanation. Newman was at his most influential; the battle was being waged on many fronts; University politics were dividing colleges and senior common rooms. There were lectures to be given, students to be seen, manuscripts to be prepared, a magazine to be edited, piety to be exercised, sermons to be written, outside speaking engagements to be met, research to be done. The *Tracts for the Times* were being reprinted, work on the edition of the church fathers was being pursued, Anglican divines were being translated and/or edited and published, works of an original nature were being produced at an astonishing rate. All this was being carried on by a small group of men. The *Lectures on Justification* appeared on the heels of the *Lectures on the Prophetical Office of the Church*. It is not beyond possibility that the work we are about to consider suffered neglect simply from the pressure of the times and the changing circumstances of the movement.

Newman's secession certainly did not help his *Lectures on Justification* find an audience. In many minds the leader had become the betrayer. His work could bear no test of sincerity. Coupled with the literary overkill of the 1830s, Newman's secession managed to obscure his finest Anglican work, but not completely. Owen Chadwick has unearthed a fascinating piece of information related to the reading habits of the Victorian clergy. He writes, "The catalogue of the clerical library in the Lincolnshire archives enables a comparison in shift in balance between what the clergy read in 1840 and in 1898. Just a few withdrawals are common to both ends of the reign: Newman *On Justification*, Maurice's *The Kingdom of Christ* . . ."[7]

Chadwick has helped us understand that the *Lectures on Justification* had an ongoing effect, but offers us no information as to the nature of the effect. R. W. Church, on the other hand, offers some insight into the immediate effect of Newman's lecturing:

> All this time the four o'clock sermons at St. Mary's were always going on. But, besides these, he [Newman] anticipated a freedom—familiar now, but unknown then—of public lecturing. In Advent and after Easter a company, never very large, used to gather on a week-day afternoon in Adam de Brome's

---

6. Mozley, *Letters and Correspondence of John Henry Newman*, II, 250.
7. Chadwick, *The Victorian Church*, II, 108.

Chapel—the old Chapel of "Our Lady of Littlemore"—to hear him lecture on some theological subject.[8]

While these gatherings may have been small, they were enthusiastic, and if Church himself is any indication of the quality of those who attended, they reached an audience that would mold the Victorian Church. Those present at the lectures, Church notes, found in them new ways of seeing old questions:

> The force, the boldness, the freedom from the trammels of commonplace, the breadth of view and grasp of the subject which marked those lectures, may be seen in them still. But it is difficult to realize now the interest with which they were heard at the time by the first listeners to that clear and perfectly modulated voice, opening to them fresh and original ways of regarding questions which seemed worn out and exhausted.[9]

On one point all witnesses agree: the *Lectures on the Doctrine of Justification* belong to the golden age of The Oxford Movement. They stand as a singular accomplishment in Anglican theology, dealing, as they do, with the theology of grace in a new light.

The new light which Newman brought to the old debate over justification began with the *Lectures on the Prophetical Office of the Church*. In those lectures he was seeking a principle of authority, but beyond such a principle he was seeking the famous *Via Media*, a system of doctrine for Anglicanism which was grounded in scripture and informed by scripture's patristic interpretation; a system which resorted to private judgement only when all other authorities had been exhausted. By applying this system to the historic formularies and liturgies of Anglicanism it would be possible to define a system of doctrine for Anglicanism. Newman's concern for his task was great:

> Protestantism and Popery are real religions; no one can doubt about them; they have furnished the mould in which nations have been cast: but the *Via Media*, viewed as an integral system, has scarcely had existence except on paper, it has never been reduced to practice except by piecemeal . . . it was to formulate the *Via Media*, and then to reduce it to practice, that Newman devoted his Anglican career. He believed very strongly that "though Anglo-Catholicism is not practically reduced to system in its fulness, it does exist, in all its parts, in the writings of our divines, and in good measure is in actual operation,

---

8. Church, *The Oxford Movement*, 132.
9. Church, *The Oxford Movement*, 133.

though with varying degrees of consistency and completeness in different places."[10]

Authority in the life of the Christian community, Newman argued, must begin with scripture; but scripture, taken alone, cannot be the sole authority, for too often it only intimates doctrine. Hence antiquity, the fathers and the early councils, must be consulted. Antiquity forms the tradition of the church, it gives voice to what was first a matter of uniform custom. Antiquity, far from undermining scripture, expands upon scripture and interprets it in an authoritative manner. Antiquity is our best guide because it seeks the *via media*, disregarding outright private judgement and limiting dogmatic assertion. Our appeal to antiquity is the extension of antiquity's own principle; by appealing to the ancient church we remove the error of the Protestants, the exclusive use of private judgement, and the error of the Roman Catholics, dogmatizing that of which even the apostles had been granted only a partial knowledge. "The English Church," Newman argued, "takes a middle course between these two. It considers that on certain definite subjects private judgement upon the text of Scripture has been superseded, but not by the mere authoritative sentence of the Church, but by its historical testimony delivered down by the Apostles."[11]

Newman was seeking a system of doctrine grounded in scripture, confirmed by the fathers and councils, consistent with the doctrinal and liturgical formularies of the sixteenth century, and supported by the writings of English divines. It was not a new question. Bishop Bull, Newman's favorite Anglican author on justification, sought much the same thing in the seventeenth century. Newman, and his Tractarian colleagues, managed to shift the discussion away from the kind of internecine bickering that was typical of the first third of the nineteenth century. By their extensive appeal to ancient authority and to the fathers, they reintroduced Anglicanism to patristic studies. Their search for a principle of apostolic authority was misinterpreted by Brilioth as a function of the Romantic age.[12] They may have romanticized their view of the early church, but their principle of authority was drawn directly from Vincent of Lerins.[13]

Having dealt with the question of authority in the *Lectures on the Prophetical Office* of the church, why did Newman then turn to justification? He gives us part of the reason in the advertisement to the first edition of the lectures; "It was brought home to the writer from various quarters, that a

10. Newman, *Lectures on the Prophetical Office of the Church*, 20.
11. Newman, *Lectures on the Prophetical Office of the Church*, 154f.
12. See Brilioth, "The Static View of the Church" in *The Anglican Revival*, 180–210.
13. Newman, *Lectures on the Prophetical Office of the Church*, 63.

prejudice existed in many serious minds against certain essential Christian truths, such as Baptismal Regeneration and the Apostolical Ministry..."[14] These doctrines, he argues, were being viewed with suspicion "in consequence of a belief that they fostered notions of human merit, were dangerous to the inward life of religion, and incompatible with the doctrine of justifying faith, nay, with express statements on the subject in our Formularies..."[15] Pusey had handled the question of baptismal regeneration, the question of the apostolic ministry was the subject of the first *Tract for the Times*, and continued into the *Lectures on the Prophetical Office of the Church*. Justification, given Pusey's work, seemed the next logical topic. Later, however, Pusey was to argue about the genesis of the lectures on justification. After the publication of Pusey's famous letter to the Bishop of Oxford, Newman wrote to him on August 4, 1840: "I have no remark to make on your preface of consequence, except to thank you for the extreme trouble you have taken with me... And my lectures were not suggested to me by any one, except the clamour of the subject."[16] Pusey disagreed. In a letter a week later, he wrote back to Newman, "Indeed you did write your 'lectures on Justification' at my suggestion, though you of course felt the difficulties too. It was at my request that you set yourself to remove them."[17]

Whether Newman or Pusey recalled the situation correctly we will never know, but Newman tended to follow Pusey's lead in weighty matters. This point is more obvious in the following quotation where we see Newman taking the same course in his *Lectures on the Doctrine of Justification* that Pusey had taken in *Tract Sixty-seven*:

> These considerations have led the writer on, first to deliver, then to publish, the following Lectures, in the hope that he might be thereby offering suggestions towards a work, which must be uppermost in the mind of every true son of the English Church at this day,—the consolidation of a theological system, which, built upon those formularies which were framed in the 16th century, and to which all Clergymen are bound, may tend to inform, persuade, and absorb into itself religious minds, which hitherto have fancied that, on the peculiar Protestant questions they were seriously opposed to one another.[18]

---

14. Newman, *Lectures on the Doctrine of Justification*, v, 14.
15. Newman, *Lectures on the Doctrine of Justification*, v, 14.
16. Liddon, *Life of Edward Bouverie Pusey*, II, 79f.
17. Liddon, *Life of Edward Bouverie Pusey*, II, 80.
18. Newman, *Lectures on Justification*, vi.

The suggestion to which Newman refers is that we must return to scripture and the church fathers to find the basis for a consolidated theological system. This, of course, was precisely Pusey's method.

The Heart of the Matter

Newman's literary ability has long been admired by students of nineteenth-century England. What too often has escaped notice was his ability to cut to the heart of an issue. This latter ability he exercised at the beginning of the third lecture on justification:

> Enough has now been said to make it appear that the controversy concerning Justification, agitated in these last centuries, mainly turns upon this question, whether Christians are or are not justified by observance of the Moral Law . . . That, in our natural state, and by our own strength, we are not and cannot be justified, is admitted on all hands, . . . to deny it is the heresy of Pelagius. But it is a distinct question altogether, whether with the presence of God the Holy Ghost we can obey unto justification . . .[19]

Here Newman was putting the moral side of the question. Does man cooperate in justification? Newman would answer yes, so long as we recognize the prior existence of righteousness in the individual, a righteousness which is God's work. In truth, Newman was caught in the same dilemma as Augustine had been when he wrote:

> . . . we are assured that human righteousness itself, though not arising independently of man's will, is yet to be ascribed to the operation of God. We cannot deny the possibility of its perfection, just because all things are possible for God—both that he does by his own will alone, and what he had ordained to be accomplished by himself with the cooperation of the wills of his creatures.[20]

If God first makes us righteous, then the possibility exists that we may cooperate in our justification.

Where Augustine had been writing against a single enemy, the Pelagians, Newman was trying to steer a course between two conflicting points of view. The Lutheran view, which he regarded as an outright error, stated that our nature had been so wholly corrupted that even with

---

19. Newman, *Lectures on Justification*, 62.
20. Augustine, *De Spiritu et Littera*, 7.

God's presence we could not obey the moral law. The overzealous Roman Catholic view, which Newman regarded as less of a total error and more of a perversion of the truth, made spiritual renewal the "one and only true description of justification."[21]

The difficult nature of Newman's task can be seen in the two theses that he establishes for proof. Stated briefly these two theses are: 1) that justification and sanctification are substantially the same, and 2) that justification follows upon sanctification. The first thesis had already been advanced by Pusey. The second thesis was commended to Newman by reading Bishop Bull. Bull, commenting on 1 Peter 1:2, had written, "Justification is certainly subsequent to sanctification, at least the first and yet imperfect sanctification . . . First comes the sanctification of the Spirit to obedience; then follows the sprinkling of the blood of Christ, i.e. to justification."[22] As we shall see, these two theses are interwoven throughout Newman's description of justification.

In beginning to define the term "justification," Newman labours to point out that "to justify" means "to count righteous." However, he goes on to state emphatically that counting righteous includes within itself the notion of making righteous: "the sense of the term is 'counting righteous,'" and the nature of the thing denoted by it is making righteous.[23] Thus, there is an abstract sense to justification that means "counting," but there is a deeper, concrete sense which is more adequately spoken of as "making" righteous. If one employs the narrow sense of the term "justification," then it is surely a declaration, and is distinguishable from any act which makes a person righteous. Logically, therefore, justification is the antecedent or efficient cause of renewal. This means that it is legitimate to speak of justification as accomplished through imputation. It is an outside declaration about our past, a declaration which removes accusations concerning that past. In this sense justification is a juridical act. "Justification then," Newman wrote, "is the 'Voice of the Lord' designating us what we are not at the time that it designates us; designating us

---

21. Newman, *Lectures on Justification*, 31. Alister McGrath points out the weakness of the juxtaposition that Newman constructs. He is especially critical of Newman's interpretation of Luther (see his comments on Galatians) and of Newman's ignoring the strength of the Calvinist position (which he sees as much closer to Newman's ideal). Many over the years have noted Newman's seeming reliance on later German Pietism as his way into Luther. McGrath also notes Newman's possible misinterpretation of the Tridentine decisions as creating a single understanding rather than a "range" of interpretations. See McGrath, *Iustitia Dei*, vol 2, 121–34.

22. Bull, *Harmonia Apostolica*, 14.

23. Newman, *Lectures on Justification*, 65. Later in this chapter it will be seen that Newman's own use of "thing" to describe grace should not be interpreted too literally at this early stage of the lectures.

what we then begin to be."[24] Justification is not the gift itself, but the declaration that the gift is being given. It is a statement of pardon. It is a statement of pardon which prepares us for holiness. All of this is encompassed by the logical and abstract sense of justification.

It was precisely over the question of our being prepared for holiness (and subsequently being made holy) by God that Newman took most violent objection to the Lutheran position as he understood it. Not only did he see the Lutheran definition of justification by faith as essentially defective, he saw in it the worst possible contradiction. Luther, he says, denies that we can ever be perfected in holiness; our corruption runs too deep. In a rather lengthy attack on this position Newman not only refutes Luther's position, but shows the awakening awareness of the medieval tradition that was to grip Wilberforce a decade later. Newman seems to borrow directly from St. Thomas's *Summa Theologiae*, 1a 2ae, 110, 1,[25] when he writes:

> our justification is not a mere declaration of a past fact, or a testimony to what is present, or an announcement of what is to come,—much less, as those who follow Luther say, a declaration of what neither has been, is, or will ever be,—but it is the *cause* of that being which before was and henceforth is. Strange it is, but such is the opinion of one of the two schools of divinity which have all along been mentioned, that God's calling us righteous implies, not only that we have not been, but that we never shall be, righteous. Surely it is a strange paradox to say that a thing is not because He says it is; that the solemn averment of the Living and True God is inconsistent with the thing averred; that His accepting our obedience is a bar to His making it acceptable, and that the glory of His pronouncing us righteous lies in His leaving us unrighteous.[26]

Newman insists upon the integrity of God's pronouncements, but he goes beyond that in insisting on the indissoluble link between pronouncement and activity, between saying something is so and making it so. God's word accomplishes what it declares. This accomplishment is worked out

---

24. Newman, *Lectures on Justification*, 66f.

25. "Therefore it is not just the forgiveness of sins alone which belongs to grace, but many other gifts of God as well. And even the forgiveness of sins does not take place without some divinely caused effect in us . . ."

26. Newman, *Lectures on Justification*, 78. In this manner of savaging his opponents, Newman remained consistent. Eamon Duffy recounts Newman's opposition to the Ultramontanes love of dogmatic assertions which Newman describes as *the act of a man who will believe anything because he believes nothing, and is ready to profess whatever his ecclesiastical, that is his political, party requires of him.* Duffy, *John Henry Newman*, 2.

in the arena to which the declaration speaks. Hence, justification consists of imputation, but not imputation alone. If imputation was the only factor involved in justification, then justification would be a one-sided affair in which God's word would cause no corresponding change in the arena (man) to which it was directed. "On the whole, then, from what has been said," Newman writes, "it appears that justification is an announcement or *fiat* from Almighty God . . . that it *declares* the soul righteous, and in that declaration, on the one hand, conveys *pardon* for its past sins, and on the other *makes* it actually *righteous*."[27] God's operation in justification is two-fold, both *counting* and *making* us righteous.[28] Hence, for purposes of definition, Newman has subsumed sanctification under justification while still admitting that justification, in its most limited sense, is the declaration of forgiveness, and sanctification, in its most limited sense, is the act of making us righteous. By subsuming sanctification under justification he makes the two terms almost synonymous.

This rather novel method of definition led to many confusions by those who read Newman. Newman's readers were still inclined to think in sequential terms about justification and sanctification, and Newman's desire to conform to Bishop Bull (giving prior position to sanctification), plus his desire to give logical priority to justification, did not aid his readers' understanding. Bishop Sumner of Chester warned his clergy to remember, "It is true, that, being thus accepted with God, and endued with his Spirit, man becomes a new creature. But he is not accepted with God because he is a new creature, but because Christ has made atonement for the wrath which in his old nature he had incurred."[29] Sumner went on to charge his clergy to remember, as Hooker had written, "The righteousness whereby we are sanctified is inherent, but not perfect. The righteousness whereby we are justified is perfect, but not inherent."[30] In Switzerland H. Merle-d'Aubigne was telling his theological students, "Among us justification is the cause, and sanctification is the effect. Among those doctors [the Tractarians], on the contrary, sanctification is the cause, and justification is the effect."[31]

27. Newman, *Lectures on Justification*, 83.

28. Newman understands this to be the real sense of the eleventh and thirteenth *Articles of Religion*.

29. Sumner, "Charge to the Clergy of the Diocese of Chester," in *The Judgement of the Bishops upon Tractarian Theology*, 357f.

30. Sumner, "Charge to the Clergy of the Diocese of Chester," in *The Judgement of the Bishops upon Tractarian Theology*, 358.

31. Quoted by Y. Brilioth in *The Anglican Revival*, 294, footnote 1. The text is from H. Merle-d'Aubigné, *Geneve et Oxford*, 29: "chez-nous la justification est la cause, et la sanctification est l'effet. Chez ces docteurs, au contraire, la sanctification est la cause, et

The confusion was understandable, but avoidable. The seeming contradiction was easily found, and as easily attacked. Had a deeper reading of Newman prevailed, however, it would have been more obvious that he was seeking a synthetic view in which justification and sanctification were removed from the restrictions of logical and durational priorities.

In expanding on the fullest meaning of justification, Newman goes on to say that since the proper work of justification is renewal, it stands to reason that justification and righteousness are almost identical in meaning. Justification makes us truly just, hence it renews us:

> The justifying Word, then, conveys the Spirit, and the Spirit makes our works "pleasing" and "acceptable" to God, and acceptableness is righteousness; so that the justified are just, really just, in degree indeed more or less, but really so far as this,—that their obedience has in it a gracious quality which the obedience of unregenerate man has not.[32]

Justification, therefore, is not only a principle of the simple negation of sin; it is that, but much more. Justification, for Newman, becomes the positive principle of our acceptableness to God.

Acceptableness, love, spiritual renewal, these are notions that have usually found their home in a doctrine of sanctification rather than justification. By placing them in justification Newman took another step in equating justification and sanctification. Justification, Newman argued, makes us righteous, and because it does so we have within us the power of grace whereby we may please God in what we do. Justification works in us as well as outside us. Justification changes our hearts, it imparts to us an active righteousness which allows us to cooperate with God. Justification and sanctification, essentially the same quality, are the grace of the gospel. This is the grace which "unfetters the will . . . and restores to us the faculty of accepting or rejecting that grace itself. It enables us to obey, not as instruments merely, but as free agents, who, while they obey, are not constrained to obey, except that they choose to obey . . ."[33] Obedience, therefore, which might more often have been spoken of as a part of sanctification, and subsequent to justification, now lies at the heart of justification. Newman writes:

> For these reasons, then, though justification properly means an act external to us, it may be said to consist in evangelical obedience; first, because obedience is one with God's imputation by

---

la justification est l'effet."

32. Newman, *Lectures on Justification*, 91.
33. Newman, *Lectures on Justification*, 94.

association; next, because they are one in fact, since He implants in part within us the very thing which in its fullness he imputes to us; and, lastly, because our concurrence in being justified is a necessary condition of His justifying.[34]

This constitutes the two-fold operation of grace in the life of the individual. A person must cooperate, must freely accept what God offers. God will not give what a person will not accept. By grace that person is prepared for the gift of justification. This preparation to accept justification is the renewal of the heart and will of humans. This, of course, is sanctification. Therefore, in the concrete event of total spiritual renewal, sanctification precedes justification, but justification is the all-encompassing term for everything which takes place.

Newman recognized the danger in his position. He knew that some might interpret this as a doctrine of justification by obedience. Thus, he cautioned his readers to remember that justification is primarily an act of God, a free gift. On man's side justification is a passive quality of righteousness which God himself prepares each to receive. The active agency in justification belongs to God alone; the passive, receptive agency belongs to the person who is made righteous by God's gift. The whole truth of the doctrine of justification, Newman believes, is to be found in a constant awareness of both elements: God's activity and man's receptivity of righteousness. Here, he argues, one finds the basic errors of Protestants and Roman Catholics.

The Protestants place too much emphasis on God's activity, and by so doing disregard the fact that Christ must be in us as well as have his merits imputed to us. The Roman Catholics, on the other hand, err in placing too great a reliance on the passive reception of holiness. This can lead to a notion of justification by obedience; hence, the heresy of Pelagius. In a sermon Newman commented on these errors and their common result:

> I have said that there are two opposite errors: one, the holding that salvation is not of God; the other, that it is not in ourselves. Now it is remarkable that the maintainers of both the one and the other error whatever their differences in other respects, agree in this,—in depriving a Christian life of its mysteriousness.[35]

By now Newman has introduced some of his most important distinctions, chiefly the active-passive distinction. He has introduced the notion of obedience, a central notion in Tractarian theology and piety; and, he

---

34. Newman, *Lectures on Justification*, 95.

35. Newman, "Righteousness Not of Us, but in Us" in *Parochial and Plain Sermons*, V, 140f.

has given immense breadth to the meaning of justification. By justification Newman would have us understand all of God's activity in bringing a person from a state of sin to a state of righteousness; so, too, he would have us understand that justification includes a human's faithful response to the divine activity of grace. God's declaration of our righteousness makes us righteous. God's speaking is his doing, scripture will not have them separated. In a fine synopsis of his view Newman writes:

> In like manner it seems a true representation of the Scripture statements on the subject, to say, that He does not make us righteous, but He *calls* us righteous, and we are forthwith *made* righteous. But, if so, justification, which in its full meaning is the whole great appointment of God from beginning to end, may be viewed on its two sides,—active and passive, in its beginning and its completion, in what God does, and what man receives; and while in its passive sense man is made righteous, in its active, God calls or declares. That is, the word will rightly stand either for imputation or for sanctification, according to the grammatical use of it. Thus divines, who in the main agree in what the great mercy of God is *as a whole*, may differ as to what should be called justification . . . One party, then, in the controversy consider it to be a mere acceptance, the other to be mainly renewal. The one consider it in its effects, the other in its primary idea. St. Austin, that is, *explains* it, and Protestants *define* it. The latter describe it theoretically, the former practically. The Protestant sense is more close upon the word, the ancient use more close upon the thing. A man, for instance, who describes bread as "the staff of life," need not disagree with another who defined it only chemically or logically, but he would be his inferior in philosophy and his superior in real knowledge.[36]

At first the passive side of justification appears only as acceptance, for at first justification is known only in the moment of forgiveness. As the life of obedience goes on, however, justification comes to be known more as renewal, sanctification, Christ fulfilling the law not only for us but in us. This is the real, practical knowledge for which Newman claims superiority. Real knowledge sees justification in the longer perspective of an active Christian life, the obedient life of those in whom Christ dwells. Therefore, to define justification is of less importance than to explain and describe it. A definition is an arid, static thing; an explanation, however, gives to the event an ongoing vitality built upon the real knowledge of the continual presence of the event in the life of the believer.

36. Newman, *Lectures on Justification*, 97f.

Righteousness as Union

In justification God both declares and makes a person righteous, but that says little about the state of righteousness. What does it mean to say a person is righteous? Newman puts the question this way:

> But the question is this, what is *that* which is *named* righteousness? what is that object or thing, what is it in a man, which God seeing there, therefore calls him righteous? what is the state in which a justified person is, or that which constitutes him righteous in God's sight?[37]

It cannot be something which is either a cause or a fruit of righteousness. It must be something that is in a righteous person that makes that person different than before declared and made righteous.

What Newman sought was a radical answer which cut behind the notion that our righteousness consists of either Christ's merits imputed to us or a principle implanted within us. Neither of these propositions cut deeply enough into the issue for Newman. The former begged the question of what it is *in a person* that makes her or him acceptable to God; the latter begged the question of the relationship between the renovating principle and God's freely given grace. The latter question was more difficult, for it meant that the idea of grace as a principle had to be given up. Righteousness could be neither a principle nor a thing; the answer had to be found in a more fundamental assertion.

Our righteousness is to be found in our union with Christ. It is Christ's presence in us that makes us righteous. The gift of righteousness is the gift of the presence of Christ. The way to righteousness is baptism; this Pusey had demonstrated to Newman's satisfaction. Newman sought to describe the state itself, what it is that we have entered through baptism. The extensive nature of union with Christ is well-summarized in this short homiletical passage:

> Christ himself vouchsafes to repeat in each of us in figure and mystery all that He did and suffered in the flesh. He is formed in us, born in us, suffers in us, rises again in us, lives in us; and this not by a succession of events, but all at once: for He comes to us as a Spirit, all dying, all rising again, all living. We are ever receiving our birth, our justification, our renewal, ever dying to sin, ever rising to righteousness. His whole economy in all its parts is ever in us all at once; and this divine presence constitutes

---

37. Newman, *Lectures on Justification*, 131.

the title of each of us to heaven; this is what He will acknowledge and accept at the last day.[38]

The typology of the life of Christ is extended to every regenerate person; but more than typology is extended. Christ really dwells in each person, and what makes a person acceptable to God is the presence of the whole Christ within that person. Every part of the economy of salvation is always present in the regenerate, righteous person.

Righteousness, therefore, cannot consist of faith, because faith must be made acceptable; nor can righteousness consist of an imparted quality in the soul, for the quality must also be made acceptable. These two errors (which Newman attributes to the Lutherans and Roman Catholics respectively) do have a point of convergence. Both presuppose a divine inward presence, the presence of the Spirit. It is the Spirit of Christ which gives to us both faith and renewal. The Spirit accomplishes this not by acting on us, but by operating within us. The Spirit both makes us righteous and is our righteousness. Faith and renewal are possible because of the prior indwelling of the Spirit.

To emphasize that righteousness is something which we possess and not a mere quality of mind, Newman proceeds to speak of the nature of a gift. He finds (especially in Romans 5:17)[39] that righteousness must be understood to be a gift freely given. Now a gift is something which, after it is given, is possessed by the recipient. Hence, the gift of righteousness confers something identifiable, it cannot simply be an act of the divine intellect counting us as forgiven. On Romans 5:17 Newman writes, "The word *gift* here used certainly must mean a thing given; implying that the righteousness of justification, whatever it turn out to be, is a real and definite something in a person, implanted in him, like a talent or power, and not merely an act of the Divine Mind externally to him, as the forgiveness of sins may be."[40] In fact, Newman argues, all the promised gifts of the gospel find their root in the gift of righteousness. Every gift given after the justifying gift of righteousness is a representation of justification.

---

38. Newman, "Righteousness Not of Us, but in Us" in *Parochial and Plain Sermons*, V, 139f.

39. Newman's use of scripture was typical of The Oxford Movement writers. He would amass great amounts of scriptural evidence, and from that he would try to form a comprehensive view of scriptural doctrine. Like Pusey he considered that the Protestant tradition had put far too much emphasis on certain Pauline texts, ignoring the general "sense" of scripture. Of course, scripture was read quite literally, but its interpretation was always tempered by the judgements of the early church. The importance of this is nicely outlined in Nockles, *Oxford Movement in Context*, 259f. where the intricacy of the debate becomes obvious.

40. Newman, *Lectures on Justification*, 140.

The gift of righteousness comes from outside us. We cannot know it in the sense that we know its fruits, faith, renewal, and obedience. It only admits of being accepted or rejected. Justification, as Newman openly admits, is an application of Christ's merits; but, relating this to the gift of righteousness, the application must be seen as the imparting of an inward gift. No longer is justification to be viewed as an essentially external act. With this Newman has arrived at the core of his concern:

> Now, turning to the gospel we shall find that such a gift is actually promised to us by our Lord; a gift which must of necessity be at once our justification and our sanctification, for it is nothing short of the indwelling in us of God the Father and the Word Incarnate through the Holy Ghost. If this be so, we have found what we sought: *This* is to be justified, to receive the Divine Presence within us, and be made a Temple of the Holy Ghost.[41]

Christ in us, for Newman as for Pusey, is the ultimate gift. The righteousness we have is ours because God literally dwells in us.

Newman concludes that the gift of righteousness is the indwelling of the Trinity, and specifically the indwelling of Christ through the Spirit. This is the distinctive grace of the gospel. Righteousness, then, can be said to be an inward gift which conveys not only the virtue of the atonement, but the whole of Christ's salvific life. Anything which more commonly was spoken of as a fruit of justification should be spoken of as a fruit or blessing of the divine indwelling:

> For instance, is justification *remission of sins*? The Gift of the Spirit conveys it, as is evident from the Scripture doctrine about Baptism: "One Baptism for the remission of sins." Is justification *adoption* into the family of God? In like manner the Spirit is expressly called the Spirit of adoption, "the Spirit whereby we cry Abba, Father." Is justification *reconciliation* with God? St. Paul says, "Jesus Christ is in you, unless ye be reprobates." Is justification *life*? The same Apostle says, "Christ liveth in me." Is justification given to *faith*? It is his prayer "that Christ may dwell in" Christian "hearts by faith." Does justification lead to holy *obedience*? Our Lord assures us that "he that abideth in Him and He in me, the same bringeth forth much fruit" . . . Christ then is our Righteousness by dwelling in us by the Spirit: He justifies

---

41. The extent to which Newman enters the larger nature-supernature issue at this point is not easily determined. He shows little interest in the question *per se*. His concern is more with establishing that God dwells in everything by virtue of being creator, but in the righteous in a special sense by way of his gracious presence. He styles this as mystical union, and is prepared to defend it as the central promise of the gospel.

us by entering into us, He continues to justify us by remaining in us. *This* is really and truly our justification, not faith, not holiness, not (much less) a mere imputation; but through God's mercy, the very Presence of Christ.[42]

From this it can be said that for Newman, as for the Tractarians generally, it is not correct to speak of a theology built upon the idea of growth in holiness. Perseverance through obedience is the moral key to living the Christian life; one does not grow holier, for complete sanctity is given in justification; put differently, one is, or is not, a temple of the Spirit. Thus, in sacramental theology, to say that there are two sacraments *generally* necessary for salvation means that in baptism we are made holy, and in the eucharist this holiness is continued in us. Baptism and the eucharist constitute the only two sacraments which are justifying, and therefore necessary for salvation. Both baptism and the eucharist have the one gift of righteousness at their core; they pertain to the presence of the Spirit in us.

Newman's notion of the gift of righteousness raises many intriguing questions, none more so than the question of the precise nature of the imparted gift. Brilioth was wont to speak of this notion of grace as "quasi-physical." Newman never addressed his whole attention to the question, but some features of it deserve our attention.

A first examination of Newman reveals a curious inconsistency. On the one hand, Newman speaks of the gift of the Spirit more as a talent or faculty; yet, on the other hand, he seems to insist on a somewhat tangible nature for the gift. Newman's insistence on this latter point seems directed against the idea that grace is simply a divine intellectual activity in which no real interior change takes place in humanity. Sins are forgiven, but the sinner remains as she or he was before justification.

The overall examination of Newman indicates that grace is not a palpable thing; rather it is more akin to a quality. The extent to which Newman, in this distinction, is consciously indebted to the Scholastic tradition is unanswerable; yet, as Rondet has pointed out, "in the thirteenth century, as St. Thomas explicitly tells us, the word grace was reserved for habitual grace. Justification, once seen as a psychological process, now became a metaphysical reality."[43] Nothing in Newman would indicate an overt debt to the Scholastic tradition. Given the general state of Thomist studies in the early nineteenth century it is unlikely that Newman could have been considered a student of the Angelic Doctor; but, it is obvious that Newman was attempting to give grace a reality that was more metaphysical

---

42. Newman, *Lectures on Justification*, 150.
43. Rondet, *The Grace of Christ*, 202f.

than quasi-physical. Grace, in Newman, though not a thing, is certainly more than a simple movement of one intellect responding to the needs of another intellect.

In defense of Brilioth's interpretation, however, it must be admitted that Newman is not completely clear. In the mid-1960s, Fr. Dessain unearthed an unpublished letter from Newman to Samuel Wilberforce in which Newman was attempting to clarify his position. Writing on the indwelling of the Spirit, he stated that it is "the great gift of grace, marvellous beyond words, exceeding in bounty, freely given to those whom God has chosen in Christ and brings to baptism."[44] So far that description is typical Newman; but the next sentences of the letter throw some confusion into the matter. Continuing to describe the work of the Spirit, Newman tells Wilberforce: "It is the indwelling of the Holy Spirit in the soul as in a Temple—a Spirit of adoption. In the first place it has (so to say) a physical, or (as we term it) a mystical influence on the soul, uniting it to Christ—it distinguishes the Christian from all unregenerate men."[45]

Is Newman really equating physical and mystical? It would be unfair to give an unqualified affirmative answer to this question. Taken in isolation, and as authoritative, the quotation from the letter to Wilberforce would make the answer an unequivocal yes, but that letter, coming two years before Newman began work on his lectures on justification, can hardly be the final authority. While the letter to Wilberforce lends some weight to Brilioth's interpretation, Newman's true sense is more adequately found in his notion of mystical indwelling; the use of physical influence is more likely an analogy drawn from the presence of the Spirit in the soul as in a temple.

This explanation seems more likely if we turn to another brief excerpt from Newman. In *Tract Eighty-two*, which is actually a letter addressed to an unnamed magazine which had been highly critical of Pusey's tracts on baptism, Newman defends Pusey's statement that the patriarchs had been sanctified but not regenerated. Replying to the editors of the magazine Newman writes:

> The Catholic Church has ever given to Noah, Abraham, and Moses, all that the present age gives to Christians. You cannot mention the grace, in kind or degree, which you ascribe to the Christian, which Dr. Pusey will not ascribe to Abraham; except, perhaps, the intimate knowledge of the details of Christian

---

44. Dessain, "The Biblical Basis of Newman's Ecumenical Theology" in *The Rediscovery of Newman*, 102.

45. Dessain, "The Biblical Basis of Newman's Ecumenical Theology" in *The Rediscovery of Newman*, 102.

doctrine. But he considers that Christians have a something beyond this, even a portion of that heaven brought down to earth, which will be forever in heaven the portion of Abraham and all saints in its fulness ... That special gift of grace, called "the glory of God," is as unknown to the so-called religious world as to the "natural man." The Catholic Religion teaches, that, when grace takes up its abode in us, we have so super abounding and awful a grace tabernacled in us, that no other words describe it more nearly than to call it an Angel's nature.[46]

The very notion of tabernacling gives evidence of Newman's use of physical analogies to express non-physical concepts. What is present in the soul is not a thing with which we are united, nor is the uniting itself capable of reification: the presence is that of grace, the activity of holiness making us holy through its continuing presence. Since the primary gift of righteousness is the indwelling of the Spirit, the transition from physical analogy to non-physical reality is consistent with Newman's theology of justification.

Given Newman's extended use of physical analogies it is possible to see how Brilioth could write in a summary of his own chapter on the Tractarian doctrine of justification, "It has been the object of the last chapter to show how the way to the land of purely mystical communion with God is laid down in the first instance, when the idea of grace as quasi-physical or substantial prevails over the purely personal idea, when the thought of infused grace drives out the imputed."[47] Dessain, however, was probably closer to the tradition that Newman was striving to revive when he spoke of Newman's concept of personal grace. Dessain's comments are opposed to Brilioth's, but strike closer to the mark, when he argues that Newman's grasp of the doctrine of the indwelling of God in the soul was truly unique in Western theology. Concluding that idea Dessain writes, "Grace, in Scripture, is the favour, the generous kindness of God. This is primarily and essentially *personal*. God

---

46. *Tract Eighty-two: Letter to a Magazine on the subject of Dr. Pusey's Tract on Baptism*, xv.

47. Brilioth, *The Anglican Revival*, 296. In fairness to Brilioth it should be noted that he is writing from a viewpoint which may not be as applicable to the Anglicanism of the Tractarians as he may have thought. The question of the quasi-physical nature of grace is one which rightfully belongs to the late medieval, Reformation, and Lutheran scholastic ages. Because Newman used Johann Gerhard as his main interpreter of the Lutheran tradition, it may well be that Brilioth was more familiar with the intricacies of Lutheran interpretation on the question of the nature of grace than was Newman. Newman shows no concern for understanding Gerhard, and simply accepts him as an authority, nor does he show any interest in the development of the doctrine of grace in the Ockhamist tradition.

takes possession of man and is present in him."[48] This personal presence of God in man is too easily identified as quasi-physical or substantial (an equation of Brilioth's that this writer finds less than adequate), when, in fact, it has more in common with an activity. In Newman, the presence of God in the soul is not a thing, or even a thing-like principle, it is an active force, power, and life which transfigures the believer and makes that believer new, which imparts (for this is the term Newman always prefers) that special grace which is holiness, the very glory of God.

With this understanding of the nature of grace and the gift of righteousness it becomes easier to understand what was lost at the fall. In his lecture on the "Characteristics of the Gift of Righteousness," Newman takes up the question of what it means to be "clothed with righteousness." He states, "Christ then clothes us in God's sight with something over and above nature, which Adam forfeited."[49] Adam had forfeited his supernatural endowment, the inward presence of the Spirit, which he had possessed at no price:

> Adam might probably have matured in holiness, had he remained in his first state, without experience of evil, whether pain or error; for he had that within him which was to him more than all the habits which trial and discipline painfully form in us. Unless it be presumptuous to say it, grace was to him instead of a habit; grace was his clothing within and without. Grace dispensed with efforts towards holiness, for holiness lived in him. We do not know what we mean by a habit, except as a state or quality of mind *under* which we act in this or that particular way; it is a permanent power in the mind; and what is grace but this? . . . Not till he fell, did he lose that supernatural endowment, which raised him into a state above himself, and made him in a certain sense more than man, and what the Angels are, or Saints hereafter. This robe of innocence and sanctity he lost when he fell; he knew and confessed that he had lost it; but while he possessed it, he was sinless and perfect, and acceptable to God though he had gone through nothing painful to obtain it.[50]

---

48. Dessain, "The Biblical Basis of Newman's Ecumenical Theology" in *The Rediscovery of Newman*, 102. However, as previously argued in the chapter on Pusey, it should be reiterated that Pusey's notion of divine indwelling, borrowing heavily from Greogry of Nazianzus, was the first profound Tractarian expression of what Dessain here credits to Newman.

49. Newman, *Lectures on Justification*, 158.

50. Newman, "The State of Innocence," in *Parochial and Plain Sermons*, V, 108f.

Hence, what Adam lost when he fell from innocence we can have only as a habit; this is nothing other than the habitual indwelling of the Spirit by which we are justified, i.e., righteousness. Adam's loss of a supernatural endowment is the significant point, for it demonstrates that man is not savable except through the indwelling presence of the Spirit.

The question must then arise, does Christ restore more than Adam lost? At the level of habitual grace it would seem not. What Adam lost was his righteous clothing, and what Christ brings to us through his indwelling is that righteous clothing. Being clothed with righteousness we are made acceptable in God's eyes. God looks upon redeemed humanity and sees not the corrupt human nature of persons, but Christ in them. Christ's presence makes them acceptable and enables God to count them righteous. Thus, the change effected is a real, distinctive change that transforms humanity. This transformation is especially evident in human's moral nature:

> Since, then, the gift of righteousness is a supernatural presence in our moral nature, distinct from it, yet indwelling in it and changing it, it is not wonderful that the change itself should sometimes be spoken of in Scripture as the gift or included in the gift. Thus, for instance, the garment of salvation put on us, is such as to cleave to us, and to tend to become part of us; what was at first a covering merely, becomes our very flesh. The glory of the Divine Nature, of which St. Peter says we are partakers, first hides our deformity, then removes it.[51]

The covering becomes our flesh, the garment becomes a part of us. The two-sided nature of the gift of Christ's presence, what it is as given and what it is as received, makes both the distinction between justification and sanctification, and their sameness, understandable. "In like manner the gift of righteousness, which is our justification as given, is our renewal as received."[52] Christ's presence within us cannot be separated from the renewal which it works. The analogy of clothing becoming flesh is a method whereby we can understand the movement from imputed to imparted righteousness. Humanity cannot be justified unless it is also renewed. To emphasize this Newman speaks of the cross as set up within each justified person, "Justification is the setting up of the Cross within us . . . But how does this cross become ours? I repeat, by being given; and what is this giving, in other words, but our being marked with it?"[53]

---

51. Newman, *Lectures on Justification*, 170.
52. Newman, *Lectures on Justification*, 170.
53. Newman, *Lectures on Justification*, 173.

Being marked with the cross (an obvious reference to the instrumentality of baptism in justification) involves pain. We do not come to the new life by merely noting the pain which Christ endured, we must enter into that pain. Suffering is an integral part of our sanctification. Having the cross set up within us, we suffer a separation from the world, from our former life, that inflicts not only the pain of separation itself, but knowledge of our former sinfulness as well.

Newman makes the sense of pain cut deeper. The entrance of the redeeming presence into the soul pervades the being of the redeemed. Newman despised the notion that by gazing upon the cross and contemplating it a person could apprehend the saving power of the atonement. Our identification with the atonement must go much deeper:

> Men say that faith is an apprehending and applying; faith cannot really apply the Atonement; man cannot make the Saviour of the world his own; the Cross must be brought home to us, not in word, but in power, and this is the work of the Spirit. This is justification; but when imparted to the soul, it draws blood, it heals, it purifies, it glorifies.[54]

Such is our introduction to the relationship between justification and the atonement.

Righteousness: A Gift

Anglican theology of the late nineteenth century was often criticized for too great an emphasis on the incarnation, thereby deprecating the atonement. Some have read this criticism back into the Tractarian era, but it does not apply. Newman, when speaking of the atonement, could write, "the great and awful doctrine of the Cross of Christ . . . may fitly be called, in the language of figure, the heart of religion . . . the sacred doctrine of Christ's Atoning Sacrifice is the vital principle on which the Christian lives, and without which Christianity is not."[55]

Newman's use of the imagery of the cross is not only graphic, but well illustrates the centrality of the atoning death:

> Now I bid you consider that that Face, so ruthlessly smitten, was the Face of God Himself; the Brows bloody with the thorns, the sacred Body exposed to view and lacerated with the scourge,

---

54. Newman, *Lectures on Justification*, 175.

55. Newman, "The Cross of Christ and the Measure of the World" in *Parochial and Plain Sermons*, VI, 74.

the Hands nailed to the Cross, and, afterwards, the Side pierced with the Spear; it was the Blood, and the sacred Flesh, and the Hands, and the Temples, and the Side, and the Feet of God Himself, which the frenzied multitude then gazed upon.[56]

Indeed, for Newman, the centrality of the atonement was paramount. Without the atonement there was no justification, no salvation. The crucifixion reordered our perception of the world, giving to everything its right value: "It is the death of the Eternal Word of God made flesh, which is our great lesson how to speak and how to think of this world. His cross has put its due value upon, everything which we see . . ."[57] The atonement not only interprets existence for Christians, it fosters their activities as well, it is the benchmark of Christian living: "the sacred doctrine of the Atoning sacrifice is not to be talked of, but to be lived upon."[58]

Newman's objection to the Evangelical insistence upon a strong doctrine of the atonement was that they held it in isolation, setting it up as the only truly significant Christian doctrine. For Newman the atonement was one part of the greater mystery of Christ's salvific life. The crucifixion is the great public event declaring God's power and will in the sinful world; but it cannot be understood outside of the context of the resurrection, for in the resurrection the power of the atonement is individualized.

In his discussion of the gift of righteousness Newman held that there were two titles applied to the gift, power and glory. It is in the title of glory that we come to see the relationship with the resurrection. God's glory is intimately connected with his presence. The glory which Christ has, he gives to his faithful people. As Newman speaks of this he asks:

> What is this glory which has passed from Christ to us? It is some high gift which admits of being transferred, as is evident. What it was in Christ, we see in some degree by the following words of St. Paul:—"Like as Christ was raised up from the dead by *the glory of the Father*, even so we also should walk in newness of life." Whatever else it was, it appears hence that it was a presence or power which operated for the resurrection of His body. In this connection it may be well to direct attention to a passage which, otherwise, with our present notions, we should explain (as we should think) more naturally. Before our Lord

---

56. Newman, "The Incarnate Son, a Sufferer and Sacrifice" in *Parochial and Plain Sermons*, VI, 74.

57. Newman, "The Cross of Christ and the Measure of the World" in *Parochial and Plain Sermons*, VI, 84.

58. Newman, "The Cross of Christ and the Measure of the World" in *Parochial and Plain Sermons*, VI, 90.

raises Lazarus, he says to Martha, "Said I not unto thee, that if thou wouldest believe, thou shouldest see the *glory* of God?" What He *had* said before to her was simply, that He was the Resurrection and the Life.[59]

Standing as the general reconciliation of God and the world, the Cross is the power of forgiveness spreading itself through all creation; the resurrection, on the other hand, is that same power of God individualized in those who are brought to it. The individualized power of resurrection is transferred, given over, as the gift of righteousness is given. Put another way, the glory of God resides in a person when the gift is given, for the gift is Christ who is the glory of God.

Newman expands the place of the resurrection in the lecture entitled "Righteousness the Fruit of our Lord's Resurrection." The atonement, he notes, is a once for all public event which took place in the course of Christ's mission on earth; it was the one great public event in the economy of salvation. This public character separates the crucifixion from all other events in the economy of grace; all the other events have an element of hiddenness in them. The resurrection is a partially hidden event; it is, so to speak, Christ's own justification. Christ's resurrection takes place through the Spirit; this is the connection with justification. His justification, in which he is shown to be triumphant, blameless, the true Son of God, and our justification, in which we are made to be what Christ always was, are both effected through the Spirit. It is part of the mission of the Spirit to apply the public atonement to individuals. As central as the atonement is, it must be seen in the light of its individual application through the Spirit.

In this causal relationship between the resurrection and justification we see Newman wrestling with the same problem that confronted St. Thomas in the "Tertia Pars" of the *Summa Theologiae*. Can the resurrection properly be called the "cause" of our justification? St. Thomas had argued:

> Two things are implied in the soul's justification, the remission of sins and the newness of life which is the result of grace. In both cases the effect brought about by the power of God is said to be caused by Christ's death and resurrection. More specifically in the field of exemplar causality, the passion and death of Christ are properly the causes of the remission of our faults, for we die to sin. The resurrection, on the other hand, more properly causes the newness of life through grace or justice.[60]

---

59. Newman, *Lectures on Justification*, 164.
60. *Summa Theologiae*, IIIa, 56, 2 ad 4, 75.

Newman also saw the complex relations between atonement and resurrection with regard to our justification. The resurrection's application through the Spirit is the key to understanding the individual application of the economy of salvation. Commenting on this, Webb pointed out:

> The theory of Justification, then, favoured by Newman and the Tractarians, understands by the word less the imputation to us of the righteousness exhibited by Christ in his death than the impartation to the soul and infusion into it of the righteousness of Christ, processes which depend directly on the exaltation at the Resurrection of his humanity from the state of mortal weakness which, during his life on earth, he shared with all other individual men, to the state of immortal power, in which it is able to become the principle of spiritual life within those who are mystically united to him.[61]

The centrality of the resurrection as a cause of our justification is seen by Newman in much the same way in which St. Thomas had seen it (remembering that St. Thomas was employing the term justification in a much more limited sense). Does this indicate a medievalism in Newman as so many of his critics would charge? Probably not. Indeed, it is arguable that the distinction between atonement and resurrection in the causality of justification is both biblical and patristic; and further, that both writers are simply picking up on those traditions.

In support of this, one need only recall that St. Thomas wrote before the great debates on justification, when it became the topic which captivated theology, and that Newman was trying to cut behind those debates which he believed had destroyed a good deal of the biblical doctrine. Again, Webb has provided a good analysis: "The opponents of The Oxford Movement have often tended to see in it chiefly a return to medievalism, and that certain aspects and stages of it may be so described is not to be denied. But more characteristic is its return to a primitive consciousness of organic participation in the risen life of Christ . . ."[62]

Newman's view of the resurrection as the type of our justification is wholly consistent with his sense of the depth of mystery involved in salvation, and the role of faith in apprehending that mystery. The resurrection is a hidden event which requires faith for its apprehension. Yet, a bare faith (the faith of one not yet justified) cannot apprehend the mystery of the resurrection; only a faith already nurtured by the possession of righteousness can apprehend the resurrection. Faith does not give possession of the

---

61. Webb, *Religious Thought in The Oxford Movement*, 90.
62. Webb, *Religious Thought in The Oxford Movement*, 90f.

resurrection, of power and glory, that is conveyed in baptism; rather, faith gives the individual title to the justification which baptism conveys. True knowledge (a part of the gift of righteousness) is, therefore, not present in any faith that may precede justification. True knowledge comes with the indwelling of the Spirit, and it is this true knowledge which discloses the depths of the resurrection, and especially of the resurrection as it is applied to individuals through the Spirit.

Faith promotes the promise of justification, but it cannot fulfil that promise. The role of faith is not to justify, but to lead a person to the conviction that he will be justified. As Newman wrote concerning this, "Wishing will not serve instead of coming, and faith cannot serve in the place of baptism. None are justified but those who are grafted into the justified body; and faith is not an instrument of grafting, but a title to be grafted."[63] Thus, the relationship between faith and the resurrection can be defined this way: the resurrection, a hidden event, demands a response of faith, but faith must respond with the belief that the power of resurrection is beyond its grasp and lies wholly within the province of the resurrection's sacramental equivalent, baptism.

Newman is now able to move to the heart of justification by faith:

> If justification, or the imparting of righteousness, be a work of the Holy Ghost, a spiritual gift or presence in the heart, it is plain that faith, and faith alone, can discern it and prepare the mind for it, as the Spirit alone can give it. Faith is the correlative, the natural instrument of the things of the Spirit. While Christ was present in the flesh, He might be seen by the eye; but His more perfect and powerful presence, which we now enjoy, being invisible, can be discerned and used by faith only.[64]

The "perfect and powerful presence" is invisible of itself, and in us. Therefore, faith takes on the role of the eye of the mind through which we apprehend the presence and power of the invisible Spirit of Christ. Faith becomes an antecedent or secondary cause of our justification. It must be present, but, alone, it cannot cause us to be justified. Only the indwelling of Christ's Spirit can cause our justification.

In dealing with faith's role in apprehending the in visible, Newman is really attempting to show that the change from the visible to the invisible presence of Christ makes our justification possible. Christ's ubiquitous Spirit can now inhabit all the faithful, whereas his body could only be present to a very

---

63. Newman, "Faith the Title for Justification" in *Parochial and Plain Sermons*, VI, 170.

64. Newman, *Lectures on Justification*, 214f.

few. Newman finds this point most graphically portrayed in the narrative of Christ's ascension. The imagery of the ascending Christ and the descending Spirit makes sense of the movement of grace in our justification:

> This, I repeat, is our justification, our ascent through Christ to God, or God's descent through Christ to us; we may call it either of the two; we ascend into Him, He, descends into us; we are in Him, He in us; Christ being the One Mediator, the way, the truth, and the life, joining earth with heaven. And this is our true righteousness,—not the mere name of righteousness, not only sanctification within (great indeed as these blessings would be, yet it is something more),—it implies the one, it involves the other, it is the indwelling of our glorified Lord. This is the one great gift of God purchased by the Atonement, which is light instead of darkness and the shadow of death, power instead of weakness, bondage and suffering, spirit instead of the flesh, which the token of our acceptance with God, the propitiation of our sins in His sight, and the seed and element of renovation.[65]

The resurrection and ascension stand at the center of our justification because it is in the mission of the Spirit that resurrection, ascension, and justification find their common element. Newman makes certain to note that it is a peculiarity of apostolic preaching that it holds the resurrection to be the key, central doctrine by which all other doctrines are to be understood. He finds many reasons for this, but he applies it to his own argument in a compelling way. Noting that Christ on the cross was to the world for atonement, he states that Christ in his resurrection was to the world as saviour. In the resurrection Christ was exalted, and returned to us as God, man, and sacrifice. This has direct bearing on us:

> But, if, as we have seen, the Resurrection be the means by which the Atonement is applied to each of us, if it be our justification, if in it are conveyed all the gifts of grace and glory which Christ has purchased for us, if it be the commencement of His giving Himself to us for our spiritual sustenance, of His feeding us with that Bread which has already been perfected upon the Cross, and is now a medicine of immortality, it is that very doctrine which is most immediate to us, in which Christ most closely approaches us, from which we gain life, and out of which issues our hopes and our duties.[66]

---

65. Newman, *Lectures on Justification*, 219.
66. Newman, *Lectures on Justification*, 222.

Devolution

In the period we are considering no English Anglican theologian could write on subjects included in the Thirty-nine *Articles of Religion* without reconciling his opinions to some plausible reading of the *Articles*. The Thirty-nine Articles have provided the ammunition for an ongoing controversy in Anglicanism. In the first chapter we saw Archbishop Laurence drawn into that controversy as he attempted to trace the intentions of the English Reformers. In the 1830s and '40s the battle was raging again (and this time it was linked to some aspects of university reform). At the center of this new engagement was John Henry Newman. *Tract Ninety: Remarks on Certain Passages in the Thirty-nine Articles* brought the issue to a head, but Newman had already seen the difficulty in the *Lectures on the Doctrine of Justification*. "We are accounted righteous before God, only for the merit of our Lord and Saviour Jesus Christ by Faith, and not for our own works or deservings. Wherefore, that we are justified by Faith only, is a most wholesome Doctrine . . ." reads article eleven. Newman, as we have seen, gave faith a secondary and antecedent role in the causality of justification. Justification consists primarily in the presence of the Spirit within the individual. This presence manifests itself in newness of heart (renewal) and newness of conduct (obedience). In this, the role of faith is certainly played down. Therefore, Newman had to raise the issue of faith; indeed, he had to raise it for two reasons: first, because throughout his theological career it was one of his great concerns, and he certainly recognized its place in the economy of salvation; and second, he was caught with the formularies of the Thirty-nine Articles.

Newman began by distinguishing between all faith, or faith as a generic term describing beliefs held, and lively faith which bears fruit in conduct and knowledge. It is lively faith which is justifying faith. Lively faith is instrumental in the life of the believer. The instrumentality of faith is an internal instrumentality; indeed, faith is the sole internal instrument, but not the sole instrument of any kind. Viewed objectively, baptism is the instrument of justification. Faith takes up the free gift brought in baptism. While baptism confers justification, justification is more than an event, it is a state. Therefore, justification needs a perpetual instrument through which it is secured in the individual. Faith is that instrument. "The two sacraments," Newman writes, "are the primary instruments of justification; faith is the secondary, subordinate or representative instrument. Or we may say . . . that the sacraments are its instrumental, and Faith its sustaining cause."[67]

---

67. Newman, *Lectures on Justification*, 226.

Justifying faith, like any other Christian attribute, must derive its authority from its source. While God is the origin of all faith and authority, the direct source of the authority of justifying faith is the act whereby we are justified, baptism. Baptism precedes true faith, and, because it is the event of justification, makes faith justifying. This is the point on which Newman believes all solifidianism is mistaken; it places faith before baptism. Faith can exist before baptism, but it is preparatory faith, not lively, true justifying faith.

In defense of his position Newman draws on the account of St. Paul. Paul, who has been confronted by a Christophany, must still be baptized. Though he has been brought to faith by the Damascus road experience, Paul's faith is not his justification; his faith is made justifying only after his baptism.[68] For those troubled by the seeming inconsistency of his position with that of *Article Eleven*, Newman cites the rubric concerning faith from the "Office for the Communion of the Sick"[69]: Newman's interpretation of this rubric bears quoting. This rubric, he says, "instructs us that faith, so far from superseding, is to represent the Eucharist, only when, from whatever cause, it cannot be obtained. It continues on and pleads in God's sight the sick person's former reception of it."[70] From such examples Newman concludes:

> Faith, then, considered as an instrument, is always secondary to the Sacraments. The most extreme case, in which it seems to supersede them, is found, not in our own, but in the Ancient Church; in which the faith of persons, dying in the state of Catechumenes, was held to avail to their reception on death into that kingdom, of which Baptism is the ordinary gate. How different is the spirit of such guarded exception, from the doctrine now in esteem, that faith, *ipso facto*, justifies, the Sacraments merely confirming and sealing what is complete without them.[71]

---

68. Newman also cites Acts 22:14, 16; Galatians 3:26, 27; Hebrews 10:22; 1 Peter 1:3–5; and Acts 10:47. In all these, he sees faith portrayed as the sustaining cause of justification, not its direct cause.

69. "But if a man, either by reason of extremity of sickness, or for want of warning in due time to the Minister, or by any other just impediment, do not receive the Sacrament of Christ's Body and Blood, the Minister shall instruct him, that if he do truly repent of his sins, and steadfastly believe that Jesus Christ hath suffered death upon the Cross for him, and shed his Blood for his redemption, earnestly remembering the benefits he hath thereby, and giving him hearty thanks therefor, he doth eat and drink the Body and Blood of our Saviour Christ profitably to his soul's health, although he do not receive the Sacrament with his mouth." *Book of Common Prayer 1928*, 323.

70. Newman, *Lectures on Justification*, 230f.

71. Newman, *Lectures on Justification*, 231.

The office of justifying faith is now clearer. By placing justifying faith after baptism, its office becomes a cooperating office. Faith cooperates with the sacraments to maintain and sustain the state of justification. This is the special office of justifying faith in the economy of salvation. Again, from the lecture on "The Office of Justifying Faith":

> While then we reserve to Baptism our new birth, and to the Eucharist the hidden springs of the new life, and to Love what may be called its plastic power, and to Obedience its being the atmosphere in which faith breathes, still the divinely appointed or (in other words) the mysterious virtue of Faith remains. It alone coalesces with the Sacraments, brings them into effect, dissolves (as it were) what is outward and material in them, and through them unites the soul to God.[72]

The office of faith does not end with its cooperation with the sacraments. Faith also has a symbolic office in which it magnifies the grace of God. Before justification faith magnifies grace by leading to justification, afterwards by sustaining the state of justification. The symbolic office of faith raises two issues, Newman's sources, and the nature of the symbolic office itself.

As we saw earlier in this chapter, Newman's notion of justification by faith was drawn from both Luther and Melanchthon. He considered Melanchthon to be the source of the Anglican doctrine. The Reformers, he notes, took up the notion of justifying faith as a sign, pledge, or emblem of our justification and of God's freely given grace. They reserved the clause that this is the case after baptism. Therefore, faith has a symbolic office, symbolizing justification, though it is not the direct cause of justification. This interpretation of Melanchthon and the English Reformers Newman drew from Bishop Bull who, in his *Harmonia Apostolica*, after quoting at length from Melanchthon, had written:

> From these proofs, it must be quite clear how entirely amiss most later Protestants have understood the doctrine of those early ones concerning justification by faith only, in supposing that they attributed to faith, above all other virtues, an instrumentality, strictly speaking, in the work of justification. This is a mere dream, for it is plain from their own teaching, which we have explained at length, that they ascribe no especial efficacy, and so no instrumentality to faith above other virtues in the matter of justification, but that they only meant that faith alone, of all other virtues, signified a respect to the free mercy of God

---

72. Newman, *Lectures on Justification*, 236f.

promised through Christ, which is the primary cause of our justification, and so, by a figurative, but not an improper method of speaking, we may say, "we are justified by faith only . . ."[73]

Newman employs Bull's analysis for two reasons: first, it reconciles him with the position of Article Eleven, or at least with a possible reading of it supported by an Anglican authority ; second, it aids him in establishing a two-fold notion of the office of faith which corresponds with his overall objective-subjective analysis of justification. Thus, Newman is able to say that faith "justifies only, in two ways, as the only inward *instrument*, and as the only *symbol*. Viewed as an instrument, it unites the soul to Christ through the Sacraments; viewed as a symbol it shows forth the doctrine of free grace. Hence it is the instrument of justification after Baptism; it is a symbol both before and after."[74]

In the context of justification Newman is more interested in what faith does than in what it is; yet he recognizes that he must say a word about the nature of faith. Drawing on Hebrews 1:11, "faith is the substance of things hoped for, the evidence of things not seen," Newman remarks that faith, in its most general sense, can be defined as that which makes the future present to us. Faith is a ground or medium of proof through which we are able to accept the existence of that which we cannot see.[75] In principle, faith can be either good or bad, an excellence or a despair. It has no abstract existence, it exists only in individuals. The evil and the good can possess faith. As it is in itself, faith is rather amoral.

Justifying faith, however, must be viewed as it is in the regenerate. Justifying faith is lively faith, and lively faith is the only real faith. Simple assent is a tenable description of faith, but it is inadequate. Trust, however, cannot be an adequate description of faith, for trust implies an ordering towards God, and is therefore inadequate as a general description of faith. The key to understanding the relationship between faith and justifying faith is in understanding the relation-ship between faith and love.

Faith, Newman maintains, is not justifying unless it is animated or informed by love. With this point we come to the relationship which most interested Newman. He sought the formal cause of justification. He asked if faith could justify without being informed by love. Seeking a description

---

73. Bull, *Harmonia Apostolica*, 205.
74. Newman, *Lectures on Justification*, 251.
75. See Newman, "Faith and Reason, contrasted as Habits of Mind" in *Fifteen Sermons Preached Before the University of Oxford*, 176–201. This sermon was preached less than two years after the publication of the *Lectures on Justification*, and employs the same text from Hebrews as its basis.

of this relationship Newman began and ended the *Lectures on the Doctrine of Justification*.[76]

Causality

Newman's method for determining the formal cause of justification began with constructing what he believed to be the two opposing traditions, the Roman Catholic (exemplified by Augustine) and the Protestant (exemplified by Luther). Luther, Newman argued, erred in his refusal to assign any formal cause to justification. By making faith an instrumental cause, without any formal cause for justification, faith is defined only by its office. The office of faith is to free men from the moral law which Chris fulfilled. Faith, then, is the apprehension of, and trust in, the freely given external application of Christ's merits. Since Christ has fulfilled the law, and we are thereby freed from it, every believer must have continuing perfect righteousness. This is the core of the Protestant problem in Newman's mind: the moral law need not be fulfilled in each individual. Newman always distinguished between error and defect. The Protestant view of justification by faith only was in error, the Roman Catholic view of justification by obedience had a defect. This defect, Newman concedes, is present more in popular teaching than in the best of the Roman Catholic tradition. By emphasizing the formal cause of justification to the exclusion of the justifying office of faith, Roman Catholic popular teaching underplayed the necessity of faith as a cause of justification. He writes: "Now I come to consider the opposite scheme of doctrine, which is not unsound or dangerous in itself, but in a certain degree incomplete,—truth, but not the whole truth; viz., that justification consists in love, or sanctity, or obedience, or 'renewal of the Holy Ghost."[77] We have already heard Newman say that justification includes all these qualities, but he is seeking a fuller answer, an answer which he believes is present in Augustine and the Catholic tradition.

Love is the divine motivation for our justification. God's love for fallen man is irrefutably demonstrated in Christ's ministry. God's love must be returned by works done in obedience to the new law of the gospel. Our justification makes these works righteous. Thus, in Newman's mind, the main dispute between Augustine and Luther is "whether or not the Moral Law can

---

76. The first lecture considers faith as instrumental cause, the second, love as formal cause, and an appendix "On the Formal Cause of Justification" is twice the length of any lecture.

77. Newman, *Lectures on Justification*, 30.

in its substance be obeyed and kept by the regenerate."[78] Newman's analysis of the dispute is best shown in a two column arrangement:

Augustine	Luther
1. By grace we can keep the moral law	1. Christ has done it for us
2. Righteousness is active	2. Righteousness is passive
3. Righteousness is imparted	3. Righteousness is imputed
4. Righteousness consists in a change of heart	4. Righteousness consists in a change of state
5. God's commandments are impossible without grace	5. God's commandments are impossible for man
6. Gospel is also Law	6. Gospel is promises only
7. Our highest wisdom is to know and keep the Law	7. Our highest wisdom is not to know the Law
8. The Law is Christ	8. The law and Christ cannot dwell together in the heart
9. Obedience is a matter of conscience	9. Obedience is not a matter of conscience
10. Man made a Christian by works after grace	10. Man made a Christian by hearing
11. Our best deeds are acceptable to God	11. Our best deeds are sin
12. Faith is taken in earnest of righteousness	12. Faith is taken instead of righteousness
13. Faith is the commandment of holiness	13. Faith is essential because it is a substitute for holiness
14. Loving faith renews the heart	14. Faith renews the heart
15. Inward life of grace, or love, is the tree, renewal is the fruit	15. Faith is the tree, works are the fruits

Obviously Newman is weighing his analysis in favor of Augustine, and is establishing the main ancient authority for his own opinion. His commitment to the *via media* method makes such an arrangement necessary, but the validity of his analysis of Luther is really secondary. On the other hand,

78. Newman, *Lectures on Justification*, 58.

he must set up Augustine's opinion to substantiate the existence of love as a formal cause of justification.

Newman now becomes somewhat uncomfortable and unclear. Yes, love must be seen as a formal cause of justification because loving faith is a source of renewal, and renewal yields up necessary good works. Obviously the principle of renewal stands at the heart of the development of the causality of justification; but this is exactly where Newman becomes uncomfortable, he dislikes giving any sense of independent reality to principles. The Council of Trent, Newman reminds us, taught that the mercy of God is the efficient cause of our justification, Christ on the cross its meritorious cause, baptism its instrumental cause and the principle of renewal in righteousness, and faith its formal cause; however, Newman cautions, baptism can as easily be seen as the formal cause because it immediately predisposes to justification. What, then, has happened to love? Newman does not answer the question; rather, he goes on to recast the question of formal causality. He asks, "whether Christ's merits, which are the original cause of our holiness and works, are to be considered as the medium (as it may be called) of the covenant *in which* we act, or the proximate cause of our entering into life?"[79] Newman sees four possible answers to this question: the first (which he identifies with the high Roman tradition) is that we are justified solely upon holiness and works wrought in us through Christ's merits by the Spirit; the second (which he identifies as high Anglican) is that we are justified upon our holiness and works under the covenant of Christ's merits; the third (which he identifies as not so high Anglican) is that our faith is mercifully appointed as a substitute for perfect holiness, and is therefore an interposing principle between God and man; the fourth (which he identifies as high Protestant) is that Christ's merits and righteousness are appointed as ours, and become the immediate cause of our justification. Not surprisingly, Newman is closest to the high Anglican view.

Employing his now familiar objective-subjective distinctions he offers up his conclusion on the question of the formal cause of justification:

> English divines, teach that our holiness and works done in the Spirit are something towards salvation, but not enough; or that we are justified by obedience under the Covenant of mercy, or by obedience sprinkled with or presented in the Atoning Sacrifice. According to them, then, we are saved in Christ's righteousness, yet not without our own; or considering Christ's righteousness as a formal cause, we are saved by two contemporaneous formal causes, by a righteousness, meritorious on

---

79. Newman, *Lectures on Justification*, 348.

> Christ's part, inchoate on ours ... In this then I conceive to lie the unity of Catholic doctrine on the subject of justification, that we are saved by Christ's imputed righteousness and by our own inchoate righteousness at once.[80]

Righteousness is both imputed and imparted. Justification comes from without and within; from without it comes as the free gift of Christ's righteousness imputed to us through the Spirit; from within it comes by our beginning in righteousness through the indwelling of the Spirit and our loving response of faith which yields obedience to the new law.

Newman was attempting to show that except where an outright denial of formal causality existed there was little difference between various Christian traditions. Newman's solution to the question of formal causality lay in his deep sense of the unity of Christ with redeemed humanity. The righteousness of Christ and the righteousness of justified humanity are the same. Christ's righteousness, imputed and imparted, dwells in humanity as well as establishing the possibility of salvation. Through this sense of the oneness of righteousness, Newman can speak of God viewing and judging humanity according to Christ's righteousness and humanity's righteousness. God sees in justified humanity the righteousness of Christ, and on that account he calls man blessed. How all this is accomplished is best noted, as mentioned earlier, in one sentence that could serve as a summary for the whole Tractarian doctrine of grace, "Justification comes through the sacraments; is received by faith; consists in God's inward presence; and lives in obedience."[81]

Baptism is the event in which Christ comes to dwell in man, making man righteous. The justification and sanctification that come through baptism are continued in individuals through the eucharist. It is the atonement constantly present, sustaining the justified state. Faith receives justification in many ways; related to the eucharist, though Christ is present in that sacrament regardless of the faith of the recipient, faith makes the eucharist efficacious in sustaining righteousness; faith also receives justification by glorifying the grace of God, showing man's nothingness and God's all-sufficiency (this is Newman's interpretation of St. Paul's insistence on justification by faith). Justification consists in the inward presence of the Spirit, for only an inward presence can make humans righteous, can give what God in Christ promises. These three, sacraments, faith, and indwelling we have confronted earlier in this chapter, but obedience demands a further examination.

---

80. Newman, *Lectures on Justification*, 367f.
81. Newman, *Lectures on Justification*, 278.

To Obey

"Justification lives in obedience" was one of Newman's key ideas, an idea he shared with Pusey and many other Tractarians. The importance of obedience to the Tractarians can hardly be overstated. They were men of deep and faithful piety who believed that their salvation depended on their faithful obedience to Christ who dwelled in them. Thus, obedience was the key to their understanding of the relationship between faith and works. In distinguishing between works and good works. Newman again followed Bishop Bull, who had written:

> Whoever thoroughly understands what we have advanced, will easily perceive that the works which St. Paul wholly excludes from justification, are only those which are performed without the grace of the Gospel, by the aid of the natural, or Mosaic law; . . . this then is a necessary conclusion from what has been said; for since St. Paul chiefly employs this argument against justification by the law either of Moses or of nature, because both these laws are entirely destitute of the means whereby men may be induced to true righteousness worthy of God, and agreeable to Him, it hence manifestly follows, that by Him, only that righteousness, and those works, are excluded from justification, which are produced by human weakness under the law, or in a state of nature.[82]

Newman argues in the same way, but he gives a more positive sense to the relationship between faith and works. Faith, he reminds us, is a habit of the soul, and a habit is something permanent which affects the character. This reformed character is manifested in our works. Therefore, our good works contribute to keeping us in the justified state. To bolster his argument he points out that St. Paul's illustrations of justifying faith are not grounded in "feeling" something, but in doing something unusual. Agreeing with St. James, Newman contends that faith cannot exist without works; faith is a habit, and the life of a habit is found in action. Faith provides the direction for works, but works provide the limit and completion of faith. Faith directs works, but works give faith its substance.

Had Newman have left his comments on works to what we have just seen, his critics might have been able to overlook some of their disagreements with him. However, a larger battle began when he added a "Note on Lecture XII: On Good Works as the Remedy of Post-Baptismal Sin." His intention was to clarify a part of the very dismal picture painted by

---

82. Bull, *Harmonia Apostolica*, 142.

Pusey on the seriousness of post-baptismal sin; however, the effect was somewhat different:

> From what has been said [in the lectures on faith, rites, and works], it would seem that, while works before justification are but conditions and preparations for that gift, works after justification are much more, and that, not only as being intrinsically good and holy, but as being fruits of *faith*. And viewed as one with faith, which is the appointed instrument of justification after Baptism, they are (as being connatural with faith and indivisible from it, organs through which it acts and which it hallows) instruments with faith of the continuance of justification, or, in other words, *of the remission of sin after Baptism*.[83]

The sense of Newman's argument was always that good works stem from the presence of Christ in us. Our good works are really Christ's action in us continually making us acceptable to God. The chief good work, in Newman's frame of reference, was our faithful response to the sacramental life of the Church. The good works which operate for remission of sins have the character of the sacraments in which we are continually called to repentance and amendment of life.

Even Newman's note on good works might have been acceptable to some (certainly to his fellow Tractarians), but events were also moving swiftly. Only three years after the *Lectures on the Doctrine of Justification* Newman published *Tract Ninety*. While the instrumental efficacy of sacraments and the expanded notion of justification were tolerated, and in some cases welcomed, in certain Anglican theological circles, the question concerning the efficacy and merit of good works remained a point on which most Anglicans would give up very little ground. In Anglicanism's popular exposition of Roman Catholicism the doctrine of meritorious works was the linch-pin on which the Reformation still hung. Thus, when Newman wrote the following, he placed himself beyond the support of all but a few friends:

> However, there is an intermediate state of which the Article [thirteen] says nothing, but which must not be forgotten, as being an actually existing one. Men are not always either in light or in darkness, but are sometimes between the two; they are sometimes not in a state of Christian justification, yet not utterly deserted by God, but in a state something like that of Jews or of Heathen, turning to the thought of religion. They are not gifted with *habitual* grace, but they still are visited by Divine influences, or by actual grace, or rather aid; and these influences are

---

83. Newman, *Lectures on Justification*, 304.

the first-fruits of the grace of justification going before it, and are intended to lead on to it, and to be perfected in it, as twilight leads to day. And since it is a Scripture maxim, that "he that is faithful in that which is least, is faithful also in much;" and "to whosoever hath, to him shall be given;" therefore, it is quite true that works done *with* divine aid, and in faith, *before* justification, *do* dispose men to receive the grace of justification;—such were Cornelius's alms, fastings, and prayer, which led to his baptism. If works before justification, when done by the influence of divine aid, gain grace, much more do works *after* justification. They are, according to the Article, "grata," "Pleasing to God;" and they are accepted, "accepta;" which means that God rewards them, and that of course according to their degree of excellence. At the same time, as works before justification may nevertheless be done under a divine influence, so works after justification are still liable to the infection of original sin; and, as not being perfect, "cannot expiate our sins," or "endure the severity of God's judgement."[84]

Newman's words may be left to speak for themselves. Unfortunately, the debate that ensued revolved around the issue of meritorious works. Newman had struck at a deeper theme which he never developed, the *auxilium Dei moventis*. Clearly he reorganized the issue. Preparation for habitual grace through an act of God in aid of man's justification concerned Newman, but no matter how tantalizing it would be to speculate on how he might have developed the theme, he never did so. Shortly after *Tract Ninety* Newman left Oxford for Littlemore. His Anglican career was about to close.

A New Understanding

Newman's concept of grace radically altered the use of much traditional language. Justification and sanctification came to be viewed as almost interchangeable terms. No longer could they be seen as sequential portions of a process. Such was also the case with imputed and inherent righteousness. Here Newman chose the formula imparted righteousness as being the most correct description of God's activity and man's receptivity. David Newsome recognized this latter point when he wrote of Newman:

> And in his rejection of the conflicting formulae of inherent righteousness and imputed righteousness for his own formula of *imparted* righteousness (i.e., the communication of the

---

84. Newman, *Tract Ninety*, 16f.

merits of Christ to sinful man, initially through the regenerating sacrament of baptism, and subsequently through the sacrament of the Eucharist which sustains the Christian in holiness and infuses his soul with the presence of Christ), Newman provided a sound foundation on which a tractarian theological system could be built.[85]

Clearly, everything hinges on the notion of imparted righteousness. By employing the notion of imparted righteousness Newman could speak of both justification and sanctification as realities present in the life of every baptized person.

The *Lectures on the Doctrine of Justification*, with their strong sense of imparted righteousness, changed the basis of the doctrine of grace. It opened the way for R. I. Wilberforce's work on the incarnation. Looking forward to the centennial of the Oxford Movement, C. C. J. Webb identified this factor: "It was a feature of the whole Movement, and one which was closely bound up with the dissatisfaction of its scholars with the Lutheran doctrine of Justification, that the Incarnation rather than the Atonement was the center of its theology."[86] When Newman expounded his theology of the impartation of Christ's redeeming presence, the incarnation became the obvious analogy of the redeemed life. Pusey had recognized this, and so did Newman. The union of God and man in Jesus Christ became the type of the union between Christ and man wrought by the Spirit in baptism. In Christ righteousness was incarnate, and so also it is incarnate in each justified individual. The centrality of Newman's incarnationalism is easily seen in a portion of a Christmas sermon preached on the text, "Both He that sanctifieth and they who are sanctified are all one: for which cause He is not ashamed to call them brethren" [Hebrews 2:11]: "Our Saviour's birth in the flesh is an earnest, and, as it were beginning of our birth in the Spirit. It is a figure, promise, or pledge of our new birth, and it effects what it promises. As He was born, so are we born also; and since He was born, therefore we too are born. As He is the Son of God by nature, so are we sons of God by grace; and it is He who has made us such."[87]

When speaking of baptism the incarnation was never far from Newman's mind:

> St. Paul sets this great truth before us, among other places, in the second chapter of his Epistle to the Colossians. First, he says,

---

85. Newsome, "Justification and Sanctification, *Journal of Theological Studies,* XV (April 1964), 32f.

86. Webb, *Religious Thought in The Oxford Movement,* 82.

87. Newman, "The Mystery of Godliness" in *Parochial and Plain Sermons,* V, 86.

> "In Christ dwelleth all the fulness of the Godhead bodily, and ye have fulness in Him, who is the Head of all principality and power." Here the most solemn and transporting doctrine of the Incarnation is disclosed to us, as the cornerstone of the whole Church system; "the Word made flesh," being the divinely appointed Way whereby we are regenerated and saved.[88]

Linking baptism and the eucharist are their incarnational basis and their power to justify (which Newman attributes to the atonement when he narrows his definition and separates justification and sanctification, forgiveness of sins and newness of life):

> This, then, is the characteristic mark of those two: separating them from all other whatever; and this is nothing else but saying in other words that they are the only *justifying* rites, or instruments of communicating the Atonement, which is the one thing necessary to us ... the two sacraments "of the Gospel," as they may be emphatically styled, are the instruments of inward life, according to our Lord's declaration, that Baptism is a new birth, and that in the Eucharist we eat the *living* bread.[89]

If the above seems to draw more attention to the atonement as the central theme, the centrality of the incarnation in eucharistic theology is well illustrated by the following:

> Let us pray Him to give us such a real and living insight into the blessed doctrine of the Incarnation of the Son of God, of His birth of a Virgin, His atoning death, and resurrection, that we may desire that the Holy Communion may be the effectual type of that gracious Economy. No one realizes the Mystery of the Incarnation but must feel disposed towards that of Holy Communion.[90]

Later Tractarian writing on the eucharist would center on the nature of Christ's presence, but before 1845 the concern was primarily with the virtue of the eucharist, its power to sustain justified persons in their state of holiness.[91]

88. Newman, "Regenerating Baptism" in *Parochial and Plain Sermons*, III, 277f.
89. Newman, *Tract Ninety*, 49.
90. Newman, "The Eucharistic Presence" in *Parochial and Plain Sermons*, VI, 151.
91. In *Tract Ninety* Newman took up the problem of transubstantiation and the localized presence of Christ in the eucharistic elements. Noting that a localized presence demands a concept of a material presence, Newman argues that the presence of Christ in the eucharist is not of that order, but of the order of a real, spiritual presence. It is at this spiritual level that the sacraments gain the character of a mystery. Hence, there is a localized presence of Christ at the right hand of the Father, and a spiritual presence in

Newman's interest in sacramental theology was subservient to his interest in the theology of grace. By writing the Lectures on the *Doctrine of Justification* he both supported Pusey's efforts in the theology of the means of grace and set the course which Wilberforce would pursue when writing on the incarnation. Above both those factors, Newman contributed a new framework for Anglican theology. He broke out of the sequential notion of justification and sanctification (whichever was placed first), and offered a theology based on an immediate, complete indwelling of Christ's Spirit through the imparting of the gift of righteousness. This, alone, would have earned him a place of respect in the history of Anglican doctrine. *The Lectures on the Doctrine of Justification* were the high point of Newman's Anglican career. His solid theological productivity after 1838 became bogged down in the innumerable controversies which preceded his departure from Anglicanism. Of the two works which came after 1838, *Tract Ninety* was clever and somewhat devious, but not weighty. *An Essay on the Development of Christian Doctrine* was his intellectual bridge out of Anglicanism as "The Parting of Friends" had been his emotional bridge.

Of all the Tractarians Newman was singularly gifted as a systematic theologian. He recognized that no Christian doctrine stands in isolation, that is must be related to all other Christian doctrine and to the life of the faithful. Alf Hardelin, though he tends to isolate the eucharist from baptism, put this last point well in the following, with which this chapter closes:

> Now we have also seen that justification, according to Newman, consists in the indwelling of the incarnate and glorified Christ in the soul through the Spirit. The instrument most fully and perfectly conveying the gift of justification is the eucharist. This sacrament is, in other words, the focus where the christological and soteriological aspects of redemption come together. Between the doctrines of the Incarnation, sacrifice, and resurrection of Christ, the real presence of His body and blood in the eucharist, and the real justification of the individual Christians in the Church there is a mutual reciprocity: they support each other.[92]

---

the eucharist: both are real, because Christ is present in both. "In answer, then, to the problem, how Christ comes to us while remaining on high, I answer just as much as this,—that He comes by the agency of the Holy Ghost, in and by the Sacrament. Locomotion is the means of a material Presence; the Sacrament is the means of His spiritual Presence. As faith is the means of our receiving It, so the Holy Ghost is the Agent and the Sacrament the means of His imparting It; and therefore we call It a Sacramental Presence. We kneel before His heavenly Throne, and the distance is as nothing; it is as if that Throne were the Altar close to us." *Tract Ninety*, 60.

92. Hardelin, *The Tractarian Understanding of the Eucharist*, 154.

4

Robert Isaac Wilberforce

The Incarnational Basis of Grace

Robert Isaac Wilberforce is the third Tractarian with whom we must be concerned. Born the second son of the great Evangelical reformer, William Wilberforve, Robert Isaac was the elder brother of Samuel Wilberforce, Bishop of Oxford and Winchester. Unlike Samuel, Robert Isaac was a retiring individual. Most of his adult life was spent in the parochial ministry; but his ties to Oxford remained strong until he left the Church of England in 1854, in a final protest against the Gorham judgement.[1] Even in his boldest act, submitting to the Roman Catholic Church, he deferred to his more prominent brother and accomplished his secession in Paris.

Wilberforce's position in the development of Anglican doctrine in the nineteenth century is more difficult to place than that of Pusey or Newman. He left Oxford in 1831, and was not a part of either the golden age of The Oxford Movement in the 1830s, or the bitter battles of the 1840s. His major works all appeared after Newman's secession, and in that respect belong to the dark hours of the late forties and early fifties. He wrote none of the tracts, nor was he involved in University politics. Yet, he had been among those who spent the "Long Vacation" of 1823 with Keble, he was an intimate of Froude and Newman,and was reckoned among the strongest supporters of the Movement.

Since Wilberforce's death in 1857, few have engaged in a deep way with his theology, but those who have continue to laud his accomplishments,

---

1. Others, most notably Archdeacon (later Cardinal) Manning, had left the Church of England in 1851, shortly after the Gorham judgement was rendered.

placing him among the most gifted of the Tractarians.² In "Tractarianism and the Bible" A. T. Lyttleton wrote that Wilberforce was "the greatest philosophical theologian of the Tractarians."³ A little later S. L. Ollard wrote, "He had been a Fellow of Oriel and was a man of commanding ability, a really great philosopher, a profound theologian, and of a most severe and saintly life."⁴ Some rehabilitation of Wilberforce was accomplished by Eric Mascall when he wrote, in the introduction to *Christ, the Christian, and the Church*, "And I cannot but regret that the books which Mr. Robert Wilberforce wrote in his Anglican days have been allowed to lapse into obscurity; they contain in germ most of what has been written in recent years by such authors as Abbot Vonier on the Eucharist and Mersch and de Lubac on the Mystical Body of Christ."⁵ It is this suggestion of Mascall's that is employed in the book *The Tractarian Understanding of the Eucharist*.

A more recent appreciation of Wilberforce's largest work which is also supported by Newsome in his even later *Victorian World* was given by E. R. Fairweather in *The Oxford Movement*:

> *The Doctrine of the Incarnation*, published in 1848, is both Wilberforce's finest theological work and one of the most distinguished pieces of the nineteenth century Anglican divinity. Indeed, with the exception of Frederick Denison Maurice's *Kingdom of Christ*, published ten years earlier, it is hard to find another English theological production from the first half of the nineteenth century that shows a comparable grasp of the basic pattern of Christian doctrine. Even Newman's systematic works, for all their insights and their moments of brilliance, seem rather casual beside Wilberforce's *magnum opus*. To say nothing more, *The Doctrine of the Incarnation* is unquestionably the great synthesis of Tractarian teaching.⁶

Given Fairweather's evaluation, it is surprising to note how limited reference to Wilberforce has been. F. J. Hall, in his monumental *Dogmatic Theology*, refers to him occasionally; Brilioth relegates him to a few footnotes; other Anglican writers studiously ignore him. Surely,

---

2 For two books that do reveal the way Wilberforce's (and Pusey's) eucharistic theology grounded changes in eucharistic practice, see Herring, *What Was the Oxford Movement?* (especially 201) and Morris, *The High Church Revival in the Church of England* (especially ch. 3).

3. Lyttleton, "Tractarianism and the Bible" in *Pilot*, III (March 23, 1901), 362. This was the first of two articles on the subject.

4. Ollard, *A Short History of The Oxford Movement*, 65.

5. Mascall, *Christ, the Christian, and the Church*, viii.

6. Fairweather, *The Oxford Movement*, 285.

his conversion to Roman Catholicism made his writings (like those of Newman) unacceptable to some of his Anglican contemporaries. His doctrine of the eucharist (which so influenced Bishop Forbes and other later Anglo-Catholics) struck many as too accommodating to the idea of transubstantiation. His involvement in the Gorham controversy, and his close association with Manning, would have put off many more moderate Anglicans. On the whole, there were a number of factors that contributed to his rapid movement into obscurity.

On the other hand, there are elements of Wilberforce's writing that commend him to our attention. Above all the Tractarians, he seemed to have the greatest appreciation for the best of the scholastic tradition. His use of scholastic material was neither enthusiastic nor deprecating; rather, he sought from it those elements of logical analysis which could shed light on the development of Christian doctrine. His dispassionate use of Anselm and Aquinas do not remind the reader of Froude's unabashed enthusiasm for the middle ages; rather, his use of the Schoolmen is reminiscent of the dispassionate truth-seeking of Hooker.

Wilberforce's writings are the most ecumenical of the Tractarian productions. He drew from every period and party in Christian history. He shared with Pusey an appreciation of the German Protestant tradition, and was fond of quoting Olshausen. Though he never dealt directly with the issue of doctrinal development, Wilberforce's grasp of the movement of Christian history was at least as great as that of Newman.

Wilberforce also commends himself to our study because he marks the end of the period of great theological productivity amongst the Tractarians Pusey and Keble continued to write, and their works (especially Keble's *On Eucharistical Adoration*) cannot be ignored; but by the time of Wilberforce's last work the issues were becoming old issues, and the controversies old controversies. By the early 1850s the Movement had changed.

Of the many forces which played on Wilberforce, two stand out as important for this work, the Gorham controversy and Newman. In 1847 the Rev. George Cornelius Gorham was refused induction to the parish of Brampford Speke by the Rt. Rev. Henry Phillpotts. Bishop Phillpotts, never one to avoid a controversy, was an adamant defender of the doctrine of baptismal regeneration. Gorham was not. Phillpotts' refusal led to a four-year controversy that culminated in a victory for the Evangelicals. One of the leading Evangelical writers in aid of Gorham was the Rev. William Goode. It was to refute Goode's denial of baptismal regeneration that Wilberforce published *The Doctrine of Holy Baptism*. Of all his works, *The Doctrine of Holy Baptism* is Wilberforce's least successful effort. It is a polemical work, and, unlike Newman, Wilberforce was not a gifted polemicist. *The Doctrine of Holy Baptism* was a learned, but undistinguished historical survey of the doctrine of baptismal regeneration. More than anything else, it appears as the capstone of the revived baptismal controversy of the first half of the nineteenth century. Interestingly, the same controversy gave rise to Wilberforce's brilliant *Sermons on the New Birth of Man's Nature*, one of the finest sets of theological sermons produced in the nineteenth century.

Wilberforce's involvement in the baptismal controversy was not simply one of party loyalty. His concern was to preserve a sense of the reality of supernatural acts. Whether supernatural realities were diminished by rationalist philosophy or by sentimentalism mattered little; the effect was the same, to rob the Christian faith of its intrinsically supernatural and mysterious character. Indeed, to preserve the supernatural character of the Christian mysteries of faith may be seen as the motivation behind every word Wilberforce published. Nowhere is this clearer than in the introduction to *The Doctrine of Holy Baptism*:

> The question at issue in the present day is the reality of Our Lord's Mediation; the truth of that system of spiritual influences, which was bestowed by the recreation of man's race in the Person of the Son of God; and that whole doctrine of grace, which is characteristic of the Gospel. If it should be true, as was always believed in ancient times, and as will be stated in these pages, that "sacraments are the extension of the Incarnation;" that through their agency the Son of God effects that great work, which He took our nature to discharge, it will not seem surprising that where the sacramental system has been undervalued, those great truths to which it bears such near relation, should also be forgotten. Hence is a true belief in Baptismal grace as intimately allied in theory to the doctrine of Atonement and of Mediation, as history shows they have been practically connected.[7]

Following Fairweather's suggestion concerning the synthetic nature of Wilberforce's greatest work, it can rightly be said that Wilberforce desired to place the incarnation at the center of all Christian doctrine. To do so was not to devalue the atonement (as was thought by Wilberforce's Evangelical opponents), rather it placed the atonement in the larger perspective of Christ's total ministry of mediation. Mediation, for Wilberforce, was the key to understanding every act of God from creation to the eschaton; it is both the principle of synthesis and the explanatory fact of the Christ event and its extension in the life of the church. In a striking passage from the close of the

---

7. Wilberforce, *The Doctrine of Holy Baptism*, 9.

introduction to *The Doctrine of the Incarnation*, Wilberforce ties his Evangelical background (with its emphasis on the atonement) to his present concerns, thereby setting the stage for his investigation of the incarnation:

> But if we be truly surrounded by a world of unseen beings, if we actually "come unto Mount Sion, and unto the city of the living God, the heavenly Jerusalem, and to an innumerable company of angels, to the general assembly and church of the first-born, which are written in heaven, and to God, the JUDGE OF ALL, and to the spirits of just men made perfect, and to Jesus the MEDIATOR of the new covenant," then, surely, it cannot be immaterial whether we rightly apprehend those mighty realities which press upon us so nearly, and whether our acts and language are fitted for that hallowed intercourse to which we have been admitted. Otherwise, we are intruding, like unconscious dreamers, into the sacred presence of the Great King. Hence the desire of the present writer, as being bound by education and hereditary attachment to those evangelical principles in which he was nurtured, to call attention to the external truths, on which the doctrines of grace are dependent. For it is no system of idle words which is made known by the holy Apostles, "concerning Jesus Christ Our Lord, which was made of the seed of David according to the flesh, and declared to be the Son of God with power."[8]

In the above we find a glimmering of the debt to Newman and a hint of their shared concern for an objective grounding for the doctrine of grace. The debt of Wilberforce to Newman can be seen much more explicitly in two other short passages. First, concerning the nature of authority in Christian doctrine, Wilberforce wrote in a manner highly reminiscent of the *Lectures on the Prophetical Office of the Church*:

> The authority of Holy Scripture is first referred to, and its infallible decision set forth. When its meaning is disputed, reference is made to the Primitive Fathers, as providing the best means of settling the dispute. So that those who maintain that Scripture is the only authority, can find no fault with the line here adopted. Scripture is referred to as the paramount authority, but when its meaning is disputed, the judgement of early ages has been taken, as being a safer exponent of its real purpose than mere logical arguments.[9]

---

8. Wilberforce, *The Doctrine of the Incarnation of Our Lord Jesus Christ*, 7.
9. Wilberforce, *The Doctrine of the Holy Eucharist*, 2.

Secondly, in employing Newman's favorite technique of dividing each question into an objective and a subjective part—what God does and how it affects us—Wilberforce shows his deep indebtedness to Newman's whole doctrine of justification:

> Now, as faith is a process in our minds, to discriminate between a true or living faith, and a dead or feigned one, is to inquire into the subjective part of the doctrine of justification—into the part, that is which belongs to us, who are the subject matter of its operation. But, then, our faith must have an object to rest upon—the oblation of Christ upon the cross once for all; and unless this event had truly happened, unless this great deed, external to ourselves, had an actual place in the world of realities, our inward feelings would be only a delusive dream.[10]

Newman had examined the nature of justification, and he had hinted at its grounding in the larger reality of Christ's incarnation; Wilberforce would take up where Newman left off and place the incarnation at the center of the mystery of man's salvation.

Wellspring of Grace

Writing in the 1840s Wilberforce could still proceed on the basis of the tradition of Adam as the direct parent of all men. Men were sinful because they inherited corruption from Adam. All of man's weaknesses, moral failures, and misery resulted directly from the sin of Adam. Given the deep corruption of man's nature Wilberforce could find scant cause for rejoicing in the fruits of progress that the industrial revolution was beginning to bring to his homeland, "for the accumulation of riches, and the increase of inventions produce no real augmentation in the happiness of mankind. Love, joy, peace, longsuffering, meekness, gentleness—these do not grow as society advances, and learning is increased."[11] Indeed, the lot of mankind, rather than being aided by this new spirit, is made worse as the tempo of life increases. It is, as it were, a compounding of yet greater crimes and guilt, robbing man of the serenity in which he may freely contemplate higher truths.

Yet, no matter what progress may be brought by the devices of men, the underlying fact of sinfulness by descent from Adam remains the basic fact of human existence. "Adam must still reproduce himself in those who are born

---

10. Wilberforce, *The Doctrine of the Incarnation*, 5.
11. Wilberforce, *Sermons on the New Birth of Man's Nature*, 3.

his children. And thus, notwithstanding all the varied contrivances of skill and artifice, is there a perpetual propagation of misery and guilt."[12]

What man receives from Adam is his corrupt nature, a nature shared by every human being. This nature is the objective side of man's existence, as his will is the subjective. What it is, therefore, that makes any given person what he is is a complex blend of nature and will. The will is the seat of human personality, the accidents which distinguish individuals. Corporate responsibility is linked to Adam's nature and his sin, individual responsibility is linked to personality, seated in the will. In the fall of man Adam's sin corrupted both his nature and will; but since will is the wholly personal quality of existence, our natural corruption is derived from the corruption of Adam's nature without regard to will.

Such a division into the principles of individuality and commonality is simply a preface enabling Wilberforce to speak of that which Christ comes to recreate. He writes, "The new creation in Christ Jesus was that reconstruction of all its principles, which implied the recasting of every thing in man's nature, except what was bound up with the indestructible identity of the heirs of immortality."[13] It is to restore man's original nature that Christ comes. While it is surely true that men's wills stand in need of conversion, that conversion is not to be confused with man's regeneration. The former applies to his personality, the latter to his nature. This distinction allows Wilberforce to give a high place to conversion without compromising his stand on the necessity of regeneration through baptism. Put differently, regeneration applies to the natural universe, conversion to the moral. Both are necessary to salvation, neither should admit of confusion with the other. Of this confusion of the two he wrote:

> There has been no greater impediment than this confusion to a due appreciation of the nature of either. Men have spoken of conversion as though it were another form of regeneration: of regeneration, as though conversion were implied as its necessary result . . . Conversion is that change or turning in man's individual being, whereby his will is altered, and in place of the love of sin comes the love of holiness . . . Regeneration, on the other hand, is the specific gift of the Gospel. It is that new birth of humanity, of which the prophets had obscurely spoken, and which was bestowed in the fulness of time through His coming, who was the true heir of the household of God . . . Regeneration, therefore, is essential to Christian conversion, because that alteration of heart, whereby every individual obeys the Gospel,

12. Wilberforce, *Sermons on the New Birth of Man's Nature*, 3f.
13. Wilberforce, *Sermons on the New Birth of Man's Nature*, 33.

derives its impulse from the divine renewal of humanity at large . . . For as regeneration is the re-creation of man's common nature, so is conversion the acquiescence of each single heart in the perfect law of the Divine Will.[14]

This pattern of nature and will goes even deeper in Wilberforce. To understand nature as our common inheritance is to understand that God created man not by several acts of individual creation, but by the creation of a type or model by which we inherit all our common characteristics. Natural descent is, therefore, a matter of great concern in Wilberforce's analogy of salvation. Just as our created nature descends from Adam, and with it its corruption, so also our new nature descends from Christ by way of recreation. "The common stream of humanity had been defiled and vitiated through the sinfulness of those through whom it had descended: it was poured, therefore, into His Manhood, as into an incorruptible fountain, that it might flow forth again with greater purity and lustre than when at first it was declared to be 'very good.'"[15]

In creation God's nature is reflected in man, man is the image of that nature as well as the product of the divine will. Christ, in turn, takes on that perfect man's nature which was present in the type and model of all humanity. Christ's humanity being perfect humanity is the humanity for which man was created, a humanity in which the conformity of perfect human nature and perfect human will are to be found. From Christ these again flow out into creation.

Thus, the first function of grace is restorative; it brings man back to a healthful relationship with God. The re-creation of man, his regeneration, is thereby linked with his first creation. Hence, the source of grace and the source of creation must be the same, the love of the Father. God the Father who through his love called into being that which was not also calls into new being that which through the sin of Adam was destroyed. Grace springs from God's love, and that love is creative. God's love is an active attribute, effecting a real change in the common nature of mankind. In a rather tightly knit passage Wilberforce argues:

> So that God's grace is wholly other than the grace of man: it has its root in His own nature, it is a producing cause of goodness in those whom His mercy favours. Its fountain is that unfathomable ocean of love, which is stored up in His Infinite Being. Thence it issues to bring forth into existence the objects which it desires . . . It comes forth like the sun's light for the

---

14. Wilberforce, *Sermons on the New Birth of Man's Nature*, 47f.
15. Wilberforce, *Sermons on the New Birth of Man's Nature*, 34.

renewal of the world. Thus *creative* is that love of God which is the principle of grace. It is Himself in action, going forth through that most precious attribute of His nature, to effect the work which it is His pleasure to perform . . . Such then is the nature of grace—God Himself working through His highest Attribute—the love of God in action.[16]

It must be admitted that Wilberforce is not overly interested in the causes of grace, the brief statement just quoted being as close as he ever comes to a discussion of the issue.

What does come through in his writing is a profound sense of concern for a doctrine of God as loving Father who, in all his relationships with man, is actuated more by a sense of love than of justice or retribution. By placing the acts of creation, incarnation (and its resulting sanctification of man's nature), and regeneration at the heart of his writing, Wilberforce comes to understand the subsequent mediatorial acts of Christ in the light of God's love for his creation.

Wilberforce's refusal to speak at length, in any abstract way, on grace is occasioned by his profound sense of the personal nature of grace. He has little interest in discussions of causality. He desires to set before his readers a deep sense of their personal relationship with God occasioned by the incarnation as the supreme event of mediation. Everything revolves around the incarnation, and our resulting union with Christ. The incarnation is the means of grace to which all other means are related, just as the love of God is the cause of the incarnation to which all other causes of grace are related. For this reason it is difficult to abstract a doctrine of grace in Wilberforce without linking it, at every point, to the incarnation. In a series of Easter sermons this point is made with some force. Christ's glorification in the resurrection is the glorification of his humanity, the product of his incarnation: "it was by the power of His humanity that our Master triumphed. He gave a new root to man's being, but it was through the virtue of that real manhood, whereby He lived among us."[17]

In a second Easter sermon Wilberforce deals directly with the topic of justification. He poses the question, what is meant by justification, and what was done towards it in the resurrection? Justification, he argues, was not required in the original state of creation, but is now required to effect a general change from a state of incurring God's wrath to being admitted to his favor. It is the peculiar office of the atoning death of Christ that it reconciles God to man; likewise, it is the office of the resurrection to complete the atonement,

---

16. Wilberforce, *Sermons on the New Birth of Man's Nature*, 199f.
17. Wilberforce, *Sermons on the New Birth of Man's Nature*, 161f.

providing the means whereby a man may be reconciled to God. In a manner reminiscent of Newman, Wilberforce writes, "what is before us is this, that our salvation depends as plainly on that influence upon our inner man, which Christ was raised from the dead to exercise, as it does on that satisfaction for our sins which He died to offer. Without the last our debt to God could not be discharged: without the first we could have no heart to profit by God's mercy."[18] Obviously this is related to the common Tractarian notion of the nature of baptismal regeneration. Behind (and, in a sense, above) this stands the incarnation which, Wilberforce reminds us, was the greatest act precisely because it was the least natural, there being nothing natural in God joining himself to the flesh of humanity.

The key to understanding Wilberforce's variety of statements on the various salvific events is to understand the complex role of Christ's humanity in the scheme of salvation. The economy of salvation is caused by the love of God, actuated by the incarnation, based on the principle of mediation, and effected by the humanity of Christ. Of the first we have already spoken, of the second and fourth we will soon speak, to the third, the principle of mediation, we must now direct our attention.

Introducing the subject in a sermon Wilberforce wrote:

> The doctrine of a Mediator holds a leading place in the re-creation of mankind. "For if by one man's offence death reigned by one; much more they which receive abundance of grace, and of the gift of righteousness, shall reign in life by one Jesus Christ." The meaning plainly of this doctrine is, that under the Gospel covenant, the God-man, Jesus Christ Our Lord, is the sole channel through which God and man are brought into connexion. Whatever God bestows upon man, whatever man offers to God, passes through this medium.[19]

Thus, the mediatorial office of Christ is two-fold. First, he is the channel of all the gifts of grace; second, he is the medium of all the human offerings of prayer, intercession, and praise.

Mediation is the cause of the incarnation. It is the particular office of Christ to be the mediator between God and man. As Wilberforce puts it, "The blessing which is to regenerate man's nature must have an external source, and it cannot be obtained, therefore, except through one who is a real channel of intercourse with God. This is what we speak of then as Our Lord's Mediation. We speak of an office which belongs to Him by nature, and results

---

18. Wilberforce, *Sermons on the New Birth of Man's Nature*, 179.
19. Wilberforce, *Sermons on the New Birth of Man's Nature*, 267.

from the constitution of His Being."[20] The incarnation finds its basis in the principle of mediation; but we must recall that Wilberforce has little respect for principles that have no concrete reality. Thus, while it is proper to speak of mediation as the principle behind the incarnation, it is more proper to speak of the incarnation as that act which gives substance to the idea of mediation. The idea may exist in sacred history before the incarnation, but only in the incarnation does the idea take on an understandable character. Only in the person of the mediator does mediation find meaning.

This fact is bound to the peculiar nature of the mediator. To be not *a* mediator but *the* mediator is beyond the grasp of normal, sinful humanity. Even sanctified humanity before the fall could not wholly suffice, for while it was in a state of righteousness and holiness it was not in a state of perfection, and it is this perfect humanity, present only in the God-man, that can intercede for us. In that Adam was created as model and type of humanity he stands for humanity, but he stands as wholly human; the type of our corrupt nature as well as our original nature. A new order enters with Christ which radically alters all previous relations between God and man. Thus, the superiority of Christ's humanity, which is the agent of mediation, is to be found in its relationship to the divine Son in the incarnation. How critically Wilberforce viewed this point is well illustrated in the following passage:

> And upon the reality of this fact [that in the incarnation God took to himself actual humanity] is built that peculiar connection between God and man, which is expressed by the term Mediation. It looks to an actual alteration in the condition of mankind, through the admission of a member into its ranks, in whom and through whom it attained an unprecedented elevation. Unless we discern this real impulse which was bestowed upon humanity, the doctrines of Atonement and Sanctification, though confessed in words, become a mere empty phraseology. That "God was in Christ reconciling the world unto Himself," implies an actual acceptance of the children of men, on account of the merits of one of their race; as well as an actual change in the race itself, through the entrance of its nobler associate. The work of man's redemption and renewal is a real work, performed by real agents. It is not only that the Almighty was pleased to save appearances, if we may so express it, by conceding to the representations of a third party, what he did not choose otherwise to yield or to acknowledge . . . but Christ's Incarnation was

---

20. Wilberforce, *The Doctrine of the Incarnation*, 214.

a step in the mighty purposes of the Most High, whereby all the relations of heaven and earth were truly affected.[21]

The peculiar connection to which Wilberforce refers, and on which mediation is grounded, is that which we referred to earlier, God taking manhood (humanity's common nature) to himself. This connection also points to the singular difference in the old Adam and the new Adam. The old Adam (though type and model) did not possess common humanity, rather he was a particular instance of that humanity. In Christ, on the contrary, common humanity, human nature as it was created to be, is present. The manhood of the God-man is perfect manhood (the very idea of God) present among men. This gives substance to the assertion of Christ's office as mediator. "What Christ associated to himself, therefore, was no individual man, but that common nature of which Adam was "the first example."[22]

If Christ takes into himself our common nature, it is necessary to ask what separates that nature which he assumes from that instance of common nature to be found in each of us. Put differently, exactly what did Adam lose? Man is created not only a "living soul", but a living soul in the image of the creator. God being a spirit, the image of God must speak, in some manner, to the constitution of man's mind. Thus, conscience and will, those qualities which pertain completely to man's spirit (mind), are the direct beneficiaries of creation in the image of the creator. Wilberforce then goes on to extend the implications of this:

> Yet the language of Scripture leads us to give it [God's image] yet a wider scope, as embracing all the excellencies, both outward and inward, with which man's nature was endowed. For, from the supremacy of his mind proceeds the power of which even his lower nature is possessed. Herein lies that mysterious principle of Will, which renders his senses and members its instruments. So that three effects are derived especially from the gift of God's image: first, Lordship over the earth and lower animals; secondly, Knowledge of God's works in creation, with which the possession of language was intimately connected; thirdly, Intercourse with God, from whom man received direct instructions concerning his conduct. Now, of these three things, the last seems to have been that of which sin most completely deprived him.[23]

The gift of creation, lost in the fall, is the image of God through which communication and conformity are possible. What sin renders impossible

21. Wilberforce, *The Doctrine of the Incarnation*, 53.
22. Wilberforce, *The Doctrine of the Incarnation*, 54.
23. Wilberforce, *The Doctrine of the Incarnation*, 65.

is the knowledge of God's will, and hence conformity through that knowledge with the divine will of the creator. But that is an effect of the gift of supernature, not the gift itself. The image of God, in some sense, remains in the constitution of man after the fall. Drawing upon the distinctions of Cyril of Jerusalem and Tertullian,[24] Wilberforce draws the distinction between God's image and his likeness. The image of God remains in man after the fall, but God's likeness is destroyed. The image lives on in the principle of conscience, but the likeness dies so that we no longer have a true knowledge of God from which right judgement can be said to flow. While this ability to judge is impaired, it is not destroyed. The real question is whether this remaining principle of conscience, this law written upon the heart, is an implanted power or an imparted gift; "is it a power of judging with which God endowed men, and then left them to themselves; or is it the result of his remaining presence?"[25]

As this gift pertains to the principle of creation through the eternal Word, the power of judging must be an imparted gift. The power of judging comes from the direct presence of the creator in the creature, more correctly defined in the concept of divine illumination. The presence of the creative Word in the creature gives to the creature the power of judging and willing. This power conforms to the judging and willing of him who, in later times, came to be our judge. Thus, that which orders human existence in its most original form is that which was superadded, the divine illumination wrought by the presence of Christ in the creature. As Wilberforce writes, "the guiding light then of original humanity, was not merely that perfection of natural understanding, which resulted from the happy constitution of man's inherent powers, but a special and supernatural indwelling of the great author of all knowledge."[26] This superadded indwelling is the perfection of our human nature, the perfection with which human nature was created, but which is not inherent in it; it is a gift of supernature added to human nature.

Therefore, to answer the question last put: what Adam lost was that divine light, granted to our common human nature, whereby we were guided into the true knowledge of God's will. The effect of this loss is not an inability to judge right from wrong, for the principle of conscience remains in us as does the now obscured image of God; rather, what is lost is the principle by which our being is ordered and governed. We come to be guided by the law of sin because our higher nature suffers the confusion of the loss of its

---

24. See Cyril of Jerusalem, *Catechetical Lectures*, 14e 10; Tertullian, *De Anima*, 41.
25. Wilberforce, *The Doctrine of the Incarnation*, 214.
26. Wilberforce, *The Doctrine of the Incarnation*, 68.

guiding light; and thereby, our lower nature is left to fight its battle with our now confused and disordered higher nature.

Without overly complicating this issue, it must be observed that in Wilberforce we are witnessing another transition characteristic of the developing Anglo-Catholic theology. In the above paragraphs it becomes obvious that Wilberforce's debt to the scholastic tradition is greater than that of any of the writers we have yet examined. The extent to which Wilberforce was indebted to particular medieval authors is not easy to assess, but conceptually he is moving in the general direction of the scholastic theology that would be more the province of the twentieth-century Anglo-Catholics. His analysis of what was lost in the fall and the direct effects of that loss strikes one as somewhat similar to the analysis of St. Thomas. In St. Thomas the formal loss is seen as a privation of original justice, whatever the individual effects of that privation may be. The sense of the orderliness of creation which is lost through the fall is quite similar in the two authors. Harmony in man's being exists only so long as sin is not present; but beyond that, this harmony comes from the presence of God. In turn, "this wonderfully ordered state of man is called original justice . . . This state was granted to man, not as to a private individual, but as to the first principle of human nature, so that through him it was to be handed down to his descendants together with human nature."[27] Thus, the effect of the fall is the privation of original justice, that principle by which our common humanity is ordered. In Wilberforce this translates into the loss of that divine light which ordered human existence. It should not go without notice that while Wilberforce was not concerned to expound a theory of divine illumination, his concept of the role of the loss of the divine guiding light stands as an almost pure equivalent to St. Thomas' privation of original justice as the formal loss incurred in the fall.[28]

Another short excursus seems in order here. Up to this point we have gone to some length in discussing Wilberforce's doctrine of original man and the fall. The attention which he pays to this theme as it relates to the humanity of Christ provides us with two key insights; first, the humanity of Christ is, for Wilberforce, the central theme in the whole soteriological process. To understand humanity's common nature and the supernature imparted to it in creation is to understand the nature of God's gracious action in the redemption of the world through Jesus Christ.

27. Thomas Aquinas, *Compendium of Theology*, 205.
28. The immediate source of Wilberforce's notion of privation is Richard Field, Dean of Gloucester, who published *Of the Church* in 1606. Wilberforce gives one reference to the appendix to Book Three, Chapter Five. See Wilberforce, *The Doctrine of the Incarnation*, 72, footnote 53.

Secondly, and more to the immediate point, this attention to the nature of humanity and the fall locates Wilberforce's thought quite well. We have noted in earlier chapters that The Oxford Movement concentrated its efforts on the patristic period. Though the language and methodology of the scholastics becomes increasingly apparent, the movement is deeply rooted in the language, imagery, and thought of the fathers. The previous paragraph notwithstanding, Wilberforce fits this model as well as Pusey and Newman. To understand this placement of Wilberforce it is necessary to recall one point about the patristic period.

In a revealing bit of commentary J. N. D. Kelly wrote that there were three particularly interesting concepts (he styled them theories) of the basis of the scheme of salvation apparent in the fathers. The first was built upon a mystical (also called physical) theory which placed the incarnation at the center. Christ's becoming man changed human nature, sanctified it, elevated it. The second was a theory built upon the notion of ransom, and the third upon the notion of sin and suffering which placed the crucifixion at the center as the atoning act. Obviously Wilberforce stood in that first tradition; but that is not wholly our point. A little further on Kelly spoke of the possibility of a single underlying notion. He wrote:

> There is a further point, however, which is not always accorded the attention it deserves. Running through almost all the patristic attempts to explain the redemption there is one grand theme which, we suggest, provides the clue to the Fathers' understanding of the work of Christ. This is none other than the ancient idea of recapitulation which Irenaeus derived from St. Paul, and which envisages Christ as the representative of the entire race ... The physical theory, it is clear, is an elaboration of it, only parting company with it when, under the influence of Platonic realism, it represents human nature as being automatically deified by the incarnation.[29]

If one assumes Kelly's basic observation to be correct, it is not out of place to ask what use Wilberforce makes of the notion of recapitulation. Clearly he sees Christ in the role of the man whose manhood is not a single instance but rather the common humanity of every man. The following passage, demonstrative of Wilberforce's appreciation of Irenaeus, is quoted with Wilberforce's own footnote in brackets:

> Now, it is set forth in numerous places of Holy Writ, that the peculiar gift of the Holy Ghost, which is bestowed in the Gospel, is that through union with the Son of God, we may regain the

---

29. Kelley, *Early Christian Doctrine*, 376f.

perfect image of the Creator. Christ "became the head [*Recapitulavit*. Ἀνακεφαλαιόω was, no doubt, the original word of St. Irenaeus,—iii.18, 1] of man's race," says Irenaeus, "that in Him we might recover the likeness of God, which in Adam we had lost." Inasmuch, then, as the gift of union with Christ, which is bestowed by the Holy Ghost, is plainly a supernatural blessing, and that through it we are to recover the likeness of God which man originally possessed, it follows that the likeness of God must have been some Divine presence, superadded to primitive nature. This presence of a superior Being was what gave perfection to that likeness of God in which man was created.[30]

Indeed, Wilberforce's basic christology, as we have seen up to this point, is predicated on the notion of recapitulation. In Christ the fullness of humanity is present, and through the presence of full humanity Christ takes into himself all that has been before the incarnation. The incarnation stands at the center because it is the great event of re-creation. Christ takes up common humanity and makes it new in the incarnation. With his usual homiletical force, Wilberforce makes this point in a Christmas sermon: "Do you see, then, the greatness of this gift? Do you see how man's being was altered? Do you see that by the birth of today there was a regeneration of man's nature?"[31] The whole of humanity is summed up in Christ, and is made new in the act of incarnation. The original order is re-established, but not without its being extended to each of us through sacraments. Christ's incarnation does not make us less the inheritors of Adam's corruption; rather, it re-creates the order of things, and institutes the manner whereby we may regain the likeness which our common nature lost at the fall.

The emphasis on Christ as the "pattern man" reveals the centrality of the humanity of Christ in the theology of Wilberforce. Christ restores that which Adam, through his will, gave up, i.e., the superadded divine light by which man knew God and his divine will. The insistence on this aspect of divine illumination appears, therefore, as wholly consistent with the Tractarian concern for our moral existence. To lead the morally upright life requires the superaddition of the divine light to our nature. We are guided by that light to the knowledge of God's will so that we may be obedient to it. Superadded guidance is what Adam lost, and so it is the primary gift of which we stand in need. We gain this gift from the re-creation of our corrupt nature (in which the image of God had been effaced and our likeness to God destroyed). In Christ's humanity the perfect image and likeness of

---

30. Wilberforce, *The Doctrine of the Incarnation*, 69f.
31. Wilberforce, *Sermons on the New Birth of Man's Nature*, 111..

God are restored; but in Christ the divine light dwells with his humanity in perfect unity, whereas in Adam it was superadded. Therefore, Wilberforce can speak of the greater gift wrought by the incarnation: "God's likeness must first be restored, before we can truly draw near to our Creator. It lies not in strength of intellect, more than in strength of limb, but in that divine gift, which, having been forfeited by the first Adam, was more than given back by the second."[32]

Incarnation: The Possibility of Our Union with God

In the previous section we have commented on the strong soteriological element in Wilberforce's incarnational theology. The incarnation is the salvific event *par excellence*; it stands at the center of all Christian doctrine, and all doctrine is understandable only in the light of Christ's becoming man. This does not mean that Wilberforce did not appreciate the importance of proclaiming those benefits which were won through Christ's earthly obedience, culminating in the crucifixion. In no sense could he be accused of demeaning the value of Christ's atoning act; rather, he saw the atonement as bearing a relationship to humanity quite distinct from that borne by the incarnation. In the atonement efficient sacrifice is offered by Christ, who is both perfect priest and perfect victim. The incarnation, on the other hand, bears a direct relationship to the re-creation of our nature. Wilberforce distinguishes the topics in this manner:

> The present subject is not the glory which Christ gained for man's nature by His Obedience, but that which he conferred upon it by His Incarnation. For by that act were Godhood and manhood brought into contact with one another. The question, therefore, is not what was gained for man's nature by Christ's Obedience; but of what it was made capable by His coming in the flesh. For from this capacity did all His acts as man result. Adam's nature, even had it retained its early purity, had been incompetent to support them.[33]

Renewal of the divine light is the major effect of the regeneration of humanity; but Wilberforce is more concerned with speaking of the actual change wrought by the incarnation. It is this change which offers the possibility of union with Christ. The incarnation stands as the supreme example of the possibility of our union with God, for in Christ the eternal Son and

---

32. Wilberforce, *The Doctrine of the Incarnation*, 82.
33. Wilberforce, *The Doctrine of the Incarnation*, 200f.

perfect humanity are united. But, the incarnation is more than a supreme example, it is an actual event of union between man and God. It takes place within the perimeter of human nature, demonstrating that human nature retains within itself enough of the divine image to make it a vehicle for union. The divine power, always present in the eternal Son, is conferred upon Christ's humanity with which it is joined. This union of manhood with divinity is, therefore, a permanent union which does not cease with the crucifixion or the resurrection; rather it becomes an everlasting union whereby the full image of God is restored to mankind through a permanent change in re-created human nature. This is the power of the incarnation that exceeds the power of the first creation. The gift of power received by Christ's human nature is that which the eternal nature has by its own, but once received it is never lost, for the human nature continues in perfect obedience to that divine will with which it is joined. Thus, the power of salvation which is inherent in the eternal Son becomes one with the full humanity of Christ. This full humanity, in turn, becomes the instrument of our salvation through its mediation on our behalf. Mediation is the function of Christ's humanity permanently joined with the divine will. Therefore, Christ is capable of pleading on behalf of mankind as its perfect example. The full extent of this mediatorial function must now engage our attention.

We have observed before that the notion of mediation in Wilberforce is crucial. He places it at the center of his doctrinal movement from the person of Jesus Christ to the effect of the incarnation on humanity. It is best to let him introduce this crucial point:

> The second part of the subject proposed, was the effect which has been produced upon the condition of mankind by our Lord's Incarnation. This, in other words, is the Doctrine of Our Lord's *Mediation*. For His name of Mediator is not bestowed by reason of any work in which he was occasionally or partially occupied; it sets forth that office, which resulted from the permanent union in one person of God and Man. For the benefits which he bestows upon man's nature result from His being the link which binds it to Deity. The salvation of Adam's race depends upon the influence of that higher nature, which has been introduced into it from above. This gift was first bestowed upon humanity in the Person of Christ, that from Him it might afterwards be extended in degree to all His brethren.[34]

---

34. Wilberforce, *The Doctrine of the Incarnation*, 211f. Wilberforce adds a footnote on 212 (footnote 1) to the last sentence referring to Bishop Andrews and St. Leo. From Andrews he quotes the *Sixth Sermon on the Nativity*: "Since sure it is that the Son of God is made the Son of Man, it is not incredible but that the sons of men may be made

Wilberforce begins by drawing the distinction between Christ and Moses. Moses acted as a mediator for his people, but Christ is the mediator for all people. Christ's office as a mediator belongs to him alone by virtue of his being the second Adam, the "pattern man." Christ not only reconciles God and man, he is that reconciliation in his one person. The office of mediator comes to Christ through his constitution as the God-man. This central fact of Christ's office as mediator, by nature the only possible mediator, has numerous implications. Foremost, Christ is the sole channel of all that flows between God and man. On God's part every grace bestowed on mankind comes through the office of Christ's mediation. On man's part every prayer prayed, every intercession offered, and every thanksgiving offered up enters the divine presence through the mediation of Christ. This mediation is not simply a function of Christ's earthly ministry given up after the return to the Father; it is a permanent, everlasting office which continues until all things are finally resolved at the last day. The humanity of Christ, taken up into God, now pleads for every person.

Wilberforce realizes that the difficulty of placing the mediatorial office directly on the results of the incarnation is that the value of the earthly ministry of Christ may be diminished; but this he sees as only a superficial difficulty. So long as the earthly ministry was in progress (right from birth to ascension) the humanity of Christ was being perfected. The humanity Christ took was perfect, sinless humanity; but in that it possessed a human will, it was subject to the temptations of the lower nature. Thus, the earthly ministry must be seen as the time of the perfection of Christ's human will, the time in which it conformed perfectly to the divine will which was its counterpart in the one Christ. As we have noted elsewhere, this is the moral equivalent of that which was the perfect humanity present in Christ's human nature; "therefore His Mediation may be referred to different periods, and considered under those several conditions, in which he successively displayed Himself. Now, that which made the most marked difference in His human character, was His ascension into glory. For then was the obedience of His earthly life rewarded by a heavenly crown."[35]

Wilberforce's chronological division of mediatorial acts makes it possible for him to consider the atonement as the ultimate earthly event of Christ's mediatorial office, without bringing it into conflict with the incarnation (which belongs to a different order altogether). But the division goes deeper, for since Christ was of two natures, so those two natures imply

---

the sons of God." From St. Leo he quotes the twenty-fifth sermon: "Filius hominis est factus, ut nos filii Dei esse possimus [He became the Son of man, so that we might be the sons of God]." This is as close as Wilberforce comes to the language of divinization.

35. Wilberforce, *The Doctrine of the Incarnation*, 218.

a two-fold aspect of ministry, one directed towards man, and one towards God; "For to man He was manifested as a teacher and an example, while He offered to God the perfect sacrifice of our redemption."[36] The former is fairly obvious, the latter requires a little explanation.

Towards God the mediatorial role may be seen as that of meeting every duty that had been wanting in the rest of humanity. The perfect obedience of the Christ is his submission to the will of the Father, the will for which was present in him by his divine nature. We have spoken of the conformity of the two wills, and this is the central point. The perfecting of Christ's humanity is the perfecting of his human will by obedience to his divine will. This perfect obedience could only be evidenced in an ongoing, earthly ministry, and could only be culminated in the final act of sacrificial death, the ultimate test of human will. Both the human and divine natures must participate in that final act. In Christ's divine nature we find that which equips him to be both the priest and the victim; priest in that he is the consecrated one in whom God dwells and acts, victim in that he is the pure one in whom no sin is present which would render the sacrifice impure. When dealing with the essential component of Christ's manhood in the act of atonement, Wilberforce's argument becomes somewhat more complex. Rejecting the notion of an abstract concept of justice (which he attributes to St. Anselm) Wilberforce nonetheless opts for a somewhat Anselmian view of the role of manhood in the atonement.[37] Christ comes as the new head of mankind. As the new head he alone is sufficient in manhood to be a part of the sacrifice for all men. Whatever may be the abstracted reasons concerning justice, it was the will of God that the atonement be in this manner. Human nature must participate in its own redemption through the atonement of the perfect man, or else the event of atonement becomes a kind of transaction worked out on a plane that has no intersection with human existence. Thus, the incarnation is the indispensable preparatory act for the redemption of mankind. The whole scheme of salvation is caught up in the one person of Christ who not only acts in his humanity on our part, but is in his eternal nature a part of that divine will which decrees that this must be the way in which the atonement is made. "If He had not been the Head of our race, in whom Manhood was set forth in its widest and most universal character, He would not have been so exactly fitted to be that perfect sacrifice, in which humanity at large finds its propitiation."[38]

36. Wilberforce, *The Doctrine of the Incarnation*, 219.
37. Wilberforce, *The Doctrine of the Incarnation*, 235–43.
38. Wilberforce, *The Doctrine of the Incarnation*, 240f.

The mediatorial office of Christ is thus best known to us in the atonement of the cross, the atonement being effective only because of the incarnation; but since this is a permanent office of Christ it must relate to the realm of eternity through Christ's perpetual intercession for us. Again this is seen in two lights, as it regards God and man. In Christ's exaltation in heaven humanity is introduced into the realm of God's kingdom: it is the manhood of Christ that pleads the perpetual intercession for us just as it is the Godhead of Christ that distributes to us, the race with which it is united, the benefits of Christ's sacrifice. This manhood is most fully revealed in the offering of Christ's own body, the offering of his perfect manhood, which is the offering he pleads before the Father. Wilberforce writes:

> No, to act on our behalf towards God is to discharge a Priest's function, and a Priest implies an offering; but it is still His man's nature which furnishes forth the victim which is presented, as well as the Priest who offers it. For what he pleads before God is that perfect sacrifice of His own body, which He offered once for all upon the Cross for the transgressions of a world. And with these functions of His man's nature does his Godhead perpetually co-operate, by consecrating His man's nature to be a perpetual Priest, and by rendering His sacrifice an inestimable offering.[39]

Finally, the principle of mediation can be summed up in the following manner. We come to know Christ as our mediator through the works of his earthly ministry culminating in the sacrifice of his perfect manhood which he offers upon the cross, and which in the resurrection and ascension is taken up into the divine kingdom, there to stand as the perpetual sacrifice for all sins and to plead for us. The manhood of Christ is divinized, and so opens a real possibility of our becoming individually the children of God. But this act of mediation on our behalf by the person of Jesus Christ begins, in one sense, in the incarnation wherein human nature is dignified and re-asserted as it was intended to be; but, in another sense, this role of mediation has been forever present in the Godhead's own existence in the person of the eternal Son: for the Word is the agent of creation itself, mediating the divine gift of existence. Thus, what the Father sees and pronounces good in creation is that which he also sees in reborn humanity, the image of the Son. The principle of mediation, in which is grounded all communication between God and his creatures, is therefore present in the whole divine plan of creation and re-creation. The incarnation, as the ultimate intersection of the human and the divine, is the key to our understanding the whole scheme of salvation. It provides, as it were, not

---

39. Wilberforce, *The Doctrine of the Incarnation*, 247.

only the ultimate example of the concern of God for the world, but also the analogue by which we are able to understand the full scope of human nature and its possible participation in the divine life.

The unity of nature and grace is found in the incarnation of Jesus Christ, and most especially in Christ's manhood. In the perfect human nature of Christ we find the fountain of all graces. It is his humanity which mediates those graces to us through its presence (co-extensive with the divine presence) in the world and in believers. The presence of that manhood is spiritual after the ascension, but it is the *manhood* which is present. This manhood is the perfected manhood of Christ's perfect nature which was always obedient. In it all grace dwells, not only as gift, but by the indwelling person of the eternal Son within the incarnate Lord. Hence, all mediation, all contact between the divine and the human, all creation and re-creation, is contained in the central event of the Word becoming flesh. The unity of nature and grace in the supernaturalization of nature through the incarnation is a theme that Wilberforce not only encouraged but left as a legacy. Eric Mascall (one of the few writers to encourage the study of Wilberforce), writing a century after Wilberforce, has said:

> And theologians have seen the union of manhood with the Person of the Son of God in the Incarnation as providing the supreme example of the supernaturalization of nature by grace, for there is no way conceivable by which human nature could be so ineffably exalted as by becoming the very medium in which God himself lives the life of man. Thus in the Incarnation we see the supreme honor conferred by God upon human nature; in no way could God have honoured it more than by himself becoming man. Yet we must not allow ourselves to think of the Incarnation in purely honorific terms. God became man not simply in order to honour mankind but to perfect and elevate and heal it.[40]

It is not our purpose to cite a number of Anglican writers of the twentieth century who sound like Wilberforce. That would be easy enough to do, and while it would demonstrate his influence, or at least that of The Oxford Movement, it would be little more than a recital of names; what is of far greater significance, and what the above short passage from a leading Anglican of the twentieth century does indicate, is that in 1845 Wilberforce was dealing with an issue that would become a critical portion of twentieth-century theology, and that he was doing so in a way that seems remarkably modern, i.e., by basing the doctrine of grace on the doctrine of the incarnation.

40. Mascall, *The Importance of Being Human*, 94.

The spiritual presence of the humanity of Christ among men is directly attributable to the agency of the Spirit. Christ's presence is the presence of his spiritual power, the power of his manhood among humans in an immaterial manner, and this presence is brought about by his divine nature. Thus, both natures participate in the ongoing work of salvation to which Christ's continuing presence is ordered. Wilberforce sketches the scheme of salvation in this manner:

> What He received in that He was human, that He had power to give, because He was Divine. The consecration of His man's nature, made it the fountain from which grace should flow forth into His brethren. So soon as that exaltation of humanity, which it gained by His Incarnation, was perfected by His consequent Obedience, He bestowed as Mediator that renewing power which the Third Person in the Ever blessed Trinity was the willing agent to convey.[41]

It is the Spirit that effects the unity between Christ and the believer. The Spirit is the agent of Christ's manhood with which we are united and through which we are brought within the realm of the divine life. Such a standard exposition of the role of the Spirit is actually leading Wilberforce to the major point he is trying to make concerning the spiritual presence of Christ as mediator. He asks: "What is the especial end and purpose of that union with the man's nature of the Son of God, which it is the office of the Holy Ghost to bestow?"[42] Our union with Christ's manhood in the Spirit is the only way of salvation. To be united with Christ's manhood is to be united with manhood not just perfect in its natural state, but raised beyond that natural state by the grace given in and through dwelling with the eternal Son in the person of Christ. This, Wilberforce argues, corresponds to the order of nature. In the order of nature we are what we are by virtue of our relationship to Adam, we have a common humanity which determines us in that order. So, also, in the order of supernature, we are determined not by natural descent but by spiritual descent:

> Now, this rule which God has made the law of nature, is transferred by Revelation to the Kingdom of grace. For here too we see a Pattern Man, who comes in as the type of restored, as our earthly father of fallen manhood. He brings with Him from above a pure and perfect, as the other transmitted a corrupt and

---

41. Wilberforce, *The Doctrine of the Incarnation*, 283.
42. Wilberforce, *The Doctrine of the Incarnation*, 290.

debilitated nature . . . Through Him is given back that perfect image of God, wherein man was originally made.[43]

Our union with Christ, therefore, is of the same method, though a different order, as our union with Adam. We are made new by the transmission of that supernature which Adam possessed and lost, and which Christ, by his incarnation, reintroduces to human existence. It is transmitted to us by the agency of the Spirit. This is the special end of which Wilberforce speaks. The purpose of our being united with the manhood of Christ is that we may receive the perfect image which makes us acceptable to God. Thus, it is from Christ's manhood that all graces flow, just as it is the office of the Spirit to convey those graces to us and make Christ spiritually present in us. The work of Christ's mediation on our behalf is first a work of re-creation, renewing us so that we may conform ourselves to the obedience of Christ's manhood dwelling in us, and thus persevere to the kingdom of grace. How this is accomplished in us, how it is that the Spirit conveys these blessings, is the next subject to concern us.

The Mystical Body

Incarnational theology has always had a special fondness for the doctrine of the Church as the mystical body of Christ. In this tendency Wilberforce was no exception. The working-out of the mediation of Christ is accomplished within the church. Integral to this mediatorial office within the church is the sacramental system of grace. In a sermon preached at Oxford in 1850 Wilberforce offered this concise statement on the basis of sacramental doctrine:

> For since the doctrine of Our Lord's Mediation is founded upon His taking our flesh: since its primary law is the re-creation in His person of our common nature, the entrance of divine graces into humanity in its Head and Chief;—therefore some medium is required, by which those things, which were stored up in Him, may be distributed to His brethren. To speak of the Head as the fountain of grace, is to assume the existence of streams, by which it may be transmitted to His members. Now this function is so plainly assigned to Sacraments, that nothing else can be alleged to supply their place. If union with Christ be union with His manhood, it is clearly through those means, whereby we become members of His Body that we are united to Himself.[44]

---

43. Wilberforce, *The Doctrine of the Incarnation*, 295.
44. Wilberforce, *Sermons on the New Birth of Man's Nature*, 227f.

It is of this sermon, "The Sacramental System" that David Newsome wrote that Wilberforce's whole systematic scheme was "summed up", and that "for comprehensiveness and clarity [it] must rank as one of the most revealing documents in Tractarian history."[45]

In the ordinances of the church alone are to be found the means whereby we are united to Christ's manhood. Yet, neither the church nor the sacraments have about them a reality that is separate from the other. One cannot speak of the church existing without those divine means whereby individuals are linked to their mediator; nor can one speak of the means of grace operating (in any regular or normative manner) outside of the mystical body. Wilberforce writes, "The two relations hang inseparably together. By the mystical body of Christ, is meant the whole family of those who by the Holy Ghost are united in Church ordinances to His man's nature. Our real union with each is what gives us a part in the other."[46]

In earlier chapters we have spoken of the centrality of the notion of union with Christ in the theology and piety of The Oxford Movement. In Wilberforce this theme is raised to the level of systematic interpretation. The church is Christ's body because he dwells in it and in all its members. There is a direct relationship between the body which Christ took in the incarnation and the body which we now call the church. The unity of the church is, therefore, dependent on the union of the body of the incarnation with that which scripture reveals to be Christ's mystical body. In a statement both concise and provocative Wilberforce writes of the unity of God, Christ, and the church: "For the union of Godhead with manhood in Christ is a real, perfect, and lasting union, of which the union of Christ with men is the appointed effect. So that these mysterious relations are cumulative and not consequent only, leading us down by successive steps to things on earth from things in heaven."[47] This sense of the incarnation and mediation as the fulcrum of salvation is carried further by Wilberforce's argument that the necessity of the incarnation for our salvation proves the necessity of sacraments. Just as the eternal Son had to take flesh as the instrument whereby humanity is sanctified, so also there must be instruments whereby the regeneration of our common nature is brought to bear on each person. Christ continues his mediation for mankind in the mystical body. Prayers offered to the Father through Christ's manhood arise from the mystical body; within the mystical body Christ's presence descends from heaven

---

45. Newsome, *The Parting of Friends*, 375. As well, see all of ch. 8, pt 2, "Robert Wilberforce and the Theological Synthesis". Hardelin refers to R. I. Wilberforce as the Movement's "first systematic theologian", *Tractarian Understanding*, 21.

46. Wilberforce, *The Doctrine of the Incarnation*, 311f.

47. Wilberforce, *The Doctrine of the Incarnation*, 320.

through the means of grace which it is the duty of the church to extend to the world. The church and sacraments are literal extensions of the incarnation because in the church and sacraments Christ's manhood is present as mediator (just as it was present in the incarnation as mediator). The grand design, therefore, finds its completion in the regenerating and sanctifying acts of sacramental grace which extend out from the church giving greater and greater scope to the effects of the incarnation. The chief effect of sacraments, in turn, is to re-unite individuals to God through regeneration and continually strengthened obedience. This obedience is the same as the obedience of Christ which was the sanctification of his manhood, the manhood which now intercedes for us. The reunion with God through the manhood of Christ, accomplished and sustained in baptism and the eucharist, is the closing of that great circle wherein God is both beginning and ending. It would be too much to say that Wilberforce consciously employed the pattern of the golden circle of John of St. Thomas in his exposition, but the similarity is striking in passages such as the last quoted.

The instruments of our union with Christ's manhood are, as we have noted, the two dominical sacraments which are the direct extension of his mediatorial office. Wilberforce's doctrine of baptismal regeneration bears no significant difference from that of Pusey. Regeneration is the primary effect of baptism, it is the action of God upon human nature that re-constitutes that common nature, and which demands a response of faith on the part of the baptized that will alter the will as the nature has already been reborn (this, Wilberforce tells us again and again, is the difference between regeneration and conversion). However, Wilberforce's greater concern for systematic completeness compels him to tie the regenerating effect of baptism to the central principle of mediation in a way that Pusey would only intimate. He writes in that polemical work published during the Gorham controversy:

> What is regeneration? It is the effect of that gift of grace, which the Father of all mercies was pleased to embody in the Manhood of the Incarnate Son, that thereby Humanity at large might be re-constructed; and which, in Him and by Him, is received by those happy members of the family of man to whom the Gospel comes, and by whom it is not rejected through unbelief or impenitence. It is not, therefore, the general influence of the Divine Power, but the gift bestowed through the Mediator: neither is it the mere promulgation by Christ of a better law, but His re creating presence. Nor yet is it attained by all men, nor even by all to whom it is offered; but by those to

whom it is given of God, and who do not reject it. It is *Christ taking up His dwelling in man.*[48]

In some ways we see in Wilberforce the culmination of the baptismal regeneration controversy. Indeed, it may be that while maintaining the high view of sacraments Wilberforce goes further in accommodating a larger scope of opinion than had any of his allies. Wilberforce's acknowledgement of the rightful place of faith and conversion in the process of salvation, while in theory no more accommodating than that of Pusey, has about it a ring of greater compassion for the opinions of the Evangelicals. There is in Wilberforce no disparaging of those who treat conversion with utmost seriousness. His phrases of consideration show a conciliatory tone that was hardly characteristic of the period. C. C. J. Webb has spoken of what was the more prevalent tone of the controversy, "But some of us can remember Tractarian households in which it [conversion] could not be mentioned without explanation, and without apology for the supposed implication of the phrase."[49] Wilberforce attempts to transcend a great deal of that long controversy:

> Regeneration is that work, whereby God renews man's nature. Its immediate process is the substitution of that new nature, which has been re-constructed in Christ, for that old nature which was corrupted in Adam. That the process thus mercifully provided for our recovery reaches to the whole man—that no part of him is untouched by that renewing power of grace, which has its source in God's love, and its channel in the Manhood of the Mediator—is not inconsistent with the truth, that in man resides a power of will, which must yield to the suasion of these better principles. The process whereby the will makes this surrender is conversion. Look at the motive principle by which the will is swayed to good, and it is God's grace; look to the action itself, and it is man's faith and repentance . . . There is no reason, then, for denying Baptismal Regeneration, on the ground that it is incompatible with the doctrine of conversion.[50]

Wilberforce's insistence on the necessity of regeneration, conversion, and faith did little to ease the growing storm surrounding Mr. Gorham, but it is a model of balance seldom achieved in the midst of bitter controversy. Of more importance is its firm insistence that the doctrine of baptismal regeneration is grounded in the incarnation and mediation of Christ. Our union with Christ truly begins at baptism, for at baptism Christ comes to dwell in

---

48. Wilberforce, *The Doctrine of Holy Baptism*, 28.
49. Webb, *A Century of Anglican Theology and Other Lectures*, 34.
50. Wilberforce, *The Doctrine of Holy Baptism*, 118.

us, thereby effecting the new birth of our nature. We are, therefore, made holy, sanctified, by his presence in us. That sanctified presence in us then increases our desire to be obedient as Christ was obedient. The chief form of this obedience is to be found in our participation in the common worship of the church, and, most especially, in our participation in the eucharistic life of the church in which the mystical body participates in Christ's own body in the highest way open to earthly humanity.

The efficacy of baptism and the eucharist, more properly the efficacy of the whole sacramental system, Wilberforce argues, is built on a strict analogy to nature. He writes:

> If there has been a real re-creation of man's nature; a true reconstruction of his ancient being; and this renewal began in the divine Son of Man, that from Him it might be transmitted to all His members; some means must be provided, whereby we hold to Christ, even as by the course of nature we hold to Adam. That Sacraments should be ordained as the medium of such union—that outward elements should be the channel through which the new Head extends His life-giving presence through the line of His children, instead of contradicting, is accordant to that natural system, whereby we inherit the inward qualities as well as outward organization of our earthly sire.[51]

The analogy goes further. The use of the common elements in baptism and the eucharist demonstrate the link between the system of nature and that of supernature. Water purifies, the water of baptism recreates through cleansing. Bread and wine feed, the consecrated elements of the eucharist preserve the life of grace.

At the core of all sacramental doctrine in Wilberforce is the doctrine of mediation. Christ, the sole channel of grace, gives to sacraments their salvific effect by making himself present in them. Sacraments, therefore, do not replace the presence of Christ, rather they extend the presence of Christ. In baptism that presence, as we have seen, is extended in the indwelling of Christ in the baptized, thereby bringing them into strict relationship with Christ's mystical body; but, then, what is the distinctive gift of the eucharist? Any review of the literature of the 1840s and '50s shows how deeply the questions of eucharistic presence and the centrality of eucharistic worship were being felt. In a sense, Pusey's censure in the 1840s had begun a process of enquiry which would extend well into the twentieth century. The Oxford Movement theologians, typical of earlier High Churchmen, refused to speculate on the manner of Christ's presence in the eucharist. Later

---

51. Wilberforce, *Sermons on the New Birth of Man's Nature*, 42.

Anglo-Catholics would not be so cautious. Yet, that Christ was truly present in the eucharistic elements, and that those same elements were truly means of grace extending the presence of Christ to every recipient, were matters of great concern to the Tractarians. We spoke in the preceding paragraph of the distinctive gift of baptism; so, also, does Wilberforce speak of the distinctive gift of the eucharist as being the presence of Christ. Christ's giving of his body and blood in the institution of the Last Supper does, once again, signify the central position of his perfect manhood for the manhood of those made new in him; but Wilberforce points out that Christ's human nature can never be separated from the divine nature with which it was *hypostatically* united. Hence, to receive Christ's body and blood is to be united with his manhood in which his Godhead is also present. He wrote, "When Our Lord, then, spoke of His Body and Blood as bestowed upon His disciples in this sacrament, He must have been understood to imply that He Himself, Godhead, Soul, and Body, was the gift communicated. His Manhood was the medium through which His whole Person was dispensed."[52] Again the analogy of the bestowal of the gift of the eucharist is strict. From Adam's flesh we inherited corruption, from Christ's flesh we inherit incorruption. Since Christ stands as the sole channel of all grace, all necessary grace can be viewed as present in his divine and human presence among men. This presence is best known to us in two ways, in the incarnation, and in the eucharist. Wilberforce sees the bond as indissoluble; admit the truth of the incarnation and you must admit the real presence of Christ in the eucharist, bestowing the gracious blessings first brought to mankind in the re-creation of common nature accomplished at the incarnation. Therefore, it can be said that the primary gospel gift of grace is the same gift in the incarnation, baptism, and the eucharist: the renewing, indwelling presence of Christ through his appointed means.

Holiness and Knowledge

Enough has been said to allow us to agree with Fairweather's assessment of Wilberforce's *Doctrine of the Incarnation*. Indeed, it does stand as the magnum opus of the Tractarians. The centrality of incarnation and mediation reasserted by Wilberforce was, for a season, forgotten in the light of his movement to Rome, and, more especially, in the rather unique development of the 1860s when the challenge of science and developmentalism captured the interest of every faction of the Church of England. It is arguable that not until the appearance of a conservative form of Anglo-Catholicism well

---

52. Wilberforce, *The Doctrine of the Holy Eucharist*, 64.

after *Lux Mundi* did the principles on which Wilberforce's doctrine were grounded find acceptance.[53]

In closing it would be appropriate to ask what the effect of this mediatorial incarnationalism was upon the individual. In many ways the effects which are brought to each individual in the sacraments are the expression of the whole of Tractarian piety:

> Looking then at the effect of Christ's mediation on mankind at large, it may be affirmed to be the producing principle of holiness and of knowledge . . . We have no original right in them; but by virtue of our being engrafted into the Body of Christ, we participate in them from Him. And since it is by aggregation to the body of the faithful that we become members of Christ, therefore our personal blessedness is the result of that family union, which gives us a share in its collective rights.[54]

The effect upon the individual begins with the church. The church as Christ's body mediates the gifts of the gospel to the individual, so that what each of us can be said to possess is held by virtue of the ministry of the body of Christ. In a short summary statement Wilberforce says:

> God's presence in Christ is the beginning of our regeneration: the union of all believers in the one Body of Christ is its second stage: the third is that influence of the Word on every individual heart, which is bestowed through the public ordinances of the Gospel. This process is not set down, of course, according to the order of time, but according to the order of causation. God calls individuals to enter His Church before they are members of it; but when they are thus called, His gifts proceed downward from that which is collective to that which is individual . . .[55]

Holiness and knowledge are the gifts which God bestows on his church and her members, and they are both infused and imparted. Infused holiness is the presence of the Spirit in each member of Christ's body, imparted holiness is that objective, external holiness which Christ gives to his church through his

---

53. One of the natural effects of radical new movements is how they become the conservatism of the next (or second to next) generation. This reminds the writer of the possibly apocryphal story of the arrival by train from London of W. R. Inge, Dean of St. Paul's, London. A young undergraduate had been dispatched to collect the "gloomy Dean," no Anglo-Catholic to be sure, and his luggage. The student noticed a well-known person on the platform, and when the Dean arrived, the student blurted out. "That's Dr. Darwell Stone. It's said of him that what he doesn't know about theology isn't worth knowing!" Inge is said to have replied, "The same might be said of what he does know."

54. Wilberforce, *The Doctrine of the Incarnation*, 457.

55. Wilberforce, *The Doctrine of the Incarnation*, 458.

continual intercession, the pleading of his perfect sacrifice. The latter Christ applies to his faithful, the former he ingrafts in them through the sacraments. Neither suffices alone; both are necessary to the life of grace.

As in holiness, so also in knowledge we require both that which is imparted and that which is infused. Imparted knowledge is that gift of the scriptures, wholly external to us, in which the gospel is made known to us:

> But His gift of knowledge was not confined to an external truth: truth, like holiness, required also to be infused into the inner nature of mankind. Not only was the body of Christ enriched with that imparted treasure of truth, the Holy Scriptures; but likewise with the engrafted principle whereby it was able to comprehend them. The first was an object committed from without to the Church's keeping: the second was a gift of wisdom, bestowed along with other graces on that collective body, which the Head of the renewed race enlightened by His presence.[56]

Holiness and knowledge are the gifts that come from Christ's mediatorial office and which aid our salvation. To the church is given not only holiness, but the means whereby it is extended to individuals. So, also, to the church is given knowledge in the form of the recorded gospel tradition, but more than that the church is given the principle whereby that knowledge is guarded and interpreted.

We have come full circle. Early in this chapter we noted the similarity of Wilberforce's principle of authority to that in Newman's *Lectures on the Prophetical Office of the Church*. To the church it is given to guard sacred truth, and to do so it is given the grace of knowledge through the mediation of Christ and through the extension of that mediation in the church's own life. The objective and the subjective meet in the church, the place of Christ's continuing mediation and the place where that mediation dwells as an inner reality, not only given but received in each individual believer's nature.

---

56. Wilberforce, *The Doctrine of the Incarnation*, 479.

5

Critics and Opponents

In July, 1838, the *British Critic* published a lengthy review article on Newman's *Lectures on the Doctrine of Justification*. While many critics and opponents would comment on Newman's work, few did it so impartially or so well as Charles Webb LeBas, Principal of the East India College, Haileybury.

LeBas, of French Huguenot extraction, had served as tutor to the family of Bishop Tomline. In that capacity he surely was brought under the influence of the older High Church school. But his association with moderate high churchmanship did not end in the Tomline home. Later, at Cambridge, he was most closely associated with J. J. Blunt, W. H. Mill, and especially Christopher Wordsworth and Hugh James Rose (to whose *British Magazine* he contributed). LeBas published over eighty articles in the *British Critic*, making him one of the most prolific of contributors. His review of Newman was one of his last contributions.. "The theory of Mr. Newman," LeBas wrote,

> takes a middle course between the Romish and Lutheran extremities. He conceives that we are justified not by the infusion of a moral quality into the soul, as the Romanists maintain;—not by a mere imputation, as affirmed by Luther and his followers; but that our justification consists in the presence of the Saviour within us, as effected and administered by the mysterious agency of the Spirit. We are accounted righteous in the sight of God, because, by his gracious and mighty working, there is within us, after baptism, the very author and finisher of our salvation,—the very source of all pardoning mercy and sanctifying grace,—the very fountain which cleanseth from all sin,—the very well-spring which gushes out unto everlasting life. In short,

justification is, with Mr. Newman, a comprehensive name for every imaginable spiritual blessing, which the Christian dispensation can possibly confer on man.[1]

LeBas had identified the strength and weakness of Newman's exposition. Justification was the all-encompassing term that LeBas thought it to be: the strength of such a use of the term was in fulfilling Newman's intention of cutting away from the notion of grace much of the technical terminology that he felt encumbered it; the weakness of such a use of the term was in confusing readers whose minds brought to the subject the long history of controversy. Newman used justification as his generic term for all that divine activity by which humanity is led to salvation.

While LeBas had correctly gleaned Newman's intention, he did not seem able to grasp its full importance. By trying to apply an older use of the terminology employed by Newman, LeBas, and many after him, lost the thread of Newman's thought and criticized Newman for a confusion that existed not so much in his writing as in their reading:

> No orthodox Christian, for instance, that we are aware of, disputes that every blessing above enumerated by Mr. Newman, is actually comprised and wrapped up in the covenant of Grace. On this point, there, surely, cannot be a moment's dissension between the most rigid Protestant, and the purest Catholic. But then, the Protestant has been taught and accustomed to observe that, in the Covenant of Grace, there are certain things which Christ has promised to do *for* us; and certain other things which he has promised to do *in* us. The things which Christ has promised to do *for* us, in the Protestant nomenclature, are generally denoted by the term *justification*; those which he has promised to do *in* us, by the term *sanctification*.[2]

No doubt LeBas's explanation of the Protestant use of the terms is oversimplified in the extreme, but the real point is that even a sympathetic reviewer such as LeBas could not grasp that Newman was trying to get beyond a sequential notion of grace in which either justification or sanctification had to come first. Newman's idea was one of comprehensive salvific activity acting continually in every individual from the moment of baptism.

The great weakness of the review we have been citing was its use of a linear symbol to aid in explaining Newman's position. LeBas represented Newman's concept of perfect obedience as a straight line under which ran a wavy line representing obedience in regenerate humanity. The very fact

1. LeBas, *British Critic*, XXIV (July 1838), 89f.
2. LeBas, *British Critic*, XXIV (July 1838), 90f.

that he could liken Newman's concept of our response to God's activity by a linear example points to the inability of many readers of the time to break out of a sequential notion of grace.

LeBas recognized one very important feature of Newman's thinking that was to elude most of his less impartial readers: the formal cause of justification does not rely on an infused moral quality; rather,

> what he does contend for, is, the inward presence of Christ in the soul, as the formal cause of our *justification*; under which term he comprises all the gifts and blessings of the renovated state: not only the remission of sins, but also, everything which is usually contemplated by those, who speak in the loftiest and most vivid terms of the righteousness of *sanctification*.[3]

LeBas, as we have noted, represented a sympathetic style of criticism. The older High Church position had a much more Lutheran ring to it, but its insistence on the necessity of good works after regeneration made an alliance with the emerging Anglo-Catholics seem plausible if not desirable.

LeBas stood outside the movement and viewed with sympathy its developing theological stance; but there were those within the movement who, though strongly allied to its principles, seem never to have fully appropriated its theological stance. William Palmer (whose main interest was the doctrine of the church) could not tolerate Ward's *Ideal of a Christian Church* and drifted away from the Tractarians in the darkest hours of the 1840s. Another, who never drifted away, but whose position never developed as far as the position of those of whom he stood in awe, was Charles Marriott. Marriott's case is much more complex than that of Palmer of Worcester. Marriott was both a friend and follower of Newman; and, as Church tells us, when Newman made the final break Marriott's allegiance was transferred to Pusey.[4] Marriott's greatest contribution (not only to The Oxford Movement but to theological scholarship in general) was editing large parts of *The Library of the Fathers*.

Little of Marriott's own theological reflections ever found its way to the printer. It seems that he had planned to publish a major commentary on Romans, but that project was abandoned as illness overtook him. His early death leaves us with only a small volume of lectures on Romans delivered at St. Mary-the-Virgin, Oxford, while he was its vicar. Delivered in 1854–55, they were never completed due to the recurring illnesses to which he finally succumbed in 1858.[5]

3. LeBas, *British Critic*, XXIV (July 1838), 116.
4. Church, *The Oxford Movement*, 62–67.
5. Marriott, *Lectures on the Epistle to the Romans*, vi.

The only other indication we have of Marriott's moderate theological stance is an interesting reading list appended to a published lecture at Chichester. For a brief time Marriott served as the principal of the theological college of that diocese. In 1840 he offered the following reading list under the heading of "Doctrine":

> Bishop Bull's *Defensio Fidei Nicaenae, et de Necessitate Credendi*; Hooker's *Ecclesiastical Polity* and *Discourse on Justification*; Bishop Beveridge on the *Thirty-nine Articles*; Bishop Burnet on the *Thirty-nine Articles*; Hey's *Divinity Lectures*; Archbishop Magee on the Atonement; Waterland on the Athanasian Creed and on Justification; Bishop Cousin on Transubstantiation.[6]

No one would want to make a case based on such a few titles, but it is of interest to note that he wants students to be familiar not only with Hooker on justification, but with Waterland as well. In the latter case it would seem that Marriott was trying either to avoid controversy or that his position on that key issue was not nearly as advanced as that of his close friend and leader, Newman. Indeed, the latter seems to be the case when we look at the evidence afforded in Marriott's lectures on Romans.

One approaches these lectures with interest, and in the hope that they will shed more light on the Tractarian concept of justification, but the lectures bear little resemblance to his more famous predecessor's work. There is little doubt that Marriott's lectures express a growing conservatism on the subject that might well have caused a rift to develop had Marriott lived longer. Given all that had happened to Oxford High Church theology by the mid-1850s it is tame stuff indeed to comment on the sixth chapter of Romans: "But the spiritual act [of baptism] is always the same, a renouncing of the carnal life, and an acceptance of the spiritual, a surrender of ourselves to Him who is alive from the dead, that we may be taken out of the old life, whose end is death, and placed in the everlasting life of grace."[7] One must ask, given the very recent blow of the Gorham decision, if this was as much as Marriott could have said.

Indeed, the next paragraph shows a marked desire to avoid the language so powerfully employed by Newman, Wilberforce, and Pusey; the language of Christ coming to dwell in the newly-baptized, of Christ tabernacling with the baptized, entering their souls. Marriott writes:

---

6. Marriott, *A Lecture Delivered at the Diocesan College, Chichester, At the Opening of Lent Term 1840*.

7. Marriott, *Lectures on Romans*, 143f.

> When Christ had made a complete atonement for our sins, He was raised from the dead by the glory of the Father, that is, by the manifest power and goodness of the Father. And in like manner we, when we become partakers of Christ's death, receive the Divine influence which is needed to raise us to a new life, the glory, or manifested power of the Holy Ghost, with which it is said in the eighth chapter that God glorified those whom he justified.[8]

Marriott, it would seem, never appropriated Newman's understanding of justification being raised up in us; rather, he saw righteousness as being applied to us, not in a precisely forensic manner, but still in some sort of external manner:

> And whom He thus calls, he also justifies. Those who obey His call, and forsake their sins by true repentance, are justified by His grace, and accepted as free from all guilt, whether of original sin or actual sin, through His infinite mercy, and through their washing in the Blood of the Redeemer. Upon their obeying His call, this gift is straightway theirs. They are justified; they are accepted as righteous before God, through the obedience and atonement of Christ their Head; they are in Christ, and are accepted in Him. Such are the very terms of their calling, such is the offer of grace and mercy which they accept; and when they accept it, they are accepted of God through Christ.[9]

Justification, Marriott would probably have admitted, is more of baptismal instrumentality than of faith; but his concept of the life of justification lacked the sense of interior renovation which made the Tractarian doctrine a source of spiritual growth.

Marriott saw the role of the indwelling of the Spirit as pertaining primarily to our advancement to glory. God in Christ justifies, and this justification is the beginning of the road to glory. In justification the Spirit comes to dwell in man, but hardly in the sense of the all-encompassing indwelling of Christ we saw in Newman; there is no real sense of the indwelling of the Trinity. The Spirit's mission is to aid each person in conforming to the image of Christ, but the image does not seem to abide in the individual. "This," writes Marriott, "is glory; and to this glory we ought to be conformed more and more, day by day; for there remains nothing more to be done than to conform us to it."[10] Marriott never developed this hint at a deeper sense of justification.

---

8. Marriott, *Lectures on Romans*, 144.
9. Marriott, *Lectures on Romans*, 220.
10. Marriott, *Lectures on Romans*, 222.

He seemed to sense that justification was the first event of true righteousness, giving some claim to eternal glory. Likewise, he seemed prepared to affirm that the Spirit is the agent of grace, preserving us in obedience; but, this is more than he said. Marriott never broke through the older understanding of justification and sanctification. He never saw them, as did Newman, as almost identical terms. His lectures on Romans have the ring of the first two decades of the 1800s rather than of the middle decade. He remained a proponent of the older High Church opinion; indeed, it may be fair to say, he was the most influential hold-over of an earlier age.

Striking Back

> The sacraments again are holy. They are means of grace, especially instituted by our Lord himself for our regeneration and strengthening in the life of righteousness which we live in Him. They form, therefore, essential constituents of the religion of the gospel. They cannot be dispensed with by any, who are within the reach of them, and are able to obtain them. The wanton or careless neglect of them, we must believe, will incur the forfeiture of our Christian privilege of having the Lord for our Righteousness. But, for that very reason,—*because* the sacraments are appointed means of grace,—because we cannot expect that, without them, the seed of the spiritual life will be implanted and grow in us,—the Christian must watch against the notion of justification *by the sacraments*. In their place he cannot estimate them too highly. As means of grace he cannot cherish them too much. But he must remember, at the same time, that they cannot justify him,—that, though they are channels of the spiritual life and strength obtained for us by the merits of Christ, they are not in themselves communications of *His Merits*, (as the Church of *Rome* speaks,) to the soul,—that Christ is the *Lord our Righteousness*, independently of anything we do, however religious and holy,—that we are accordingly justified "freely," as the Apostle says, and by no other instrument, therefore, than that faith, which simply owns the freedom of the gift, and reserves the exclusive glory of our salvation to Christ.[11]

Some like LeBas, Marriott, William Palmer, and even J. B. Mozley in his earlier years, were sympathetic critics. Their criticism was generally grounded in the notion that the Tractarians went a little too far beyond

---

11. Hampden, *The Lord our Righteousness: A Sermon Preached before the University of Oxford, 1839,* 19f.

the Anglican heritage. Others, such as R. D. Hampden just quoted, were outright opponents. By the time Hampden preached the sermon just quoted justification through baptismal instrumentality was a firmly established Tractarian doctrine. The tone of Hampden's sermon serves to indicate how explicit the battle in Oxford had become. Hampden had a particular reason to pick at Tractarian teaching. So resoundingly had he been attacked (and at some points, doubtless, misunderstood) by both Tractarians and Evangelicals that he probably saw such statements as both attacks and defenses. "The Lord our Righteousness" makes Hampden sound almost evangelical in his desire to maintain the supremacy of faith in the process of justification. He was not an Evangelical, but rather a Liberal in the tradition of Arnold. The Liberals had been the individuals first attacked by the Tractarians, but the Evangelicals had been the ones to return the fire.

The real battle began after the publication of *Tract Ninety*; yet it should be noted that Newman said nothing that differed in substance in *Tract Ninety* from what he had said in earlier writings on justification, sacraments, and the efficacy of good works. The storm provoked by *Tract Ninety*, if we are to believe Dean Church, had its origins more in the calculated way in which fashionable opinions concerning the articles were pared away than in the doctrinal content of the tract. Church writes:

> But the Tract had sufficient novelty about it to account for most of the excitement which it caused. Its dryness and negative curtness were provoking. It was not a positive argument, it was not an appeal to authorities; it was a paring down of language, alleged in certain portions of the Articles to be somewhat loose, to its barest meaning; and to those to whom that language had always seemed to speak with fulness and decision, it seemed like sapping and undermining a cherished bulwark. Then it seemed to ask for more liberty than the writer in his position at that time needed; and the object of such an indefinite claim, in order to remove, if possible, misunderstandings between two long-alienated branches of the Western Church, was one to excite in many minds profound horror and dismay.[12]

One of those in whom such horror and dismay was excited was Daniel Wilson, a disciple of Charles Simeon, and Bishop of Calcutta. Wilson belonged to the party of Evangelicals which was responsible for so much of the overseas evangelization accomplished in the early nineteenth century; yet, he kept a close eye on theological movements in England. After the

12. Church, *The Oxford Movement*, 196.

publication of *Tract Ninety* Wilson warned his diocesan clergy of the dangers inherent in the emerging High Church opinions:

> *So the grand central doctrine of our reliance upon Christ by faith, for pardon and justification* is acknowledged; but then, observe how the error steals in. The word indeed remains—Justification is continually spoken of; but it is explained away by the Tractarians. It is no longer the Justification of the New Testament, but of the Council of Trent. It is made to consist of an infused righteousness within us, as well as of pardon without us; and thus the entire body of scriptural theology is silently corrupted, the ground of our acceptance with God shifted; and though faith is still spoken of, yet when we come to the practical question as to what is the instrumental cause of justification, we are told that the sacraments, not faith, are the grand connecting link. Thus "faith is made void, and the promises made of none effect;" perpetual doubt and fear are engendered, hope is extinguished, the corner-stone of salvation is dug up, and the glory of Christ transferred to man's miserable doings.[13]

Polemical attacks such as Wilson's were commonplace during the period; but there were those among the opposition that went much further than polemics. To offer but two examples of such statements, and both from the period before *Tract Ninety* when it seemed that reason might still prevail, we turn to one obscure writer, the Rev. Henry McGrath of St. Ann's, Manchester, and one rather better-known writer, the Rev. George Stanley Faber.

McGrath was writing to the wider audience when he prepared his lecture on justification. He was concerned to contrast the Roman and Anglican positions. His position is typical of the Evangelical—now merging with the Low Church—position of the day. "The justification of a sinner in the sight of God," he wrote in 1840, "is a judicial declaration by the Lord himself of the party's innocence, his being absolved from the charge of guilt brought against him, and his being pronounced perfectly righteous in reference to a law, of which he was a transgressor, or accused of being so."[14] But since God's law is twofold, not only condemning evil but enjoining good, justification must be two-fold. It not only forgives, counts righteous, but it sets a pattern for us as well. This pattern comes only by faith and helps preserve that which was accomplished in justification.

---

13. Wilson, *Tractarianism Subversive of the Gospel*, 4f.

14. McGrath, *The Doctrine of the Church of England as Contrasted with That of the Church of Rome*, 7.

Recognizing an issue that in the twentieth century would later trouble some Roman Catholic writers,[15] McGrath draws a distinction for which he should have been given greater attention:

> The Church of Rome confounds together in this decree [Chapter 7, Trent on Justification] two doctrines essentially distinct—Justification and Sanctification:—and by making sanctification a part of justification, she nullifies the doctrine of the text, justification by faith only. We maintain the necessity of Sanctification as well as of Justification, but not to justify. Justification consists in remission of sins through the imputation of Christ's righteousness; Sanctification is the renovation of nature by the Holy Ghost. The one is the reception of the sinner into favour, and his adoption into the family of God; the other is, as it were, the affection and behaviour of the child as the member of the family when he is so adopted.[16]

The distinction he draws he considers the most important difference between Roman Catholic and Anglican formularies. There is nothing on which justification builds; and further, sanctification is a long (probably lifelong) process:

> Justification is the title of admission of a sinner into the family of God—Sanctification the effect produced by this blessed relationship. The one is his acceptance into the favour of the Lord ; the other is the work which subsequently but assuredly goes on in his heart, the process by which the sinner is gradually restored to the likeness of his Maker.[17]

In the course of four years G. S. Faber published major works on justification, regeneration, and election. Of the three the first, on justification, is not only his best effort but also the only one which really merits our attention. Faber's *The Primitive Doctrine of Justification Investigated* was not a rebuttal of Newman; rather, it was written to counteract the influence of the Irish Layman, Alexander Knox.[18] Faber argued that Knox represented a purely Roman Catholic position concerning the issue of infused righteousness, while he, Faber, affirmed a forensic notion of imputation. Faber's

---

15. See especially Rahner, "Some implications of the Scholastic Concept of Uncreated Grace," *Theological Investigations*, I, 319–46.

16. McGrath, *The Doctrine of the Church of England as Contrasted with That of the Church of Rome*, 29f.

17. McGrath, *The Doctrine of the Church of England as Contrasted with That of the Church of Rome*, 31.

18. See Chapter One of this book.

volume was primarily concerned with adding up the biblical and Anglican material supporting the forensic notion, and, at that level, added little to the ongoing development. However, because his work on justification and Newman's work on the same topic appeared almost simultaneously Faber added two appendices in reference to Newman. Faber's deepest criticism of Newman has some validity to it. He contends that Newman makes two different sets of statements: in the first set Newman argues that God justifies before he sanctifies; that justification is a declaring righteous; that it is an imputation, a perfect act, and has a judicial quality, is forensic. In the second set Faber sees Newman arguing the opposite position, that justification is a continual work; that we can have no righteousness before God justifies us, but our righteousness after justification is such as to be the ground on which God justifies us; that justification is an imparting act making us righteous; that justification and sanctification are substantially the same thing.[19] We have already seen and noted this tendency in Newman; however, Faber fails to see that it is the second set of propositions that Newman affirms more vigorously. Faber's criticism was well-founded, but incomplete. He was content to point out the logical disparities without pressing his case. Likewise, in a more general criticism of Newman's position, he saw Newman arguing for the necessity of good works after justification, but he did not make the case that if justification is a continuing process, virtually identical with sanctification, then does not this mean that we can, in some sense, merit justification? Faber alluded to the notion, but never developed it as a criticism.[20]

If the reaction to Newman's stance on grace was mixed in the academic and parochial centers of England, it was perhaps less mixed (and more negative) in the episcopal palaces. Most bishops and deans remained silent until after the publication of *Tract Ninety*, but then the storm broke. Musgrave, the Bishop of Hereford, warned his clergy, "But beware of a mistake in mixing up Sanctification as an element in Justification . . . While insisting on the absolute necessity of Sanctification, this Master in Israel [Hooker] denies entirely that it has any share in the former; and he calls Justification by inherent grace,"a perverting of the truth of Christ."[21]

Hugh Nicholas Pearson, the Dean of Salisbury (Sarum deans have the authority, by ancient canonical right, to charge the clergy), wrote in 1842 concerning Newman's doctrine, "The Doctrine of Justification by an inherent righteousness infused by the Spirit of God, is here plainly expressed;

---

19. Faber, *The Primitive Doctrine of Justification Investigated*, 411.

20. Faber, *The Primitive Doctrine of Justification Investigated*, 393–408.

21. Musgrave, "Primary Charge to the Clergy of the Diocese of Hereford" in *The Judgement of the Bishops upon Tractarian Theology*, 362.

and I need only point out the contrast which it exhibits to that of the great Apostle to the Gentiles, and of the Reformers of the English Church."[22] Invoking Hooker to make his point, Pearson goes on to argue, "The righteousness of Sanctification, which is interior and our own, is thus, as the profoundly-learned Hooker has elaborately shown, confounded with that of Justification, which is exterior and not our own, but imputed to us by faith in Jesus Christ."[23] On the issue being attacked by both Musgrave and Pearson, Newman's position changed very little between the *Lectures on the Doctrine of Justification* and *Tract Ninety*. In the former Newman had written, "Justification comes *through* the sacraments; is received *by* faith; *consists* in God's inward presence; and *lives* in obedience."[24] Later, in *Tract Ninety*, Newman expressed substantially the same notion when he wrote, "A number of means go to effect our justification. We are justified by Christ alone, in that He has purchased the gift; by Faith alone, in that Faith asks for it; by Baptism alone, for Baptism conveys it; and by newness of heart alone, for newness of heart is the life of it."[25]

Others were not so whole-hearted in their condemnation. Connop Thirlwall, Bishop of St. David's, saw the whole problem as essentially verbal, different terms being used to express the same reality. Bishop Blomfield of London, though uncomfortable with most Tractarian language, was wont to allow that there might be some instrumental efficacy involved in baptism which, in turn, might be related to some inherent righteousness, though it is questionable to what extent he understood the implications of such an affirmation.

On the whole, official acceptance of Newman's views was slow in coming. Most Bishops viewed Newman with suspicion, and occasional hostility. Critics of the Tractarian doctrines of grace and its means far outnumbered advocates. Certainly the furor over *Tract Ninety* and Newman's eventual secession to Roman Catholicism slowed the process of acceptance even further. By the time any measure of acceptance was won in episcopal residences, Newman was far beyond caring.

---

22. Pearson, "Charge to the Clergy in the Diocese of Bricknell" in *The Judgement of the Bishops Upon Tractarian Theology*, 367.

23. Pearson, "Charge to the Clergy in the Diocese of Bricknell" in *The Judgement of the Bishops Upon Tractarian Theology*, 367.

24. Newman, *Lectures on the Doctrine of Justification*, 278f.

25. Newman, *Tract Ninety*, 130.

F. D. Maurice

The opponents and critics who have been cited throughout this chapter are, for the most part, forgotten. While a few of them emerged as leaders in the Church of England, they added little to positive doctrinal development. They offered more ready reaction than reasoned response. One individual, however, demands our attention because of his prominent place in nineteenth-century Anglicanism. Frederick Denison Maurice stands out among the critics of The Oxford Movement as one who attempted a different positive synthesis of the Christian tradition. His influence has been widely felt both in the late nineteenth century and since. He is popularly considered to be the father of Christian Socialism in England. His influence on thinkers such as Jowett, Westcott, and the Liberal Catholics has been well documented. In this regard he can easily be considered as equally influential when compared with the Tractarians; his influence, however, comes more from his social thinking than from his specific contributions to the development of Anglican doctrine. Even today the theology of Maurice remains difficult to assess. He seemed more willing to offer up clues than answers, to seize upon certain aspects of doctrine with little regard for the wider scope of systematic construction. He deserves attention in this chapter because, after the Tractarians, he was the most famous product of the mid-nineteenth-century Church of England.

In most controversies concerning grace and it's means it is possible to trace the line of development through the shadings of meaning given to certain key terms—justification, sanctification, regeneration, etc. Authors occasionally emerge, however, who so radically alter the basic definitions that their works bear investigation even though their doctrinal notions win few adherents. F. D. Maurice presents just such a case when he deals with grace and baptism.

For Newman justification had been the central theme; for Maurice it was righteousness. Every man, according to Maurice, possesses a sense of righteousness to which he clings no matter what may happen. Maurice found this sense of righteousness supremely evident in Job:

> His [Job's] confidence that he has a righteousness, a real substantial righteousness, which no one shall remove from him, which he will hold fast and not let go, waxes stronger as his pain becomes bitterer and more habitual. The deepest acknowledgements of sin come forth from his heart. But he speaks as if his righteousness were deeper and more grounded than that. Sin cleaves very close to him; it seems as if it were a part of himself. But his righteousness

belongs to him still more entirely. However strange the paradox, it is more *himself* than even that is.[26]

Job senses that righteousness is at the core of his existence. He possesses a righteousness that all his sin cannot destroy. Is it an inherent righteousness? Yes, but not in the traditional sense of an infused virtue. For Maurice righteousness inheres more deeply than that. It is a real righteousness that precedes any other act of grace, and, indeed, may precede any act of grace at all:

> . . . we say boldly to the man who declares that he has a righteousness which no one shall remove from him—That is true. You have such a righteousness. It is deeper than all the iniquity which is in you. It lies at the very ground of your existence. And this righteousness dwells not merely in a law which is condemning you, it dwells in a Person in whom you may trust. The righteous Lord of man is with you, not in some heaven to which you must ascend that you may bring Him down, in some hell to which you must dive that you may raise Him up, but nigh you, at your heart.[27]

Maurice's special notion of inherent righteousness helps unfold the theological world in which he lived.

The righteousness which each man can claim as inherent is not so much a principle or an infused virtue as it is a person. Righteousness, we are told, dwells in a person in whom we may trust. "The righteous Lord of man: is with you . . . at your heart" is the fundamental statement. This is the presence of Christ within each person. It yields the sense of righteousness which every person, including Job, senses; it is, however, not from baptism or justification, but from creation.

Maurice's theology was always Christocentric. Our sense of righteousness comes from Christ's indwelling which is a part of creation. Every created being has the special indwelling of Christ. Christ, as the agent of creation, dwells in humanity producing a sense of Christ's presence which is the sense of righteousness, sin notwithstanding. In this affirmation of Christ's indwelling Maurice believed that he had found the mistake of most theologians; they regarded righteousness as a possession, when they should have regarded it as an act of being possessed. Early in his career he stated the principle in the *Kingdom of Christ*:

26. Maurice, *Theological Essays*, 55f.
27. Maurice, *Theological Essays*, 62.

> Everyone must have been struck with these words of St. Paul—"that I may be found in him, not having my own righteousness, which is of the law, but that which is by the faith of Christ; the righteousness, that is, of God by or upon faith" (ἐπί τή πίστει). What is remarkable in these words is, of course, their connexion. St. Paul is speaking of some very high attainment, some end which was to be the consummation of all his strivings. And this attainment, this end, is what? Having an individual righteousness? No; but precisely the *not* having it.[28]

Man possesses no righteousness, but is possessed by Christ. Through the acknowledgement of this being possessed man has a sense of righteousness. This sense of righteousness, therefore, is the acknowledgement, both vestigial and partial, of his creaturely dependence. High spiritual attainment becomes the acknowledgement of total dependence.

Twenty years after the *Kingdom of Christ* Maurice continued to stress this same point. Commenting on the third chapter of Romans, Maurice saw St. Paul employing levelling language, language that put all humanity under the single heading of sinful. St. Paul afforded no comfort to the Jewish believer; both Jew and Gentile exhibited good and evil, neither was superior in either:

> When, therefore, he goes on to speak of God justifying the Jew and the heathen equally, he has prepared both to understand that they can have no real righteousness but that which they derive from God; and that they possess it in Him by renouncing it in themselves; that they have it when they trust Him; that they have it *not* when they distrust Him.[29]

Trust and distrust become central in Maurice's scheme of salvation. To trust God is to acknowledge that one is possessed by God, and, therefore, to have righteousness. But, then, where does justification fit in this economy? The introduction of the notion of trust helps answer this question. Maurice followed Luther in the idea that faith is simple trust in God. He was a defender of Luther, and expounded what he felt was the true basis of Luther's theology:

> Love, they [the Roman Catholics] said, is a higher grace than faith, by the testimony of your [Luther's] own St. Paul, and yet you make the grace of faith and not of love the ground of justification. I do not, he would answer, make what you call the grace

---

28. Maurice, *The Kingdom of Christ*, I, 88.
29. Maurice, *The Doctrine of Sacrifice Deduced from the Scriptures*, 150.

of faith and not of love the ground of justification. I do not tell a man that he is to ask himself, how much faith he has, and if he have so much, to call himself justified. What I tell him is precisely that he is not to do this, that this is the very trick which he has been practicing upon himself, while he has been under your teaching. He is not to think or speculate about his faith at all. He is to believe, and by believing, to lose sight of himself and to forget himself. And, therefore, I cannot allow that he is justified by his grace of love, though I admit that to be the highest of all graces. Trust is the beginning of love, the way to love.[30]

To trust in the power of Christ is at the root of Maurice's interpretation of St. Paul, as well as his own theology of justification.

This is borne out in an examination of Maurice's essay on justification in his *Theological Essays*. The design of the essays places the essay on justification at the center of the volume, and indicates Maurice's acknowledgement of the centrality of the debate over justification. In the first few essays Maurice builds his christocentric system, and then tackles the issue of justification. Maurice's deep conviction on universal salvation made him very critical of those who used justification as a way of dividing up the world between the saved and the damned. He saw the long centuries of debate (including St. Paul's part in it) over justification as a history of man's desire to claim something as his own which he would deny to others. The positive side of justification, he argued, begins by acknowledging that simple, total trust is at the heart of justification. This lesson is learned in Christ's earthly trust of the Father:

> If we start from the point at which we arrived in the last Essay, and believe that the Christ, the King of man's spirit, having taken the flesh of man, willingly endured the death of which that flesh is heir, and that His Father, by raising Him from the dead, declared that death and the grave and hell could not hold Him, because He was His righteous and well-beloved Son we have that first and highest idea of Justification which St. Paul unfolds to us. God justifies the Man who perfectly trusted in Him; declares Him to have had the only righteousness which He had ever claimed—the only one which it would not have been a sin and a fall for Him to claim—the righteousness of His Father—the righteousness which was His so long as He would have none of His own, so long as He was content to give up Himself.[31]

---

30. Maurice, *The Kingdom of Christ*, I, 92f.
31. Maurice, *Theological Essays*, 147.

The justification of the humanity of Christ is the basis for all justification. The man Jesus Christ, trusting absolutely in his Father's love and righteousness, is justified by virtue of that trust. We, in turn, are justified because Christ was justified. From our human perspective justification can be rooted only in trust, a trust gained by witnessing what God has done in Christ.

Christ is righteous in that he claims no righteousness of his own, but claims only the righteousness of the Father. When men are possessed by this righteousness, then, is it properly imputed, imparted, or infused? Torben Christensen has argued that it must be imputed since it is based on trust,[32] but the issue appears to be rather more difficult to resolve. It is true that men are not righteous outside of Christ, that the only righteousness they have is Christ's; this righteousness, however, is given by Christ in a particular way. Christ's righteousness comes to all not only in justification, but in creation as well. Creation brings righteousness with it; justification, it would seem, is the realization that this righteousness is the righteousness of Christ. We are justified because we trust in God's merciful dispensation to justify us as he justified his Son. Therefore, it is possible to say that faith alone justifies. In this, Maurice becomes the champion of his own brand of Lutheranism:

> He [Luther] did not call upon men to acknowledge either a new doctrine or an old one, to believe either in a certain opinion concerning justification or in a certain opinion concerning the atonement. He called upon them to believe in God the Father Almighty—in Jesus Christ His only Son our Lord, and in the Holy Ghost. He said again and again that the *Credo* was justification. He told men that union with Christ was deliverance from sin and condemnation, that that union was claimed and maintained by faith; that faith was therefore justification.[33]

Still, the question of the nature of that union with Christ lingers on. It is obvious that the union with Christ does not begin at justification (whether it is the cause or effect of the union), but at creation. Christ is always present in the individual; thus, justification begins to resemble a theory of consciousness in which justification itself is the point of realizing that which has always been true. This impression is heightened by Maurice's description of the critical turn in St. Paul:

> All his zeal as an Apostle of the Gentiles, all his arguments against his own countrymen, have this ground and no other; the one would have worn out from contempt and persecution,

---

32. Christensen, *The Divine Order: A Study in F. D. Maurice's Theology*, 45.
33. Maurice, *The Kingdom of Christ*, I, 94.

> the other would have fallen utterly to pieces, if he had not been assured that Christ's resurrection declared Him to be the Son of man, the Head of man, and therefore, that His justification was the justification of each man. He had not arrived at this discovery without tremendous personal struggles. He had felt far more deeply than Job did, how much he was at war with the law of his being, the law which he was created to obey; he had felt far more deeply than Job, that there was a righteousness near him, and in him, in which his inner mind delighted. He had been sure that there must be a Redeemer to give the righteous the victory over evil; to deliver him out of the power to which he was sold, to satisfy the spirit in him which longed for good. He had thanked God through Jesus Christ his Lord. And now he felt that he was a righteous man; that he had the only righteousness which a man could have—the righteousness of God—the righteousness which is upon faith—the righteousness which is not for Jew more than Gentile—which is for all alike.[34]

Paul delights in the law we were created to obey, the righteousness in and near a person, Maurice contends. This is a retrospective delighting, however, for it becomes apparent only after Paul comes to faith in Jesus Christ. Maurice, it would seem, is making justification an event ordered to the mind. Justification imparts understanding, especially an understanding of righteousness.

Righteousness, for Maurice, is not just a passive principle in men's lives which is brought to the fore by justifying faith. Righteousness is the Righteous One, an active, effective person: "the righteousness of God manifests itself in another way than by Law, namely, in the Person of Jesus Christ; and that, so manifested, it is effectual to make men righteous; it is effectual to confer a blessing."[35] The first effectual manifestation of righteousness is the forgiveness of sins. Forgiveness is at the heart of justification. Sin, therefore, must be connected to knowledge, or rather its lack, because justification brings knowledge of righteousness. These interconnected ideas become much plainer in Maurice's short comment on Romans 3:

> And now comes in the Justification. The sin has consisted in the man not liking to retain the invisible and righteous God in his knowledge; God has made him conscious of that sin; the deliverance from it, the restoration of man to a right state, must be the justification. How is it effected? St. Paul declares that God has manifested the Righteousness of which the law testified, but

34. Maurice, *Theological Essays*, 147f.
35. Maurice, *The Doctrine of Sacrifice*, 148f.

which the law could not produce, in the Person of Jesus Christ. He says that His Righteousness is manifested in the forgiveness of sins.[36]

We come, then, to see that Maurice is rather more traditional than he appeared at first. Justification is the forgiveness of sins, the removal of an obstacle to the restoration of the divine order in human existence.

Finally, it is dangerous to interpret Maurice by the use of traditional categories, but it seems possible to say, with Christensen, that in Maurice righteousness is imputed and not imparted. This is possible only because of Maurice's constant insistence on the one righteousness of Christ. Humanity cannot possess this righteousness, it can only be possessed by it. This righteousness cannot, in any sense, be thought of as humanity's own. It was this point that made Maurice an admirer of Luther, a defender of the Reformation, and an advocate of the Thirty-nine Articles of Religion.[37]

F. D. Maurice: Become What You Are

> To Pusey the context of Baptism was the sinful world on the one hand and the Church as the ark of salvation on the other; in Baptism we are brought from the sinful world into the Church, we are given a new nature by regeneration and we receive the infusion of the Holy Spirit. To Maurice the context was a world not ruled by the evil one but already redeemed by Christ: every child that is born is born into a world already redeemed, and in Baptism this truth is proclaimed and the child is put into relation to it.[38]

More has been made of the conflict between Maurice and Pusey than the situation warranted. Indeed, from Maurice's first reading of the Tracts on Baptism he knew that he could not support Pusey's position. Archbishop Ramsey put his finger on the reason in the excerpt just quoted. Maurice saw

---

36. Maurice, *The Unity of the New Testament*, II, 22.

37. In *The Faith of the Liturgy and the Doctrine of the Thirty-Nine Articles* Maurice wrote: "It was my object in the first Sermon to show that the Prayer Book does not lead us to formal or exclusive worship, but has been and is the great witness to Englishmen for spiritual and common worship. It was my object in the second Sermon to show that the *Thirty-nine Articles* do not contain 'a ground-plan of the Universe,' but are a warning to us against various ground-plans which confused and limited the thoughts of clergymen in former days respecting Earth and Heaven, and their relation to each other; which are likely to have the same effect upon Clergymen in our days." v.f.

38. Ramsey, *F. D. Maurice and the Conflicts of Modern Theology*, 35.

the world as already redeemed in Christ, Pusey certainly did not. Moreover, to carry on for a moment with Ramsey's analysis:

> Pusey seemed to Maurice, no doubt unjustly, to postulate a change in the divine favour elicited by Baptism. Maurice seemed to Pusey to deny that anything *happened* in Baptism, and to reduce it to a public affirmation that the child was already a son of God. It is certain that Maurice believed that much happened in Baptism, but he subordinated this to what had already happened in the redemption of mankind by the Son of God.[39]

It is this "subordination" that makes Maurice's baptismal theology difficult to understand.

Maurice constantly argued that the bane of theology had always been the desire to separate the saved and the damned. Catholic theology had done this in its baptismal doctrine, Protestant theology had done it in its theology of faith and conversion (or, in Calvin's case, in the doctrine of election).[40] So long as the desire to create two separate societies exists in the Church and in theology, the gospel is denied. Christ who has created all humanity has as surely redeemed all humanity. Redemption is something accomplished, it is something which binds persons to Christ. In this context baptism assumes the character of the first sign of Christ's kingdom on earth, the church. Here Alec Vidler's analysis is helpful:

> Baptism is the first of these signs. It is the witness, the pledge, the assurance, to every man and to every child who receives it that he is a member of Christ, the child of God, and an inheritor of the kingdom of heaven. It is the sacrament of initiation into the new covenant. It is the enacted proclamation and assertion that what is true for mankind is true for this man and that man.[41]

To understand Maurice's position requires that we realize that in Maurice an assertion or an affirmation indicates something happening; yet, on this point, which was the basis of Pusey's difficulty with Maurice, Maurice seems vague at best. Note how he described the effects of baptism:

> First, as to the effect of baptism. I have contended that baptism affirms a man to be in a certain state, and affirms the presence of a Spirit with him, who is able and willing to uphold him in that state, and to bring his life into accordance with it . . . But this state, I have contended, precludes the notion that goodness,

---

39. Ramsey, *F. D. Maurice and the Conflicts of Modern Theology*, 35.
40. See especially *The Kingdom of Christ*, I, 258–88.
41. Vidler, *F. D. Maurice and Company*, 92.

> purity, holiness, belongs to any creature considered in itself. To be something in himself is man's ambition, man's sin. Baptism is emphatically the renunciation of that pretence. A man does not, therefore, by baptism, by faith, or by any other process, acquire a new nature, if by nature you mean, as most men do, certain inherent qualities and properties. He does not by baptism, faith, or by any other process, become a new creature, if by these words you mean anything else than that he is created anew in Christ Jesus, that he is grafted into him, that he becomes the inheritor of his life, and not of his own.[42]

Maurice is arguing against an infusion of virtue which becomes the possession of the baptized. This much is clear. What is not so clear is what it is that God does in baptism which distinguishes the baptized from the unbaptized. It is obvious that in baptism God calls persons out of themselves and into himself. This is the only interpretation left open to being "created anew in Christ Jesus". Can this be related to regeneration?

Maurice argues that it can, but only if regeneration is understood as a corporate term. The stress is again placed on the importance of the whole divine order. Regeneration is the term which describes the return of the divine order in the corporate life of humanity. Regeneration is the re-assertion of the divine plan over against the plan of the world. In stating this positive principle, Maurice wrote:

> Regeneration may mean the renovation or restitution of that which has fallen into decay, the repair of an edifice according to the ground-plan of the original architect . . . There being a certain constitution intended for man by his Creator, and certain influences about him or within him which weakened or undermined it, the author of the work might lovingly look upon it, and devise certain measures for counteracting those influences, and bringing it forth in its fulness and order.[43]

From this it would appear that the effect of baptism is to draw men out of themselves and into a knowledge of the order for which they were created. Regeneration, then, would pertain as much to the whole order as to any individual.

Maurice's baptismal theology was thoroughly moral. We have seen that he denied any change in nature through baptism. The change wrought through baptism is in the moral direction of the baptized. It is a renewal of the ability to conform to the divine order, effected by a renewed sense of the

---

42. Maurice, *The Kingdom of Christ*, I, 283.
43. Maurice, *Theological Essays*, 163.

presence of the Spirit who leads men out of themselves. Thus, to be in Christ through baptism is to be emptied of one's own concerns for the sake of the moral life: "the operation of this Spirit upon him [the baptized] is to draw him continually out of himself, to teach him to disclaim all independent virtue, to bring him into the knowledge and image of the Father and the Son."[44]

Maurice placed great emphasis on his baptismal theology, but it did not receive much attention in wider circles. Despite all the emphasis which Maurice put on it, it was subservient to his theology of divine order. As was the case with his theology of grace, so in baptismal theology he would not exclude the unbaptized from the general redemption of humanity. Maurice's considerable effort to include all humanity among the redeemed makes it difficult to see baptism as more than the individual and particular affirmation of what is generally and universally true.

Baptism's great effect, according to Maurice, is inclusion in the recognizable family of God. All persons are children of God, but baptized persons recognize this and witness to it by individual inclusion in the true universal society, the church. As Maurice wrote:

> By your baptism you have been admitted into the family of God; the right of calling God your father has been conferred upon you; the right of believing that he has redeemed you and reconciled you to himself; the right of approaching him at all times and in all places through his well-beloved Son.[45]

Archbishop Ramsey has argued that Maurice's guiding principle in baptism was "become what you are." This appears to be the case, for in baptism Maurice would have us claim and assert our place in the family of God. In so doing we renounce what Maurice called our "evil nature", the nature which tends to self-centeredness rather than self-abnegation. But it is not the nature which is evil, rather it is certain tendencies within that nature. We are all subject to these evil tendencies. Again, Maurice's language is confusing:

> Baptism asserts for each man that he is taken into union with a divine Person, and by virtue of that union is emancipated from his evil nature. But this assertion rests upon another, that there is a society for mankind which is constituted and held together in that Person, and that he who enters this society is emancipated from the world—the society which is bound together in

---

44. Maurice *The Kingdom of Christ*, I, 284.
45. Maurice, *Christmas Day and Other Sermons*, 26.

the acknowledgement of, and subjection to, the evil selfish tendencies of each man's nature.[46]

Maurice's baptismal theology leaves the reader hanging, wondering exactly what it is that constitutes the change in individuals. The implications of Maurice's theology seem much greater than its language will allow. Maurice disavows any change of nature being accomplished in baptism, and yet he espouses a real divine act taking place. Baptism, according to Maurice, makes one an inheritor of the kingdom, but one is already a member of the kingdom by virtue of Christ's creation and redemption of the whole order. Alec Vidler has argued that above everything else Maurice's baptismal theology is a theology of baptism as the "sacrament of constant union", a phrase borrowed from the first edition of the *Kingdom of Christ*. Yet, it is not a popular phrase with Maurice, and, it would appear, it does not appear in the second edition which Maurice claimed more adequately expressed his own thinking.[47]

In the end, it may be that Maurice's theology of baptism, like his theology of grace, was indistinct. He was a masterful apologist, a good historian, but not a very constructive thinker. At points where one would expect a constructive systematic statement Maurice leaves the subject and goes on to another. This open-ended quality has surely accounted for some of his prophetic reputation—he admits of many interpretations; but, it frustrates every effort to place Maurice in a particular historical and doctrinal context. If this criticism seems too severe, given the high esteem in which Maurice has been held by many over the last few generations, it may be that his reputation is due more to his role in founding Christian Socialism than to his theology. The fairest way to end these comments on Maurice, therefore, is a brief conclusion by one who might be thought to be far more sympathetic, Torben Christensen:

> In 1964 W. Merlin Davies stated: "The importance of Maurice as in some sense the 'father of modern English theology' has been sufficiently demonstrated." Considered as a summing up of what so many have said about Maurice's importance and influence, this statement might seem to be justified. Yet it ought to be added that nobody has demonstrated the impact Maurice has actually had on the development of English theology. The naked truth is, however, that apart from his having contributed to the downfall of Victorian orthodoxy through his criticism, the

---

46. Maurice, *The Kingdom of Christ volume 1*, 331.

47. See the editor's introduction to the edition of *The Kingdom of Christ* already cited. Note that the editor is A. R. Vidler!

influence which Maurice wielded on the theological thinking of his own day was negligible. This was also the case after his death. Maurice found no new followers in what he had considered the essentials of his teaching, nor did it become a formative influence in the religious or theological debate of a later age.[48]

The End of the Beginning

Robert Isaac Wilberforce, in an admirable if somewhat biased conspectus of the first half of the nineteenth century, outlined the major themes of that period. The century began, Wilberforce reminds us, with an increase in religious fervor which was the result of the Evangelical movement. The repeal of the Test and Corporations Act, and other political events, gave rise to The Oxford Movement. The Tractarians sought a new principle in the old doctrine of apostolic succession. Yet, only so much could be said concerning the historic episcopate before the fundamental question "how are men saved?" arose again. This basic question, put first by the Evangelicals, gave rise to two systems or theories. These two constituted the two schools, Evangelical and Catholic:

> Some have imagined that since the sacrifice of Christ has atoned for sin, men may apply the remedy to themselves by an act of faith, and thus bring themselves into relation with their maker. Without denying that such acts result from the influence of Almighty God—for all human acts result, indirectly from his power—they yet affirm that persons come to God as individuals, and afterwards fall within the range of those relations which bind together the members of Christ. The Church system, on the other hand, supposes the first movement to come from God, when, in the person of the Word, He unites to Himself man's nature. Its primary principle is, that those spiritual gifts which, but for sin, would have been the original inheritance of man's nature, were embodied in the humanity of the Word made flesh, that from Him they might be communicated to His brethren. In this manner did grace find its way from heaven to earth, diffusing itself through the body of the Church, and extending to all its members. That which dwelt first in Christ in that He was full of grace and truth by nature,

---

48. Christensen, *The Divine Order*, 300. The quotation Christensen uses is from W. Merlin Davies, *An Introduction to F. D. Maurice's Theology*, ix–x.

was to be extended as a gift to His servants. "For of his fulness have all we received, and grace for grace."[49]

Later in the same charge, Wilberforce drew out more plainly his impression of the critical issue:

> The true point at issue is whether there be any substance in the ordinances of grace—whether any real thing is conferred upon men, when they are made members of Christ, or when they receive their Maker. And this will be found to depend upon the notion which is entertained of Him—whether His Incarnation is understood to be a permanent fact, exercising a present influence upon the condition of His servants.[50]

Throughout this chapter we have heard the dissenting opinions from those who, in the minds of the Tractarians, would in lesser or greater degree diminish what was given first in the incarnation and subsequently in the means of grace. The debate over grace and its means found its highest expressions in the period 1833–53. By the latter date (except for eucharistic doctrine) the debates were becoming stale, and the issues were changing. Despite all that has been written about the controversies and changes that affected the Church of England in the 1860s and '70s, very little constructive theology would be written on the incarnation and grace until the last decade of the century.

Pusey's view of the matter was too optimistic, yet in an 1853 sermon he could dare write what thirty years before many would have considered unthinkable:

> Further, all agree that God, in justifying us, not only *declares* us, but *makes* us, righteous. He does not declare us to be that which he does not make us. He makes us that which we *were* not, but which now, if we are in Him, (what ever there still remain of inward corruption,) we by His gift are, holy. He does not give us an untrue, unreal, nominal, shadowy righteousness, "the righteousness of God in Christ;" for which, being unrighteous still, we are to be accounted righteous. But what He imputes, that He also imparts. He creates in us an inchoate and imperfect, yet still a real and true righteousness; inchoate and imperfect, because "we all," while in the flesh, "in many things offend;" yet real and true, because it is the gift of God, and the first fruits of His Holy Spirit.[51]

---

49. Wilberforce, *The Evangelical and Tractarian Movements*, 12f.
50. Wilberforce, *The Evangelical and Tractarian Movements*, 16.
51. Pusey, "Justification, a Sermon Preached before the University at St. Mary's, on the 24th Sunday after Trinity, 1853" in *Nine Sermons*, 7f (pagination is by sermon).

We have seen that agreement was hardly widespread, but the Tractarian doctrine of grace had made significant inroads into the understanding of God's activity by the mid-nineteenth century. In the same sermon as was just quoted, Pusey mentioned a theme that would become increasingly important in the life of the emerging Anglo-Catholic parishes and institutions. In a rare, remarkably beautiful passage he wrote:

> All is of Christ. His is the grace, which brought us out of the mass of our natural corruption in Adam. His was the new principle of life, which in baptism He imparted to us. His the grace which cherished, nurtured, enlarged, that first gift, or if unhappily we wasted it, through repentance, brought us back, converted, renewed, restored us. His, each gift of superadded grace, whereby He rewards the use which, through His grace, we make of each former grace, bestowing grace for grace. And life eternal, too, will be from Him, grace for grace.[52]

"Through repentance" was to become a hallmark of the Tractarian doctrines of grace and its means as they spread into the life of the Church of England.

---

52. Pusey, "Justification, a Sermon Preached before the University at St. Mary's, on the 24th Sunday after Trinity, 1853" in *Nine Sermons,* 43 (pagination is by sermon).

6

Penitential Ministry

The Tractarian Experiment

Writing just before the centenary of The Oxford Movement C. P. S. Clarke made a point too important to be overlooked. Speaking of the common interpretations of the movement he wrote:

> I cannot help feeling that some eminent historians of the Movement have been led astray by its dramatic character. It does in its Oxford days present all the features of a great tragic drama. In the first act there is the unfolding and developing of the plot; in the second the period of triumph and success; in the third the set-back of *Tract 90* is followed by a series of reverses culminating in the reverberating crash of the departure of the hero, upon which the curtain falls. Dean Church, indeed, made no attempt to bring the story beyond 1845. Others have told us most interesting things about later developments but rather leave the impression that what follows is in the nature of an epilogue, like the conclusion of a book telling us what happened to the principal characters, rather than the gradual unfolding of a story... In my own mind 1845 was a stage, not a climax. It is the end of the first canto of an epic, not the last act of a drama.[1]

Clarke, S. L. Ollard (to whom Clarke dedicated the work just cited), and other High Churchmen of the same period, tended to see the line of development primarily in the revival of Catholic liturgical practice and Catholic

---

1. Clarke, *The Oxford Movement and After*, viif. See further Herring, *The Oxford Movement in Practice*, especially chapter 8, for an excellent engagement with confession as well as the continuity between the pre-1845 Oxford Movement and what followed.

sacramental doctrine. Both are among the true developments of the period; but throughout this work we have been tracing the underlying theological development of the doctrines of grace and incarnation without which the other developments would have been shallow indeed.

Surely the events after 1845 were not merely an epilogue, but rather the next stage of a movement that both developed and grew amidst great adversity. The eucharistic controversy has been most often cited as the major source of friction in the 1850s through the 1870s. Since the ritualist controversy belongs to the larger eucharistic controversy, this is undoubtedly true; but it must be remembered that the eucharistic controversy did not begin over the issue of the mode of Christ's presence, rather it began as a controversy over the means of grace. Because it is the central controversy (with the Gorham case running a close second) it has been studied in every succeeding period; because its main feature was the mode of Christ's presence, it lies outside the scope of this investigation.

If it is valid to contend (as Clarke did) that The Oxford Movement gave rise to a continuing expression of Catholic theology and piety in Anglicanism, then it must be shown that this was worked out in the wider life of the Church. Two striking areas of endeavor stand out among the many directions in which The Oxford Movement spread in the larger Church: first, its parochial experiments; second, its involvement in the penitentiary system through its encouragement of the sisterhoods. Both of these were the result of the strong commitment of most Tractarians to work among the poor and disadvantaged, but the nature of that work found its theological basis in the doctrines with which we are concerned.

Numerous examples of parishes could be cited. The great Tractarian parishes of London, St. Paul's, Knightsbridge (and her daughters), St. Alban's, Holborn, All Saints', Margaret Street, all evidence the Tractarian style of Church life. Yet one of the earliest Tractarian parishes is often forgotten. St. Saviour's, Leeds, was an avowed experiment in which mission to the working class and sacramental principles were the motivating factors. It is to that parish that we turn for an example of doctrine and practice in the Tractarian mode. "Dr. Hook," wrote G. P. Grantham, Vicar of St. Saviour's in a later, more settled period, "had devised a plan for dividing Leeds into thirty independent parishes, one of which was to be the scene of the 'Tractarian experiment.'"[2] Hook's notion of an experiment was to install a "college" of clergy to oversee the work in this area. He proposed the idea to his good friend, Pusey, who took it up pledging a large amount for the construction of the church. The long, sad story that followed need

2. Grantham, *A History of Saint Saviour's, Leeds*, 6.

not be told in this context, but in 1845 the church was completed, and the great experiment was under way.

The experiment turned out to be much more than Hook had anticipated, for the intervening years had produced a great body of young, convinced Tractarians who desired to put into practice the doctrines given new life in The Oxford Movement. The following, written by one of St. Saviour's first clergy, illustrates the depth of doctrinal zeal that was brought to the experiment:

> Those more intimate truths which bring home to the individual soul the fruits of the Incarnation, and draw out in array the mysteries of the humiliation of the Eternal Son, had not commonly been brought home to the hearts of the people. The anti-Sacramental system, which the intercourse with foreign Reformers brought into England, starts back appalled from the sight, in its details, of the Divine Nature joined to the Human, whereof is One Christ: and deeming that the Sacramental teaching is the conversion of the Godhead into Flesh, faith fails to discern the deeper and wiser marvel, the taking of the Manhood into God. To that mind the old doctrine of Justification seems to assert an inherent righteousness in humanity apart from our Lord's Incarnation . . . In a word, they practically supposed the mystery of the Incarnation to be subservient only to the Atonement, in lieu of believing that our Lord hallowed His own Human Nature in order to impart this Its holiness to us, and by It to bind us into one with Himself and with God.[3]

The experiment promoted by such Catholic zeal found its expression in the homiletical, eucharistic, and penitential life of the parish. Whereas in some of the more famous Tractarian parishes eucharistic practice and ceremonial became the chief item of controversy, at St. Saviour's the storm mounted over the issue of confession and absolution. Nothing was closer to the heart of Pusey's ideal than the regular practice of self-examination, confession, and absolution. The octave of St. Saviour's consecration found Pusey in Leeds preaching as often as three times a day, outlining, as it were, the theological background for the practice which he is more famous for describing in *The Entire Absolution of the Penitent I and II*. Of the nineteen sermons preached, Pusey wrote ten. The others were the products of Marriott, Keble, Dodsworth, Isaac Williams, and Upton Richards (first Vicar of All Saints', Margaret Street). On the whole they form a bleak course of sermons, dwelling at length on the weight of sin.

---

3. Pollen, *Narrative of Five Years at St. Saviour's, Leeds*, 71f

Almost immediately confession became a regular part of the life at St. Saviour's. Dr. Hook was less than enthusiastic; Longley, the Bishop of Ripon, was appalled. Keble went to Leeds in 1848 to investigate the situation and reported favorably to Pusey. He thought that confession was being handled in a reasonable manner. Reflecting on the controversy Pollen wrote, "He [the Bishop of Ripon] disliked their [the St. Saviour's clergy] teaching and doubted if it were true on the doctrines of Penance and Confession, and on the doctrine of the Eucharist. These lay at the root of their work in the parish, and if once made the matter of dispute *could* not be given up, how much soever peace and unity were desired."[4]

> Just how many confessions were heard is not known, but that they were heard in the church is evidenced by the fact that the Bishop of Ripon ordered the practice stopped in 1848 when the Rev. Thomas Minster succeeded A. P. Forbes as vicar.[5]

Nor should the attitude of Pollen that confession was integral to the work at St. Saviour's be thought of as unique. The attitude was shared throughout the emerging Tractarian parishes. Good evidence of this is found in a comment of the 1860s concerning St. Alban's, Holborn:

> No wonder, then, that the St. Alban's priests, working in the locality they do, feel everything superficial that is not based on Confession; that they have their misgivings unless, like the Ephesian converts, their penitents confess and show their deeds. The parishioners may now be Confirmed and brought to Holy Communion without Confession, but they are made clearly to understand that in such a case the responsibility of a devout communion rests with themselves alone. In point of fact, few of them would desire to Communicate without Confessing first; and the number of parishioners form no inconsiderable proportion at the Festival Communions.[6]

Doctrinal questions remained central. Incarnation, grace, and the means of grace, remained the points of contention. While the controversy at St. Saviour's centered on confession, the other questions were not ignored. In censuring the clergy of St. Saviour's Bishop Longley wrote:

---

4. Pollen, *Narrative of Five Years at St. Saviour's, Leeds*, 79f.
5. Savage and Tyne, *The Labours of Years*, 200.
6. Excerpt from an article in *The Churchman's Companion for November, 1869*, which appears as an appendix in G. W. E. Russell, *St. Alban the Martyr, Holburn: A History of Fifty Years*, 354.

> Now our received notion of a sacrament is, that it is one of those means of grace which are generally necessary to salvation; and the impression naturally produced upon your minds [by preaching on the seven sacraments] must be, that it would be just as dangerous to neglect extreme unction, as to neglect Baptism or the Lord's Supper: and remembering the teaching of another of your Preachers [the Rev'd. S. Rooke], you would draw the inference that you were as much bound to come to a priest for private absolution before receiving the Holy Communion, as to go to the Holy Communion itself.[7]

The wholesale secession of St. Saviour's clergy to Roman Catholicism between 1848 and 1851 only strengthened the Bishop's dislike for St. Saviour's. In reply to the Bishop's censures a letter was composed, addressed to the vicar, the Rev. T. Minster, purportedly written by members of the congregation. In truth, no matter how well-instructed, it is unlikely that among the 660 signers, 249 of whom could not write their names, any could have been found with the acumen to compose the text; yet, if nothing else, it serves to illustrate how firmly another disputed doctrinal point had been ingrained in St. Saviour's teaching:

> the solemnity connected with your ordinary administration of Holy Baptism, has seemed nothing else to us than the necessary consequence of the doctrine which you and our other pastors have been the instruments of God's inworking in our souls, viz., that in the sacrament we are regenerate and born anew, grafted into the body of our Lord, and made the children of God. It has but fulfilled, in some measure, the gracious purpose of reminding us that we received, in our baptism, the gift of the regenerate nature, and experienced in our own persons the fruitfulness of the Incarnation of the Son of God.[8]

The practice of hearing confessions continued in St. Saviour's despite the Bishop's censure. Savage and Tyne report that "confessions were heard, initially in the church, but owing to the spying of Mr. Randall, Vicar of All Saints, (which church owed so much to St. Saviour's) this was reported to Dr. Longley and he ordered that the practice should cease . . . Mr. Minster carried on hearing confessions, but this time in the vicarage."[9] Even after the disaster of 1851 when Newman came to preach at St. Ann's Roman Catholic Church, Leeds, and a number of St. Saviour's clergy were received into the

---

7. Longley, *A Letter to the Parishioners of St. Saviour's, Leeds*, 8.
8. Appended to Longley, *A Letter to the Parishioners of St. Saviour's, Leeds*.
9. Savage and Tyne, *The Labours of Years*, 20.

Roman Church at the service, the sacramental practice of confession, absolution, and penance, did not cease at St. Saviour's. It did take a brief, bizarre twist under the leadership of the next vicar, The Rev'd. Knott who, with his sister, came to the parish after Minster's sudden departure. The bizarre twist was that for a time the Rev'd. Robert Aitken was present assisting Mr. Knott. This led to placing great emphasis on conversion, revivals, and other enthusiastic practices, followed by instruction on penance. One recorded incident bears repeating as an illustration of the combination of emerging Anglo-Catholic practices with the Aitkenite ideal:

> Miss Knott, assisted by Mrs. Hughes, ran two classes for the factory girls. There were about forty girls in each class and the two groups were kept very much apart. One class "of loose, wild girls" had activities of a mainly social and educational nature. There was just one rule of a vaguely religious type—that they must not swear; some of the girls thought this to be "devilish peculiar." Attempts were made, however, to get them to change their ways. When a girl showed signs of conversion she was sent to the incumbent and he and his two deacons, two more of Mr. Aitken's converts, would pray with her until she was ready for confession and absolution. Often these young girls would be brought to such a pitch of frenzy that their "ravings and rantings—shrieks, sobs, and shouts may be heart in the street." The girl would then join Miss Knott's other class, which she called her "devout and holy girls" or the "converted Class." The members of the "Converted Class" attended mass at 5:00 a.m. every day on their way to work in the nearby flax mills, and Evensong at 7:30 p.m. when on their way home. The girls were encouraged to spend much time in prayer, to confess their sins and to attend the Lower House [a parish school] to receive instruction.[10]

However aberrant the full practices of St. Saviour's may have been during that brief period in the 1850s, the practice of regular confession was becoming ingrained in Tractarian parishes. The above account from St. Saviour's leads us to a further point concerning the work of these parishes, the concern for the working poor and the fallen women of the cities.

The rise of penitentiary work is a narrative that cannot be told outside the larger context of the revival of religious orders in the Church of England. It is to the many groups of "sisters of mercy" that credit must go for much of the pioneering work in the urban centers of England. The story need not be retold, but the connection with the emerging Anglo-Catholic Church-manship must

---

10. Savage and Tyne, *The Labours of Years*, 30.

be made. As early as 1849 the Rev'd John Armstrong had appealed for the establishment of Church penitentiaries staffed by devoted and pious women. He published appeals in such widely circulated periodicals as the *English Review*, the *Quarterly*, and the *Christian Remembrancer*.[11]

Beginning in the mid-1840s penitentiaries had developed, some religious such as Wantage and Clewer, some secular such as the large one at Magdalen Hospital, London. By 1853 an association had been formed to foster and further this work. In its First Annual Report the members wrote, "Day after day brings to the doors . . . some poor fallen woman, anxiously yearning to leave their [sic] course of sin and misery, and to enter upon the path of penitence and virtue, and day after day sees them returning back, despairing and heartbroken, to their abodes of guilt, because the Houses already established are too small to receive them."[12] The concern was wider than the Tractarian movement, but the council of the Association reflected more Catholic sentiments than other associations of the time. Such luminaries as W. F. Hook (who, despite his Leeds problems, must be classed among the Tractarian sympathizers), W. E. Gladstone, Mr. Justice Coleridge, J. Armstrong, Thomas Keble, Bishop Forbes, Bishop Wilberforce and others, were among those convinced of the principle of the association, i.e., "to aid those Penitentiaries only which are superintended by self-devoted women, under the guidance, as to spiritual matters, of a clergyman of the Church of England."[13]

The ideal envisioned by these early leaders of the penitentiary movement is nicely summed up in the work of the sisters at Clewer and their warden, the Rev'd. T. T. Carter (who was later to be Armstrong's biographer). Carter's vision of the penitential life began with confession. While he never advocated compulsory confession, his biographer admits, "he did feel that a Penitentiary could not cure those extreme cases without this medicine."[14] So the ideal of regular confession was set not only for the sisters who did the work, but for penitentiary residents as well. Carter's model for the work was widely used, and the Community of St. John Baptist became a leader not only in England, but, as a history of their first two decades indicates, in the United States as well.[15] It is not simply in the use of Confessions that the Clewer community provided a model; it also had a wider outlook than many other penitentiaries. Those in whom devotion had truly been fostered

---

11. Armstrong, *An Appear for the Formation of a Church Penitentiary*, 14.
12. *First Annual Report of the Church Penitentiary Association*, 1.
13. *First Annual Report of the Church Penitentiary Association*, 15.
14. Hutchings, *The Life and Letters of Thomas Thellusson Carter*, 81.
15. Simpson and Story, *Stars in His Crown*, 1–33, especially 19, footnotes 7 and 8.

could aspire to be "Magdalens" in the community, carrying out much of the work of the community; again Carter's biographer writes:

> ... so in this comparatively new penitentiary system any soul, however degraded in the past, may, if persevering, still recover some genius for holiness, rise to the demands of a dedicated life, a dedication in a different form from that of a Sister of Mercy, yet having a beauty of its own, as a rose differs from a lily.[16]

The roots of the developing penitentiary life (as well as the developing conventual life) are clear enough: a sense of the need of God's grace, a sense of that need being fulfilled in the ministry of sacraments, the strong belief in the mediation of Christ evidenced in the incarnation as the basis for the sacramental ministry of grace. We have cited this brief example from the penitentiary work because it demonstrates at once both the strong sacramental aspect of the founders, and their equally strong social concerns. Twenty years after its founding the Church Penitentiary Association produced a set of papers for discussion at its annual meeting. Among many interesting points noted are: after twenty-one years (as of 1873) there were thirty-one houses in union with the association; these houses accommodated 829 penitents; they were staffed by 118 "self-devoted" women. More interesting still is the comment that reflects how much had been learned (much of which was anticipated by T. T. Carter) in the first two decades:

> Perhaps it is better not to attempt a forced system of religious training. It is of great advantage if some liberty of going outside the walls of the penitentiary can be allowed, e.g., to church, and for exercise, so that the change back to the world may not be so great ... The expediency of urging sacramental confession is more than doubtful .In most cases a very considerable time is required before the penitent can safely be trusted to make a true confession ... It seems best to let it be sought as a great privilege and favour after evidence given of sincerity.[17]

From Tractarian to Anglo-Catholic

Tracing the wider history of a movement through two principal examples of its work can lead to the conclusion that the controversy involved was worked out only at the practical level of Church life. Such was not the

16. Hutchings, *Life and Letters of T. T. Carter*, 87.
17. *Penitentiary Work in the Church of England*, 22.

case with the controversy over the practice of confession. As early as 1843 a serious written controversy began. The baptismal regeneration and eucharistic controversies received more attention in the press and courts; but the confession controversy, while less famous, received a good deal of attention in printed disputation.

In what proved to be the next to last number of the *British Critic*, Frederick Oakeley published an article on sacramental confession. Oakeley was then the minister of the Margaret Chapel (soon to become All Saints', Margaret St. with Upton Richards as its first vicar). He, like W. G. Ward, was concerned for the practice of the Catholic faith in the Church of England. Also like Ward, he tended to look at current Roman Catholic practice (especially of the French variety) as the norm for developing the practices of the Church of England.

Oakeley, like Pusey, was deeply concerned about the effect of post-baptismal sin. He, too, found its remedy in the practice of sacramental confession. The special value of confession and absolution was its sanative effect. Baptismal regeneration cannot stand alone. There must be a remedy for sin after baptism if total despair is to be avoided:

> You cannot elevate persons' notions of holiness, deepen their sense of the guilt of sin, increase tenderness of conscience, enliven the impression of the Divine Presence around and within, and realize the expectation of a Judgement according to works, without suggesting to the mind of an attentive and considerate disciple, many harassing retrospects, many perplexing doubts, many fearful misgivings, and anxious anticipations. And if your "Church principles" have not done all this, they have done less than nothing. This, and nothing less than this, is the result of carrying out, as hearers will do for themselves, even if preachers will not do it for them, the great doctrine of Baptismal Regeneration; which is, in truth, the very key-stone of all practical theology.[18]

Pusey had realized this very point by 1843, but he had chosen to avoid saying so in hopes of avoiding any controversy. Oakeley felt no such burden and went on to advocate the practice of sacramental confession to all those who wished to follow a Catholic way to salvation. Like Wilberforce, Newman, and Pusey, Oakeley knew that all Catholic sacramental theology must find its ultimate grounding in the incarnation. In an attempt to conclude the whole argument for a sacramental church by relating its incarnational base Oakeley,

---

18. Oakely, "Sacramental Confession," *British Critic*, XXXIII (April 1843), 306.

probably unknowingly, wrote a short, precise description of the emerging Tractarian incarnational theology of church and sacraments:

> From the moment that our Blessed Lord assumed the Flesh, He sanctioned, for all ages to come, the great truth upon which the whole ecclesiastical dispensation is built, that God comes to us, in the Gospel, under earthly veils. The Church is a farther, and ever-present Token, of that Condescension that dates from the Nativity, or rather from the Annunciation; God, once manifest in the Flesh, is continually manifest, though, since His Ascension, in a different form from that which He wore previously to it. He has never ceased to "dwell" (or tabernacle) "amongst us," since He first "came down from heaven and was incarnate." He is (what an awful thought!) *continually* incarnate in His Church. In the words of the Apocalypse, incorporated into the ancient Office for the Dedication of a Church ... "Audivi vocem magnam de throne dicentem: Ecce Tabernaculum Dei cum hominibus, et habitabit cum eis. Et ipsi populus ejus erunt, et Ipse Deus cum eis erit eorum Deus (Rev. 21:3)." Either, then, (if we may make such an hypothesis in the same breath with such an announcement), the great Sacramental principle of the Consecration of Matter had its first and last exemplification in our Lord's three years' ministry, or the Catholic Church, in all her developments [sic.] and ramifications (because in her very soul and essence), is an abiding personification of the same principle. Either theory is consistent and intelligible, though only one, of course, is true. But the alternative is between them; they cannot stand together.[19]

While Oakeley was emphasizing the primacy of the incarnation, his greater mentor, Pusey, was preparing to show that while the incarnation is the fundamental doctrine upon which sacramental theology is built, the atonement remains a central mystery of the Christian faith.

In chapter 2 we spoke of the immediate effect of the tracts on baptism (and Pusey's early preaching) on the sense of the serious nature of post-baptismal sin. Hugh James Rose was one of the first to notice this feature in Pusey. Writing to Pusey shortly after the publication of the tracts in question Rose queried Pusey, on the relationship between baptismal regeneration and subsequent absolution: "But again, take the power of the keys as even declaratory only. Is this connected with the doctrine of no remission

---

19. Oakely, "Sacramental Confession," *British Critic*, XXXIII (April 1843), 314.

but at baptism? We begin our daily service with confession and *absolution* as the necessary foundations for corporate prayer."[20]

Pusey's formal answer to Rose's question took ten years to formulate, and while the answer is to be found in those texts which were investigated in chapter 2, it should here be noted that at the same time Pusey was preparing to resume his role as a University Preacher, he was also preparing for the consecration of the great Tractarian experiment, St. Saviour's, Leeds. The question of sin and its remedy was certainly on his mind. It was Pusey who fixed the course of the sermons to be preached during the octave of St. Saviour's consecration, and having done so it became *A Course of Sermons on Solemn Subjects chiefly bearing on Repentance and Amendment of Life.*[21] Here the cross was not lost, rather it was held up as the powerful example of God's love for his creation. Christ, as virtue incarnate, has power which he confers upon the cross, and so the cross becomes the symbol by which men are drawn to their creator:

> Yet this power It has only, because He Who loves our souls, imparts it; He must draw us inwardly, if we are to run to Him, as He has said, "No man cometh unto Me, unless the Father Who has sent Me draw him." He saith not, "The thoughts of my Passion, meditation upon My exceeding love, thankfulness for the love wherewith I so loved them as for them to become Man, for them so to suffer," but "I shall draw all men unto Me." Himself, our Redeeming Lord, is that living centre of our souls, the Sun of Righteousness to Whom all turn, from Whom all look for and have the glow of life and love, through which they live whom God brings back into the harmony of His creation. Himself is the True Son, "from Whose heat nothing is hidden" in His new creation; Himself the Hidden Magnet, Who, having no Form or Beauty when He died for us, draws mightily to Himself, imparting to them of the Virtue which goeth forth from Him, and there by transforming them into Himself, so that the closer they are held to Him, the more His Virtue floweth into them, and the more they receive of Him, the more do they, by His indwelling Virtue, cleave unto Him, upheld not of themselves, but by His Spirit which dwelleth in them. He, through Whom are all things, Himself, through all—inspirations, Sacraments, hidden drawings, the yearnings and cravings of the soul, prayers, meditations, the Mysteries of His Incarnation, Life and Death

---

20. Pusey House Library, Chest B, Drawer 2, H. J. Rose to E. B. Pusey, March 16, 1836.

21. Pusey, *A Course of Sermons on Solemn Subjects Chiefly Bearing on Repentance and Amendment of Life.*

and resurrection, His Sufferings and His Glory,—draweth all; Himself as God, the Beginning from Whom all things are, the End to Whom all things tend.²²

The power of the cross comes from the love of God. This love (the same that is the cause of our justification) must manifest itself not only in our contrition for violating it, but also in our concern for those who need it most. Hence, the foundation of the great experiment in Leeds came from love and contrition on Pusey's part which he saw as the necessary extension of the love that caused both the incarnation and the atonement. Christ first loved us that, in turn, we might love him, which in turn must be extended:

> Real love to Christ must issue in love to all who are Christ's, and real love to Christ's poor must issue in self-denying acts of love towards them. Casual alms giving is not Christian Charity. Rather, seeing Christ in the poor, the sick, the hungry, the thirsty, the naked, we must, if we can, by ourselves, if not, by others, seek them out, as we would seek Christ, looking for a blessing from it, far greater than any they can gain from our alms.²³

Perhaps if the Tractarian ideal had been viewed more in the context of the total ideal envisioned by Pusey, rather than in the narrower context of specific controversial points, it might have met with great acceptance, Holiness of life, constant repentance, devotion to the poor and suffering, these were the foundations of Tractarian practice. The larger ideal expressed by Pusey reached out to the unchurched, the unserved, and the unsaved, because it began not with sacramental practices which focused controversy on only one element, but with missionary love. This missionary love fostered devotion, and that devotion took the form of Catholic church practice. It was the practice that brought about the confession controversy.

By the early 1850s others had entered the battle over auricular confession. Never one to avoid a battle Henry Phillpotts, Bishop of Exeter, fresh from his defeat in the Gorham case, took up the Anglo-Catholic cause on the issue of confession. Phillpotts was never an advocate of "habitual" confession, but he was a firm supporter of the validity of the practice in extreme cases. Though Phillpotts lacked the insight of Forbes he could still reason with some force.

The Dean of Exeter had preached a sermon which came very close to denying any divine commission in absolution. This Phillpotts took to be

---

22. Pusey, *A Course of Sermons on Solemn Subjects Chiefly Bearing on Repentance and Amendment of Life*, 177f.
23. Pusey, *Sermons from Advent to Whitsuntie*, 58.

both untrue and in contradiction with statements the Dean had made earlier. First Phillpotts asks the rhetorical question:

> Now, is the receiving the secret, auricular (for the words are in this instance of the same import) confession of the sins of the dying penitent, or of one who is withheld from the Lord's table by fear of his unfitness to present himself—is the receiving of such confession one of the ministrations of Christ's ministers? Our Church says that it is: you, as a high officer in that Church, have again and again declared that you unfeignedly believe it so to be. You must then, on your own principle, joyfully and thankfully acknowledge that Christ is with His minister in receiving such confession, and in pronouncing thereupon the Church's solemn form of absolution.[24]

Having quoted the form of absolution in the *Office for the Visitation of the Sick*, the Bishop takes up a point in the Dean's disputed sermon, "it is through Him, our great High Priest in Heaven, and not through the mediation of *any priest on earth*, we have access with confidence to the Father."[25] Bishop Phillpotts' reply to this point is important in that it outlines the real issue at the heart of the confessional debate, i.e. in what sense, and to what degree if any, does the priest hold a mediatory role which can be called Christ's? The entire debate over the power of the keys could easily be reduced to the question of the relationship of the mediator Christ Jesus to the ministry of the Church. Phillpotts, in his reply to his Dean, tries to strike a middle ground, but in so doing tends to obscure the issue slightly:

> Very true: but that matter before us concerns not *mediation*, but *ministry*. When we exercise the power which was conferred by Christ upon the Apostles and their successors in the text [2 Cor. 5:18f. had been the text of the Dean's sermon], we act as ministers, not as mediators—forgiving ministerially those whom Christ forgives absolutely, using us as His ministers, as dispensers of the gifts of His grace, by the means which He has appointed and empowered us to use . . . we never dare to call or think ourselves mediators to the Father in any other sense than through the mediation of Jesus Christ.[26]

---

24. Phillpotts, *Confession and Absolution: A Letter to the Very Rev. the Dean of Exeter*, 14.

25. Phillpotts, *Confession and Absolution: A Letter to the Very Rev. the Dean of Exeter*, 15.

26. Phillpotts, *Confession and Absolution: A Letter to the Very Rev. the Dean of Exeter*, 18.

The confusion that Phillpotts seemed unable to overcome was between the mediation of Jesus Christ and the relationship of the ministry to that mediation. In the final sentence of the above quotation he seems to be nearing the central issue of the extent to which priesthood is mediatorial precisely because it is an extension of the work of forgiveness in the ministry of Christ. Twenty years later the famous slum priest Charles Lowder was to offer a distinction that indicates how much the theology of absolution had been clarified in just two decades. "The very idea of priesthood," Lowder wrote to the Bishop of London, "is mediatorial, but the priest is simply the representative, the minister of the one great Mediator. God employs means, which implies something between us and God; they are His means and instruments, deriving all their efficacy from Him, and only effectual in the way which He appoints, sanctions, and blesses."

Phillpotts represented a moderate High Church position of the mid-nineteenth century. Lowder, on the other hand, represented the development of the Tractarian position into the Anglo-Catholicism of the next generation. But opinions from the other side weighed in heavily. Typical of the other side is Francis Close, whom we met in chapter 1 of this book, now Dean of Carlisle. In 1873 he published a series of sermons in which he argued (relying primarily on the 1552 *Book of Common Prayer*) that confession had no place in the Church of England. Close went further than most when he denied any biblical basis to the notion of absolution, and quite beyond the bounds of historical fact when he concluded:

> I believe that I have sufficiently proved that this "auricular confession," and "priestly absolution," however modified and restrained has no place in the Scriptures in the Word of God written—that it was unknown, or unauthorized, and unrecognized in the primitive Church for twelve hundred years after Christ: and that, as it was said by our venerated archbishops, the *reformers* "allowed it no place in the Reformed Church."[27]

One area of the controversy, as we have just seen, was the question of ministry and mediation; but another was the equally violent debate over the frequency of confession. Phillpotts could argue for the validity of the practice and still reserve it for extreme cases. Others like Pusey, Keble, Lowder, and their allies, argued that it was a deep and permanent part of their perseverance in holiness. Lowder summed up their point of view admirably when he wrote to his bishop:

---

27. Francis Close, *Auricular Confession and Priestly Absolution*, 14.

> When we consider what men like Dr. Pusey, Mr. Keble, Canon Liddon, Mr. Carter, Mr. Bennett, and Mr. Mackonochie have said and written about Confession, out of the fulness of their own spiritual experience, can it be supposed that habitual Confession, which they practice themselves and advocate, is injurious to vital religion? . . . We do not assert that the practice of Confession is absolutely *necessary to the spiritual life*, but that it is *highly conducive to its healthy development*. The Holy Spirit may supply to your Lordship and others the lack in other ways, but the Catholic priests, whom I have named, are proofs in their lives and experience that habitual Confession is not detrimental to the highest spiritual advancement.[28]

So heated did the issue of habitual confession become that the Lambeth Conference of 1878 felt compelled to deal with it. The argument represented by Close found little acceptance in the more moderate body at Lambeth. They wished only to deal with the issue of frequency. In a masterpiece of equivocation the committee charged with writing a consensus report returned its verdict:

> Further, having in view certain novel practices and teachings on the subject of Confession, your committee desires to affirm that in the matter of Confession the Churches of the Anglican Communion hold fast those principles which are set forth in the Holy Scriptures, which were professed by the Primitive Church, and which were re-affirmed at the English Reformation; and it is their deliberate opinion that no minister of the Church is authorised to require from those who may resort to him to open their grief a particular or detailed enumeration of all their sins, or to require private confession previous to receiving the Holy Communion, or to enjoin or even encourage the practice of habitual confession to a Priest, or to teach that such practice of habitual confession, or the being subject to what has been termed the direction of a Priest, is a condition of attaining to the highest spiritual life. At the same time your Committee are not to be understood as desiring to limit in any way the provisions made in the *Book of Common Prayer* for the relief of troubled consciences.[29]

Pusey fired off a published letter to his Archbishop inquiring as to the meaning of the word "habitual."[30] In truth the issue had already been

---

28. Lowder, *Sacramental Confession*, 6ff.
29. "Official 'Letter' of the Lambeth Conference of 1878," 186.
30. Pusey, *Habitual Confession Not Discouraged by the Resolution Accepted by the*

resolved, and the Lambeth letter did nothing to change practices as they had developed.

By the 1870s the practice of auricular confession, which had developed out of the complex of Tractarian thinking on grace, baptismal regeneration, incarnation, mediation, the church, and sacraments as extension of the mediatorial office of Christ, had become an integral feature of Anglo-Catholic Church life. It was a *fait accompli*. It had found its way into the practice, it had been found of great benefit, and those who practiced it would not give it up. Again, Charles Lowder, now writing of his pastoral experience:

> It is no question now of restoring the practice of Confession in the Church of England; that difficulty has been already solved. Those hundreds of clergy who know the priceless value of Confession in their own spiritual lives, as well as in their pastoral work among their flocks, and thousands of laity who owe so much gratitude to their acquaintance with it, forbid the thought. Can you suppose, my Lord, that after going to Confession myself, and hearing the Confessions of others for more than twenty-six years, and this through all the trials of an active and not uneventful career, while I have been taught by persecution and opposition to realize to the very quick the awful responsibility of each step which I have taken, both as affecting my own salvation and that of others, my mind and practice are not irrevocably fixed?[31]

Indeed, they were irrevocably fixed.

Lambeth Conference.
31. Lowder, *Sacramental Confession*, 5.

Epilogue

Looking back from almost two hundred years of interpretation and influence, one can easily identify in the practice of today's Anglicanism the continuing influence and effect of The Oxford Movement. Its leading characters were not Victorians but Georgians. Eamon Duffy has recently characterized the most famous of them as "one who died a prince of the Church, and somewhat improbably, an English national treasure, eulogized in the *Spectator* as 'the great Anglican, the great Catholic, the great Englishman.'"[1] George Herring in his introduction to *What Was The Oxford Movement?* captured a bit of the incongruities of the effect when he wrote, "then there is The Oxford Movement. So pronounced was its influence in Victorian England that today it is virtually impossible to read an account of religion in that period without coming across it."[2] Duffy's paragraph, quoted in the prologue of this book, gives it an even higher place in Anglican history, indeed the single most important force in the formation of modern Anglicanism.

Each generation has found new and greater insights into the Movement of 1833. We need look no further that Peter Nockles *The Oxford Movement in Context* to see the full influence of the Tractarians' predecessors, discussed less fully but as appreciatively in the first chapter of this work; the University of Chicago's re-issuing of Church's *The Oxford Movement: Twelve Years, 1833–1845* (and at that in a series entitled Classics of British Historical Literature) made accessible to a wider audience not only the magnificent prose of Dean

---

1. Duffy, *Newman*, 110.
2. Duffy, *Newman*, 1, footnote.

Church but the intensity of that initial period.[3] The Canadian theologian E. R. Fairweather's masterful introductions to selections from the Tractarian writings, as well as his giving over a singularly large portion to Robert Isaac Wilberforce, in *The Oxford Movement* gave a wider perspective to the influences at play in those first years; beyond that he reminds us to look back to the first centenary writings, especially Yngve Brilioth's *The Anglican Revival* and his *Three Lectures*. Fairweather's work contains one of the best select bibliographies up to the 1960s, now complemented by Lawrence Crumb's *The Oxford Movement and Its Leaders: A Bibliography of Secondary and Lesser Primary Sources*, a life-work of enormous value.[4]

The historians' thread that runs back from Duffy and Diarmaid MacCullough (who brings his massive scholarship to the expropriation of Hooker's *Laws* via Keble's edition)[5] includes the splendid works of David Newsome, whose biography of Manning and the Wilberforces, *The Parting of Friends*, is wonderfully complemented by his last work, *The Victorian World Picture*, in which he writes:

> Tractarianism . . . was a religion of the Church. Its emphasis on the priestly function, respect for liturgy and the centrality of the sacraments seemed to invert the priorities of the Evangelicals . . . Newman's teaching on the nature of justification, together with Pusey's severe strictures on post-baptismal sin, made Evangelicals seriously question whether the cherished Protestant doctrine of "justification by faith alone" was being subtly transformed into the totally unacceptable Catholic notion that "good works" might be adjudged as meritorious within the economy of grace.[6]

Beyond this we must not forget the monumental work of Owen Chadwick in his *The Spirit of The Oxford Movement* and his massive two-volume study *The Victorian Church*. So also we should be grateful, indeed, for the many briefer histories written near the time of the centenary, the reports of the Anglo-Catholic Conferences of 1923, 27, and 30; the innumerable parochial histories, and the earlier works of Sidney Ollard, G. W. E. Russell, H. L. Stewart, and so many more. Most of all, the deep,

---

3. So, also, the reader might want to look up Church's moving obituary of Newman in the *Times of London* August 12, 1890, pp. 7–8.

4. Including as it does works by the Canadian philosopher H. L. Stewart, and the American pre-Tractarian Bishop of New York, John Henry Hobart.

5. MacCulloch, *All Things Made New*, 318.

6. Newsome, *Victorian World Picture*, 193.

admittedly long, works on the lives of Pusey, Liddon, Gladstone, and, of course, almost innumerable lives of Newman.

Describing the period with which this volume has been concerned, Henry Scott Holland wrote:

> Its impulse was sincere and strong. The flame of its devotion burned keenly. There was a consuming love of souls, a great pity, a heartfelt charity, a noble spirit of self-sacrifice, a rich inspiration, a splendid confidence in the Fatherhood of God, and the power of redeeming love put out in Jesus Christ. The whole Catholic creed had become alive to thousands upon thousands of men and women, who desired nothing better than to convey to the poor and the suffering and the foolish their own sense of peace and joy that had come to them through the transfiguring efficacy of pardon and grace.[7]

We have seen all those virtues Holland so eloquently ascribes to the Tractarians. The doctrine of the "transfiguring efficacy of pardon and grace" was the very heart of The Oxford Movement. It found its first massive expression in Pusey's *Tract Sixty-seven*, with its insistence on the reality of baptismal regeneration; it found its fullest expression in Newman's *Lectures on the Doctrine of Justification*, with its insistence on the completeness of the gifts imparted to the individual when that person is both healed and elevated; it found its roots in Wilberforce's *Doctrine of the Incarnation of Our Lord Jesus Christ*, with its insistence on the incarnation as the central, abiding mystery of salvation.

From these, and other, doctrinal expressions The Oxford Movement moved out from the academic world into the life of the Church of England in the mid-nineteenth century. Parishes, convents, and penitentiaries were founded which were the visible signs of a new age in the life of the established Church. Throughout the whole period the figure of E. B. Pusey, the reluctant leader, emerges again and again as the guiding light of this new spirit.

Hopefully the reader has been left with a sense of Pusey's importance to The Oxford Movement. Pusey's role, not only as leader but as theologian, was crucial to the Catholic revival in the Church of England. He, alone, provided both intellectual depth and ecclesiastical stability in the worst hours of the 1840s and '50s. In Pusey we see the pattern of growth that is characteristic of the new High Churchmen. Baptismal regeneration sheds the aridity with which it had become encumbered and becomes a living doctrine on which the whole of Christian life can be based.

---

7. Holland, "The Nineteenth Century" in *Our Place in Christendom*, 149.

EPILOGUE

John Henry Newman, so often studied, also emerges in a new light. The *Lectures on the Doctrine of Justification*, surely Newman's finest Anglican work, take on the character of a completion of topics begun by Pusey. Newman's incisive mind cut away at centuries of dispute and offered the perceptive reader a fresh look at the way in which God acts to save humanity. So long mostly ignored, the *Lectures on the Doctrine of Justification* must now be read as a primary document in the development of Anglican theology in the nineteenth century not to mention central to the development of Cardinal—now Saint—John Henry Newman's importance for Anglicans, Catholics, and the whole church.

Robert Isaac Wilberforce, the least known of the three central figures in this narrative, must be credited with recognizing that every statement about man's salvation has its historical equivalent in the incarnation. The incarnation, standing at the center of history and salvation, operates as the supreme example of Christ's office of mediator. Wilberforce never successfully solved the problem of the relation of humanity to divinity in the one Jesus Christ; he never managed a thorough statement of the individuality of the humanity which Christ took; but, his ability to relate the corporate nature of Christ's humanity to our new birth grounded the Tractarian doctrines of grace and its means in the incarnation.

No theological movement has real substance unless its main theses find expression in the life of the church. While academic supporters, and academic critics, grew up on every side, the thrust of The Oxford Movement found its fruition in the spiritual life. Too often the theology of The Oxford Movement has been viewed as a result of its piety. It is hoped that this volume has shown that the opposite was nearer the truth. With a firm grounding in the doctrines of grace and its means the Tractarians founded a style of church life unknown in England since the Reformation. Confessions began to be heard in increasing numbers, work among the poor and the working class (too often the same in this period) was given major importance, religious orders appeared to fill a 300-year gap, and sacramental worship became central. These are some of the effects of The Oxford Movement that demonstrate its importance, as well as its vitality.

Other forces appeared which would contribute to the next period of Anglican history. F. D. Maurice, whom we noted only as a critic of the Tractarians, found a sympathetic hearing among the socially concerned. His understanding of the church, and its relationship to society, would become a major factor in the founding of the Christian Social Union, and, indeed, in the writings of the *Lux Mundi* authors. The mission of the church took on the character of one society sent to redeem another. In this the Tractarians had contributed through their slum ministries, but the Tractarian notion of salvation was admittedly more individualistic than that of the Liberal Catholics a generation later.

Biblical criticism, introduced into England from Germany, posed a major threat to the Tractarian notion of the authority of scripture. In the end, the Anglo-Catholics, with their strong sense of the place of tradition in authority, were better able to deal with the issue than were their Evangelical brethren, but the furor over the new methods of interpretation was great. The depth of emotion excited by the new biblical critics was tragically demonstrated in the rift which developed between Liddon, Pusey's most devoted disciple, and Charles Gore, first principal of Pusey House. Liddon found it impossible to accept Gore's views on inspiration as the product of one associated with the name and memory of Pusey.

Behind the controversy over biblical inspiration and criticism lay the deeper change in the intellectual climate. Darwinian evolutionary theory had challenged traditional biblical interpretation as early as the 1860s. No longer could scripture provide scientific data on creation. At first, the Church reacted with fervor and furor; but, as science developed, the Church came to appropriate its results as part of general revelation. The first full expression of this in the Church of England must also be credited to the Liberal Catholics.

Darwinism, as strong as its effects were, was only part of a larger intellectual movement which viewed the world and human history as part of a grand development. In this area Newman's name must again be mentioned. His *Essay on the Development of Christian Doctrine* is one of the most important documents of the nineteenth century, not so much for its tests of validity in doctrinal development, as for its recognition of development as a proper mode for understanding and interpreting Christian doctrine.[8]

By the time Pusey died (1882) England was transformed from an agrarian to an industrial society. The Empire was nearing its zenith, and for all the social problems that both these factors created, optimism was rather more prevalent than it had been when The Oxford Movement began. They knew the profound fear occasioned in the upper classes by the French Revolution. These, and many other better recognized factors, formed the spirit of their theology and piety. The Liberal Catholics, on the other hand, were the legatees of Tractarian piety. They tempered the emphasis on human sinfulness. They

---

8. Newman's *Essay on Development of Doctrine* has been receiving increasing attention in this regard. For a good example of this see the editor's introduction to John Henry Newman, *An Essay on the Development of Christian Doctrine*, J. M. Cameron, ed. A new printing of the first edition was issued in 2014, which gives us an easy and accessible base with which the many subsequent editions can be compared. See also, the revised preface to the third edition of 1877.

brought nature and grace a little closer to one another. They saw God working in history a little more clearly than had the Tractarians. They were, if anything, a little too optimistic about humanity's cooperation.

In trying to sketch those elements that separated the Tractarians and the Liberal Catholics we may have left the impression that the line of development was very thin. One reading of the subject, relying on the differences, could certainly produce that idea. However, it would be produced at the cost of ignoring the two great themes outlined in this volume, grace and incarnation.

The Liberal Catholics never produced systematic statements on grace and its means. Gore paid the most attention to the doctrine of grace. His analysis of St. Paul's theology of grace is the closest thing to a treatment of the subject amongst the Liberal Catholics. But Gore's interest was conciliatory. He felt too many battles had already occurred, and desired to present a theology of grace that could be accepted by all but the most devoted adherents of the older schools. In the end his theology of grace came off as rather insipid when read in the light of Newman.

A case can be made for the fact that the Liberal Catholics wrote on the incarnation and the church because they were topics left incomplete by The Oxford Movement. After all, the full title of *Lux Mundi* was *Lux Mundi: A Series of Studies in the Religion of the Incarnation*. The authors represented in that volume inherited from the Tractarians a renewal of interest in the incarnation as the fundamental mystery of Christianity. Moreover, they inherited the Tractarian concern for our union with God which is based on the incarnation. The Liberal Catholics' leading philosopher, John Illingworth, tied these themes together in a manner reminiscent of The Oxford Movement:

> For we find the desire for union with God to lie at the very basis of our being, and when once the story of the Incarnation has dawned upon our horizon, we recognize that under the conditions of the world of sin in which we live, nothing else could have so adequately satisfied this inmost aspiration.[9]

Liberal Catholics developed the incarnational theme in every direction; and with the aid of the new ideas of their age, developed it far beyond the scope possible even for Wilberforce. Yet, the concern for incarnational doctrine as the basis of the life in Christ was the same for both generations. Being "in Christ", whether exemplified by being part of an organic and more horizontal church or a hierarchical and more vertical church, whether seen

---

9. Illingworth, "The Incarnation and Development" in *Lux Mundi*, 154.

as more corporate or more individualistic, is a fundamental and characteristic doctrine of Anglo-Catholicism that found renewal in The Oxford Movement and carries on to the present day. It binds the two High Church movements of the nineteenth century.

The Tractarians had vigorously denied the idea that humanity was wholly perverted by the fall. A person remained God's good creation even though fallen originally and actually. The Liberal Catholics were able to build on this, and to incorporate a much more organic concept of nature and grace. The result was that Christ became more the consummator than in the Tractarians, but the sense of Christ as redeemer was hardly lost. Nowhere are all these themes more closely linked than in Gore's famous Bampton Lectures:

> He [Christ] is, according to those theologians of the New Testament [Paul and John], the author of the universe, and He abides in all His creation as its principle of cohesion. He is the ground of its progress and the light of its rational members. Finally, He is the goal of all its movements. When sin perverted His creation in part, He was not baffled by its ravages, but came out again to redeem, and in redeeming to consummate his previous working. By His Incarnation He inaugurated a kingdom of redemption in the heart of the old kingdom of nature. Again, He abides in that new creation as the inner principle of its life. Again, He bears along this new work, and with it the old work which it completes, to its final goal in Himself. In creation and in redemption He is author and inherent life, and final cause.[10]

This statement, alone, provides sufficient material to demand a closer study of the relationship between Tractarian and Liberal Catholic incarnational theology. No reader can help but be struck by the similarities of the two schools.

And Finally

The impression left by many writers is that the era of the Liberal Catholics was, in many ways, an Anglican zenith. This volume has, hopefully, corrected a few misunderstandings about the preceding period. For too long the Tractarians have been viewed as pietists, who left a legacy of spirituality and devotion to the sacraments, but who were without a living, dynamic theology.

---

10. Gore, *The Incarnation of the Son of God*, 45.

More and more the central theme of our incorporation in Christ comes to the fore as the greatest theological contribution of The Oxford Movement. This theme provided the Liberal Catholics with their strong theology of the church. In this the Tractarians cannot be assumed to have been proto-Liberal Catholics. They were Anglo-Catholic theologians and churchmen whose contributions far exceeded a mere paving of the way for the next generation.

Perhaps the purest stroke of genius was Pusey's choice of baptism as his inaugural theme. He seemed to sense that our being in Christ must be the fundamental gift we have received. Everything else we have been given, everything else we have received through revelation, is understandable only in the light of our becoming one with him from whom we have come and to whom we are to return.

Our unity with Christ calls forth many questions, questions that demand studies of grace and incarnation. Yet, our life in Christ remains the central concern of the Tractarians. Can it be, then, that the shy, pious Regius Professor of Hebrew was the most important Tractarian?[11] It is certainly very evident that he was much more important than many have thought. He, alone, was able to link theology, piety, and social concerns into a concrete synthesis which produced the Tractarian parishes and institutions. He, often with only Keble for support, stood firm in the belief that since we are made holy in baptism, everything else we believe, do, and think, must be ordered to our perseverance in holiness. So, too, he stood firm in the belief that our incorporation into Christ makes personal and subjective sense of everything else we believe; without the surety of baptismal regeneration we have no firm footing in the Christian life. All these factors were integrated into his single life of devotion and activity.

Pusey's life represented both the theology and the piety of The Oxford Movement. It was the embodiment of everything that Tractarians stood for. When he died many felt that he had lived beyond the era of Tractarian vitality and would be relegated to a small niche in histories of the nineteenth century. Richard Church, with typical acumen, knew differently. In a sermon preached at the opening of the Oxford term after Pusey died, Church took the liberty to speak of Pusey's life. He noted the passions and controversies in which Pusey had been embroiled, but then he struck the note that we hope has been communicated about Pusey (and about those with whom he labored), and on which we will close:

---

11. See for instance Perry Butler, ed., *Pusey Rediscovered*. For some recent works that have tried to rehabilitate Pusey's image see: Strong and Engelhardt Herringer eds., *Edward Bouverie Pusey and the Oxford Movement* (2012), and Douglas, *The Eucharistic Theology of Edward Bouverie Pusey* (2015).

But when our confusions are still, when our loves, and enmities, and angers have perished, when our mistakes and misunderstandings have become dim and insignificant in the great distance of the past, then his figure will rise in history as one of that high company who really looked at life as St. Paul looked at it. All who care for the Church of God, all who care for Christ's Religion, even those—I make bold to say—who do not in many things think as he thought, will class him among those who in difficult and anxious times have witnessed, by great zeal, and great effort, and great sacrifice, for God and Truth and Holiness; they will see in him one who sought to make Religion a living and mighty force over the consciences and in the affairs of men, not by knowledge only and learning and wisdom and great gifts of persuasion, but still more by boundless devotedness, by the power of a consecrated and unfaltering will.[12]

---

12. Quoted from Dean Church's *Cathedral and University Sermons* in Liddon, *Life of Edward Bouverie Pusey*, VI, 390.

A Select Bibliography

Primary Sources

Alexander, John. *Letter to the Right Reverend William Skinner D.D., Bishop of Aberdeen, and Primus of the Church of Scotland; on the Eucharistic Doctrine Exhibited in the Scottish Communion Office as It Stands Affected to the School of Archdeacon Wilberforce, and the Teaching of the Great Anglican Divines.* Edinburgh: R. Lendrum, 1857.

Armstrong, John. "An Appeal for the Formation of a Church Penitentiary." 2nd ed. London: J. H. Parker, 1849.

Baring-Gould, S. *Luther and Justification.* London: Church Printing Co., 1871.

Barrett, G. S. *The Influence of the Late Dr. Pusey, and of the Oxford Movement Associated with His Name on the English Nation and the English Church.* London: Jarrod and Sons, 1882.

Barter, William Brudenell. *Tracts in Defense of the Christian Sabbath, the Church, Her Priesthood, and Her Sacraments.* London: F. and J. Rivington, 1851.

Bricknell, W. S. ed. *The Judgements of the Bishops upon Tractarian Theology.* Oxford: J. Vincent, 1825.

Bull, George. *Harmonia Apostolica.* Library of Anglo-Catholic Theology, Vol. 29. Oxford: J. H. Parker, 1842.

Carter, Thomas T. *Mere for the Fallen. Two Sermons in Aid of the House of Mercy, Clewer.* London: J. Masters, 1856.

———, ed. *Notes and Questions on the Catholic Faith and Religion. The Notes and Answers Compiled Chiefly from the Works and in the Words of Dr. Pusey.* London: A. D. Innes, 1891.

———. *Spiritual Instructions on the Holy Eucharist.* 3rd ed. London: Joseph Masters, 1871.

———. *The Treasury of Devotion.* New York: E. and J. B. Young, 1902.

Church, Richard William. *The Oxford Movement: Twelve Years, 1833–1845.* Chicago: University of Chicago Press, 1970.

Close, Francis. *Auricular Confession and Priestly Absolution Tested by Scripture, by Antiquity, and by the Formularies of the Church of England: Being Three Sermons Preached in Carlisle Cathedral on Sunday October 5th, 12th and 19th 1873.* 2nd ed. London: Hatchard and Sons, 1872.

Deacon, G. E. *Baptismal Regeneration Not Left an Open Question by the Church of England. A Sermon Preached in the Parish Church of Ottery S. Mary.* Exeter: H. J. Wallis, 1850.

Documents from the Second Vatican Council. http://www.vatican.va/archive/hist_councils/ii_vatican_council/index.htm.

Faber, George Stanley. *The Primitive Doctrine of Election: Or an Historical Enquiry into the Ideality and Causation of Scriptural Election, as Received and Maintained in the Primitive Church of Christ.* 2nd ed. London: Thomas Blenkarn, 1842.

———. *The Primitive Doctrine of Justification Investigated: Relatively to the Several Definitions of the Church of Rome and the Church of England and with a Special Reference to the Opinion of the Late Mr. Knox, as Published in His Remains.* 2nd ed. London: R. B. Seeley and W. Burnside, 1839.

———. *The Primitive Doctrine of Regeneration: Sought for in Holy Scripture; and Investigated through the Medium of the Written Documents of Ecclesiastical Antiquity.* London: R. B. Seeley and W. Burnside, 1840.

First Annual Report of the Church Penitentiary Association. London: Spottiswood and Shaw, 1853.

Forbes, Alexander Penrose. *A Primary Charge Delivered to the Clergy of His Diocese, at the Annual Synod of 1857.* 2nd ed. London: Joseph Masters, 1858.

———. *Theological Defense for the Rt. Rev. Alexander Penrose Forbes, D.C.L., Bishop of Brechin, on a Presentment by the Rev. W. Henderson, and Others on Certain Points concerning the Doctrine of the Holy Eucharist.* London: Joseph Masters, 1860.

Grantham, George Pierce. *A History of Saint Saviour's, Leeds, with a Full Description of the Church.* London: J. Masters, 1872.

Grueber, C. S. *Holy Baptism: A Complete Statement of the Church's Doctrine on the Subject.* London: J. Masters, 1850.

Hampden, Renn Dickson. *The Lord our Righteousness: A Sermon Preached before the University of Oxford November 24, 1839.* 4th ed. London: B. Fellowes, 1842.

———. *The Scholastic Philosophy in Its Relation to Christian Theology.* Oxford: J. H. Parker, 1833.

Harper, Francis Whaley. *A Few Observations on the Teaching of Dr. Fuse and Mr. Newman concerning Justification.* Cambridge: W. P. Grant, 1842.

Heber, Reginald. *The Personality and Office of the Christian Comforter.* 2nd ed. London: J. Hatchard, 1816.

Johnston, J. O., and W. C. E. Newbolt. *Spiritual Letters of Edward Bouverie Pusey.* London: Longmans, Green, and Co., 1898.

Jones, William. *An Essay on the Church.* New ed. London: SPCK, 1818.

———. *Works.* 6 vols. New ed. London: F. and J. Rivington, 1810.

Keble, John. *The Christian Year.* New ed. Philadelphia: E. H. Butler, 1864.

———. *Outlines of Instructions or Meditations for the Church's Seasons.* Edited by R. F. Wilson. Oxford : J. H. Parker, 1880.

———. *Sermons for the Christian Year.* 11 vols. London: Walter Smith, 1887.

———. *Village Sermons on the Baptismal Service.* Oxford: J. H. Parker, 1868.

Knox, Alexander. *Remains.* 3rd ed. 4 vols. London: Duncan and Malcolm, 1844.

Laurence, Richard. *An Attempt to Illustrate Those Articles of the Church of England which the Calvinists Improperly Considered as Calvinistical.* 4th ed. Oxford : J. H. Parker, 1853.
———. *The Doctrine of Baptismal Regeneration Contrasted with the Tenets of Calvin.* 2nd ed. Oxford: J. H. Parker, 1827.
———. *The Doctrine of the Church of England upon the Efficacy of Baptism Vindicated from Misrepresentation.* Part 1. 3rd ed. Oxford: J. H. Parker, 1823. Part 2. 2nd ed. Oxford: J. H. Parker, 1827.
Liddon, Henry Parry. *The Divinity of Our Lord and Saviour Jesus Christ.* 14th ed. London: Longmans, Green, and Co., 1900.
———. *Explanatory Analysis of St. Paul's Epistle to the Romans.* Oxford: E. Baxter, 1876.
———. *Life of Edward Bouverie Pusey, D.D.* 4 vols. London: Longmans, Green, and Co., 1893–97.
———. *Some Elements of Religion.* 7th ed. London: Longmans, Green, and Co., 1890.
Longley, C. T. [Bishop of Ripon]. *A Letter to the Parishioners of St. Saviour's, Leeds.* London: F. and J. Rivington, 1851.
Lowder, Charles F. *Sacramental Confession Examined by Pastoral Experience: A Letter to the Rt. Rev. and Rt. Hon. the Lord Bishop of London.* London: F. and J. Rivingtons, 1874.
Lyra Apostolica. London: Rivingtons, 1836.
Mant, Richard. *An Appeal to the Gospel: Or an Inquiry into the Justice of the Charge, Alleged by the Methodists and Other Objectors, That the Gospel Is Not Preached by the National Clergy.* 3rd ed . Oxford: Oxford University Press, 1812.
———. *Musings on the Church and Her Services.* London: F. and J. Livington, 1870.
Marriott, Charles. *Lectures on the Epistle to the Romans.* Oxford: J. H. and J. Parker, 1859.
Maskell, W. *The Outward Means of Grace. A Sermon Preached in the Church of S. Mary, Totnes, at the Triennial Visitation of the Right Reverend the Lord Bishop of Exeter. August 11th, 1848.* 4th ed. London: William Pickering, 1849.
Maurice, (John) Frederick Denison. *Christmas Day and Other Sermons.* 2nd ed. London: Macmillan, 1892.
———. *The Doctrine of Sacrifice Deduced from the Scriptures.* Cambridge: Macmillan, 1879.
———. *The Faith of the Liturgy and the Doctrine of the Thirty-nine Articles. Two Sermons the Substance of which was Preached at St. Peter's, Vere Street, on Sunday, September 9th, 1860.* Cambridge: Macmillan, 1860.
———. *The Kingdom of Christ.* 2 vols. Edited by A. Vidler. New ed. London: SCM, 1958.
———. *The Prayer-Book and the Lord's Prayer.* London: Macmillan, 1902.
———. *Theological Essays.* London: J. Clark, 1957.
———. *The Unity of the New Testament.* 2 vols. 2nd ed. London: Macmillan, 1884.
McGrath, Henry W. *The Doctrine of the Church of England as Contrasted with that of the Church of Rome: A Course of Lectures on Some of the Leading Points of Difference between the Church of England and the Church of Rome Delivered in St. Matthew's Church Manchester, in 1839.* London: Hatchard and Son, 1840.
Milner, Joseph. *The History of the Church of Christ.* Edited and expanded by Isaac Milner. 2 vols. 4th ed. Philadelphia: Hogan and Thompson, 1835.
Mozley, J. B. *Lectures and Other Theological Papers.* New York: E. P. Dutton, 1833.

———. *The Primitive Doctrine of Baptismal Regeneration.* London: J. Murray, 1856.

———. *A Review of the Baptismal Controversy.* New York: E. P. Dutton, 1883.

———. *A Treatise on the Augustinian Doctrine of Predestination.* London: J. Murray, 1855.

Neale, John Mason. *Sermons on the Blessed Sacrament.* 2nd ed. London: J. T. Hayes, 1870.

Newman, John Henry. *Apologia Pro Vita Sua.* Edited by D. J. DeLaura. New York: W. W. Norton, 1968.

———. *An Essay on the Development of Christian Doctrine.* Edited and introduced by J. M. Cameron. Harmondsworth, UK: Penguin, 1974.

———. *Fifteen Sermons Preached before the University of Oxford.* Westminster, MD: Christian Classics, 1966.

———. *Lectures on Certain Difficulties Felt by Anglicans in Submitting to the Catholic Church.* London: Burns and Lambert, 1850.

———. *Lectures on the Doctrine of Justification.* 3rd ed. London: F. and J. Rivingtons, 1874.

———. *Lectures on the Prophetical Office of the Church.* 2nd ed. London: F. and J. Rivingtons, 1838.

———. *Parochial and Plain Sermons.* 6 vols. Westminster, MD: Christian Classics, 1967.

———. *Unpublished letter to the Rev. Thomas Henderson, August 2, 1838.* Newman Letters, Bundle 11. Pamphlet Room, Pusey House, Oxford.

Newton, John. "Olney Hymns." In *The Works of the Rev. John Newton.* 2 vols. New York: Hobert Carter, 1847,

"Official 'Letter' of the Lambeth Conference of 1878." In *The Lambeth Conferences of 1867, 1878, and 1888*, edited by R. T. Davidson, 163–90. London: SPCK, 1889.

Palmer, Sir William. *A Narrative of Events Connected with the Publication of the Tracts for the Times.* London: F. and J. Rivingtons, 1883.

———. *A Treatise on the Church of Christ.* 2 vols. London: F. and J. Rivington, 1842.

Penitentiary Work in the Church of England. Papers Prepared for Discussion at the Anniversary Meeting of the Church Penitentiary Association on Penitentiary Work in the Church of England Papers Prepared for Discussion at the Anniversary Meeting of the Church Penitentiary Association, on S. Mark's Day, 1873, at the Request of the Council. London: Harrison and Sons, 1873.

Perceval, A. P. *A Collection of Papers Connected with the Theological Movement of 1833.* London: F. and J. Rivington, 1842.

Phillpotts, Henry. *Confession and Absolution. A Letter to the Very Rev. the Dean of Exeter, on a Sermon Preached by Him in the Cathedral at Exeter on Sunday, Nov. 7th, 1852, and since Published.* London: J. Murray, 1852.

Pollen, John Hungerford. *Narrative of Five Years at St. Saviour's, Leeds: to Which Is Added, an Extract from the Christian Remembrancer for January, 1850.* Oxford: J. Vincent, 1851.

Pusey, Edward Bouverie, ed. and trans. *Advice for Those Who Exercise the Ministry of Reconciliation through Confession and Absolution Being the Abby Gaume's Manual for Confessors.* Oxford: J. H. Parker, 1878.

———. *The Articles Treated on in Tract 90 Reconsidered and Their Interpretation Vindicated : in a Letter to the Rev. R. W. Jelf, D.D., Canon of Christ Church; with an appendix from Abp. Ussher on the Difference between Ancient and Modern Addresses to Saints. Oxford : J. H. Parker, 1841.

———. *A Course of Sermons on Solemn Subjects, chiefly Bearing on Repentance and Amendment of Life, Preached in St. Saviour's Church, Leeds, during the Week after Its Consecration on the Feast of S. Simon and S. Jude, 1845.* Oxford,: J. H. Parker, 1845.

———. *The Entire Absolution of the Penitent.* Oxford: J. H. Parker, 1846.

———. *Habitual Confession Not Discouraged by the Resolution Accepted by the Lambeth Conference: A Letter to His Grace the Lord Archbishop of Canterbury.* Oxford : J. H. Parker, 1878.

———. *The Holy Eucharist a Comfort to the Penitent.* Oxford: J. H. Parker, 1843.

———. *Lenten Sermons Preached Chiefly to Young Men at the Universities between A. D. 1858–1874.* Oxford: J. H. Parker, 1874.

———. *A Letter to His Grace the Archbishop of Canterbury, on Some Circumstances Connected with the Present Crisis in the English Church.* Oxford: J. H. Parker, 1842.

———. *Letter to the Right Rev. Father in God, Richard Lord Bishop of Oxford, on the Tendency to Romanism Imputed to Doctrines Held of Old as Now in the English Church.* 3d ed. Oxford: J. H. Parker, 1839.

———. Manuscript Fragment on St. John's Gospel. n.d.

———. *Nine Sermons Preached before the University of Oxford and Printed Chiefly between A. D. 1843–1845. Now Collected into One Volume.* London: A. D. Innes, 1891.

———. *Parochial Sermons. Vol. 3.[Reprinted from Plain Sermons by Contributors to Tracts for the Times].* Rev. ed. London: Walter Smith, 1886.

———. *Parochial and Cathedral Sermons.* London: Rivingtons, 1882.

———. *Parochial Sermons Preached and Printed on Various Occasions Now Collected into One Volume.* Oxford: J. H. Parker, 1865.

———. *Postscript on the Alteration of a Line in the Christian Year.* n.d.

———. *Sermons from Advent to Whitsuntide.* Oxford: J. H. Parker, 1848.

———. *What Is of Faith as to Everlasting Punishment.* Oxford: J. H. Parker, 1880.

Reminiscences of Forty Years by an Hereditary High Churchman. London: J. Masters, 1868. [Anon.]

Romaine, William. *Works.* 8 vols. London: Chapman, 1796.

Rose, Hugh James. *Letter to E. B. Pusey, March 16, 1836.* Chest B, Drawer 2, Pamphlet Room, Pusey House, Oxford.

Scott, Thomas. *Theological Works.* 5 vols. London: J. Seeley, 1805–8.

Sermons Preached at S. Barnabas, Pimlico, in the Octave of the Consecration, 1850. London: W. J. Cleaver, 1850.

Simeon, Charles. *Horae Homileticae.* 21 vols. London: Holdsworth and Bell, 1832–33.

Thirty Years Corres Correspondence between Bishop Jebb and Alexander Knox. 2 vols. 2nd ed. London: James Duncan, 1834.

Tomline, George. *Elements of Christian Theology.* 2 vols. London: T. Cadwell and W. Davies, 1815.

Tract for the Times in Reply to the Oxford Tracts on Scriptural Views of Holy Baptism, with an Appendix, Containing a Few Observations on the Chapter on the Efficacy of Baptism, in the Church of England a Protester against Romanism and Dissent. London: James Nisbet, 1833. [Anon. A Member of the University]

Tracts for the Times by Members of the University of Oxford. 4th ed. London: Rivingtons, 1834–1842.
Tyrewhitt, R. St. J. *Other Men's Labour. A Sermon on the Death of the Rev. E. B. Pusey, D.D.* Oxford: J. H. Parker, 1882 .
Venn, Henry. *The Complete Duty of Man.* New ed. London: J . Buckland and G. Keith, 1895.
Ward, William George. *The Ideal of a Christian Church.* 2nd ed. London: J. Toovey, 1844.
The Warnings of Advent: A Course of Sermons Preached in the Church of St. Bartholomew. London: J. Whitaker, 1853.
Whittingham, William Rollinson. *The Priesthood in the Church, Set Forth in Two Discourses.* Baltimore: Knight and Colborn, 1842.
Wilberforce, Robert Isaac. *The Doctrine of Holy Baptism.* London: J. Murray, 1849.
———. *The Doctrine of the Holy Eucharist.* 2nd ed. New York: E. and J. B. Young, 1845.
———. *The Doctrine of the Incarnation of Our Lord Jesus Christ, in its Relation to Mankind and to the Church.* 2nd ed. London: J. Murray, 1849.
———. *The Evangelical and Tractarian Movements: A Charge to the Clergy of the East Riding, Delivered at the Ordinary Visitation, A.D. 1851.* London: J. Murray, 1851.
———. *Sermons on the New Birth of Man's Nature.* London: J. Murray, 1850.
Williams, Isaac. *The Autobiography of Isaac Williams, B.D.* Edited by Sir G. Prevost. London: Longmans, Green, and Co., 1892.
———. *The Baptistry, or the Way of Eternal Life.* Oxford: J. H. and J. Parker, 1858.
Wilson, Daniel. *Tractarianism Subversive of the Gospel.* Whitchurch, UK: J. Walford, 1843.

Secondary Sources

Allchin, A. M. *The Silent Rebellion: Anglican Religious Communities, 1845–1900.* London: SCM, 1958.
Aquinas, Thomas. *Compendium of Theology.* Translated by C. Vollert. St. Louis: Herder, 1948.
———. *Summa Theologiae.* Oxford: Blackfriars, 1964–80.
Augustine. "The Spirit and the Letter." In *Augustine: Later Works,* edited and translated by J. Burnaby, 182–250. Library of Christian Classics 8. Philadelphia: Westminster, 1955.
Avis, Paul. *Anglicanism and the Christian Church.* Minneapolis: Augsburg Fortress, 1989.
Barth, Karl. *The Epistle to the Romans.* Translated by Edwyn C. Hoskins. Oxford: Oxford University Press, 1968.
———. *The Word of God and the Word of Man.* New York: Peter Smith, 1958.
Binns, L. Elliott. *The Evangelical Movement in the Church of England.* London: Methuen, 1928.
Bowen, Desmond. *The Idea of the Victorian Church.* Montreal: McGill University Press, 1968.
Brilioth, Yngve. *The Anglican Revival: Studies in the Oxford Movement.* London: Longmans, Green, and Co., 1925.

———. *Three Lectures on Evangelicalism and the Oxford Movement*. Oxford: Oxford University Press, 1934.
British Critic XXIV (July, 1838); XXXIII, (April, 1843).
Brose, Olive J. *Frederick Denison Maurice: Rebellious Conformist*. Athens, OH: Ohio University Press, 1971.
Brown, Stewart J., Peter B. Nockles, and James Pereiro, eds. *Oxford Handbook of the Oxford Movement*. Oxford: Oxford University Press, 2017.
Burkhard, Conrad. "The Politics of a Conversion—The Case of Robert Isaac Wilberforce." *International Journal for the Study of the Christian Church* 16:3 (2016) 182–96; DOI: 10.1080/1474225X.2016.1221591.
Butler, Perry, ed. *Pusey Rediscovered*. London: SPCK, 1983.
Capon, Robert Farrar. *Between Noon and Three: Romance, Law, and the Outrage of Grace*. Grand Rapids: Eerdmans, 1993.
Carus, William. *Life of Simeon*. New York: Robert Carter, 1847.
Chadwick, Owen. *The Mind of the Oxford Movement*. London: A. & C. Black, 1960.
———. *The Spirit of the Oxford Movement*. Cambridge: Cambridge University Press, 1990.
———. *The Victorian Church*. 2 vols. New York: Oxford University Press, 1966, 1970.
Christensen, Torben. *The Divine Order: A Study in F. D. Maurice's Theology*. Leiden: Brill, 1973.
Clarke, C. P. S. *The Oxford Movement and After*. London: Mowbray, 1932.
Clark, J. C. D. "Church, Parties, and Politics." In *The Oxford History of Anglicanism*, 289–313. Edited by Jeremy Gregory. Oxford: Oxford University Press, 2017.
Cornish, Francis Warre. *The English Church in the Nineteenth Century*. 2 vols. London: Macmillan, 1910.
Coulson, John, and A. M. Allchin. *The Rediscovery of Newman: An Oxford Symposium*. London: SPCK, 1967.
Crumb, Lawrence N. *The Oxford Movement and Its Leaders: A Bibliography of Secondary and Lesser Primary Sources*. 2nd ed. ATLA Bibliography Series. Lanham, MD: Scarecrow, 2009.
Davies, Horton. *Worship and Theology in England: From Newman to Martineau*. Vol. IV. Princeton: Princeton University Press, 1962.
DeMille, George E. *The Catholic Movement in the American Episcopal Church*. 2nd ed. Philadelphia: Church Historical Society, 1950.
Dessain, C. S. *The Spirituality of John Henry Newman*. Minneapolis: Winston, 1977.
Douglas, Brian. *The Eucharistic Theology of Edward Bouverie Pusey: Sources, Context and Doctrine within the Oxford Movement and Beyond*. Leiden: Brill, 2015.
Duffy, Eamon. *Newman: A Very Brief History*. London: SPCK, 2019.
———. *Worship and Theology in England: From Watts and Wesley to Maurice, 1690–1850*. Vol. III. Princeton: Princeton University Press, 1961.
Fairbairn, A. M. *Catholicism: Roman and Anglican*. New York: Scribners, 1899.
Fairweather, E. R. *The Oxford Movement*. New York: Oxford University Press, 1964.
———. *A Scholastic Miscellany*. London: SCM, 1956.
Fouyas, Methodios. *Orthodox, Roman Catholicism, and Anglicanism*. London: Oxford University Press, 1972.
Gillett, G., ed. *Report of the Oxford Movement Centenary Congress, July, 1933*. London: Catholic Literature Association, 1933.
Gore, Charles. *The Incarnation of the Son of God*. New York: Schribner's Sons, 1898.

———, ed. *Lux Mundi: A Series of Studies in the Religion of the Incarnation*. 15th ed. London: J. Murray, 1915.
Gorringe, Timothy. *Karl Barth: Against Hegemony*. Oxford: Oxford University Press, 1999.
Griffin, John R. "Radical Phase of the Oxford Movement." *Journal of Ecclesiastical History* 27 (1976) 47–56.
Habets, Myk. "'The Essence of Evangelical Theology': A Critical Introduction to Thomas F. Torrance." In T. F. Torrance, *The Trinitarian Faith: The Evangelical Theology of the Ancient Catholic Church*, vii–xxxii. London: T. & T. Clark, 2016.
———. *Theology in Transposition: A Constructive Appraisal of T. F. Torrance*. Minneapolis: Fortress, 2013.
Hardelin, Alf. *The Tractarian Understanding of the Eucharist*. Uppsala: Almquist and Wiksells, 1965.
Hefling, Charles. "Justification: The Doctrine, the Lectures, and Tract 90." In *The Oxford Handbook of John Henry Newman*, edited by Frederick D. Aquino and Benjamin J. King, 243–63. Oxford: Oxford University Press, 2018.
Herring, George. *What Was the Oxford Movement?* London: Bloomsbury, 2002.
Holland, Henry Scott. "The Nineteenth Century." In *Our Place in Christendom*. London: Longmans, Green and Co., 1916.
Hooft, W. A. Visser 'T. *Anglo-Catholicism and Orthodoxy: A Protestant View*. London: SCM, 1933.
Houghton, E. R. "The British Critic and the Oxford Movement." *Studies in Bibliography* 16 (1963) 119–37.
Hunsinger, George. *Reading Barth with Charity: A Hermeneutical Proposal*. Grand Rapids: Baker, 2015.
Hutchings, W. H., ed. *The Life and Letters of Thomas Thellussen Carter*. 3rd ed. London: Longmans, Green, and Co., 1904.
Inglis, K. S. *Churches and the Working Class in Victorian England*. Toronto: University of Toronto Press, 1963.
Janes, Dominic. *Victorian Reformation: The Fight over Idolatry in the Church of England, 1840-1860*. Oxford: Oxford University Press, 2009.
Kelly, J. N. D. *Early Christian Doctrines*. 3rd ed. London: A. & C. Black, 1965.
Kerr, Fergus. *Twentieth-Century Catholic Theologians*. Oxford: Wiley-Blackwell, 2006.
King, Benjamin John. *Newman and the Alexandrian Fathers: The Shaping of Doctrine in Nineteenth Century England*. Oxford: Oxford University Press, 2009.
King, Benjamin John, and Frederick D. Aquino, eds. *Receptions of Newman*. Oxford: Oxford University Press, 2015.
———. *The Oxford Handbook of John Henry Newman*. Oxford: Oxford University Press, 2018.
Lock, Walter. *John Keble: A Biography*. 5th ed. London: Methuen and Co., 1893.
Lockhead, Marion. *Episcopal Scotland in the Nineteenth Century*. London: J. Murray, 1966.
Lyttelton, A. T. "Tractarianism and the Bible." *Pilot* III, March 23, 1901.
MacCullough, Diarmaid. *All Things Made New: The Reformation and Its Legacy*. Oxford: Oxford University Press, 2016.
Mascall, E. L. *Christ, the Christian, and the Church*. London: Longmans, 1946.
———. *The Importance of Being Human*. London: Oxford University Press, 1959.

McCready, David. *The Life and Theology of Alexander Knox: Anglicanism in the Age of Enlightenment and Romanticism*. Leiden: Brill, 2020.
McGrath, Alister. *Iustitia Dei: A History of the Christian Doctrine of Justification*. 2 vols. Cambridge: Cambridge University Press, 2020.
———. "Trinitarian Theology." In *Where Shall My Wond'ring Soul Begin? The Landscape of Evangelical Piety and Thought*, edited by Mark Noll and Ronald F. Thiemann, 51–60. Grand Rapids: Eerdmans, 2000.
Molnar, Paul and Myk Habets. *T&T Clark Handbook of Thomas F. Torrance*. London: T&T Clark, 2020.
Morris, Jeremy. *The High Church Revival in the Church of England*. Leiden: Brill, 2016.
Mozley, Ann, ed. *Letters and Correspondence of John Henry Newman during His Life in the English Church*. 2 vols. London: Longmans, Green, and Co., 1891.
Newsome, David. "Justification and Sanctification: Newman and the Evangelicals." *Journal of Theological Studies*. New Series 15 (1964) 32–53.
———. *The Wilberforces and Henry Manning: The Parting of Friends*. Cambridge, MA: Belknap, 1966.
Nockles, Peter B. *The Oxford Movement in Context: Anglican High Churchmanship 1760–1857*. Cambridge: Cambridge University Press, 1994.
Ollard, S. L. *The Anglo-Catholic Revival: Some Persons and Principles; Six Lectures Delivered at All Saints', Margaret Street*. London: Mowbray, 1925.
———. *A Short History of the Oxford Movement*. 2nd ed. London: Mowbray, 1932.
Overton, J. H. *The English Church in the Nineteenth Century: 1800–1833*. London: Longmans, Green, and Co., 1894.
Pollen, Anne. *John Hungerford Pollen, 1820–1902*. London: J. Murray, 1912.
Radcliff, Jason. *Thomas F. Torrance and the Church Fathers: A Reformed, Evangelical, and Ecumenical Reconstruction of the Church Fathers*. Eugene: Pickwick, 2014.
———. *Thomas F. Torrance and the Orthodox-Reformed Dialogue*. Eugene: Pickwick, 2018.
Rahner, Karl. "Some Implications of the Scholastic Concept of Uncreated Grace." In *Theological Investigations*, Vol. 1, 319–46. London: DLT, 1961.
———. *The Trinity*. London: Herder & Herder, 1970.
Ramsey, A. M. *F. D. Maurice and the Conflicts of Modern Theology*. London: Cambridge University Press, 1951.
———. *The Gospel and the Catholic Church*. 2nd ed. London: Longmans, 1956.
Reed, John Shelton. *Glorious Battle: The Cultural Politics of Victorian Anglo-Catholicism*. Nashville: Vanderbilt University Press, 1996.
Rondet, H. *The Grace of Christ*. Westminster, MD: Newman, 1967.
Russell, G. W. E. *St. Alban the Martyr, Holborn: A History of Fifty Years*. 2nd ed. London: Allen, 1913.
Sarinsky, Darren, ed. *Theologies of Retrieval: An Exploration and Appraisal*. London: Bloomsbury, 2017.
Savae, Stephen, and Christopher Tryne. *The Labours of Years*. Cowley, UK: Church Army, 1960.
Scharlemann, R. P. *Thomas Aquinas and John Gerhard*. New Haven: Yale University Press, 1964.
Simpson, J. B., and E. M. Story. *Stars in His Crown*. Sea Bright, NH: Ploughshare, 1976.
Stewart, H. L. *A Century of Anglo-Catholicism*. London: Dent and Sons, 1929.

Storr, Vernon F. *The Development of English Theology in the Nineteenth Century: 1800–1860*. London: Longmans, 1913.

Strong, Rowan, and Carol Engelhardt Herringer, eds. *Edward Bouverie Pusey and the Oxford Movement*. New York: Anthem, 2012.

Stunt, T. C. L. "John Henry Newman and the Evangelicals." *Journal of Ecclesiastical History* 21 (1970) 65–75.

Symonds, H. Edward. *The Council of Trent and Anglican Formularies*. London: Oxford University Press, 1933.

Tickle, Phyllis. *The Great Emergence: How Christianity Is Changing and Why*. Grand Rapids: Baker, 2012.

Torrance, Thomas F. *The Doctrine of Grace in the Apostolic Fathers*. Grand Rapids: Eerdmans, 1959.

———. "Karl Barth and the Latin Heresy." *Scottish Journal of Theology* 39 (1986) 461–82.

———. *Preaching Christ Today: The Gospel and Scientific Thinking*. Grand Rapids: Eerdmans, 1994.

———. *Scottish Theology: From John Knox to John McLeod Campbell*. Edinburgh: T. & T. Clark, 1996.

———. *Theology in Reconstruction*. Grand Rapids: Eerdmans, 1965.

———. *The Trinitarian Faith: The Evangelical Theology of the Ancient Catholic Church*. Edinburgh: T. & T. Clark, 1988.

Vidler, A. R. *F. D. Maurice and Company: Nineteenth-Century Studies*. London: SCM, 1966.

———. *The Theology of F. D. Maurice*. London: SCM, 1958.

Wale, Augusta. *The Anglican Sisters of Mercy*. London: Elliot Stock, 1895.

Ward, Wilfrid. *W. G. Ward and the Oxford Movement*. London: Macmillan, 1889.

Webb, C. C. J. *Century of Anglican Theology and Other Lectures*. Oxford: Blackwell, 1923.

———. *Religious Thought in the Oxford Movement*. London: SPCK, 1928.

———. *A Study of Religious Thought in England from 1850*. Oxford: Clarendon, 1933.

Williams, N. P., and Charles Harris, eds. *Northern Catholicism: Centenary Studies in the Oxford and Parallel Movements*. New York: Macmillan, 1933.

Yelton, Michael. *Anglican Papalism: An Illustrated History*. London: Canterbury, 2005.

You may also be interested in:

Anglo-Catholicism
A Study in Religious Ambiguity

by W.S.F. Pickering

A revised and enlarged edition of the most powerful and polemic critique of the Anglo-Catholicism movement. This penetrating and highly readable study has established itself over the years as the standard text on the subject.

Rising in the wake of the Oxford Movement, Anglo-Catholicism can be seen as a deliberate attempt to catholicise the Church of England and to make its doctrines and services similar to those of the Roman Catholic Church. Early followers were persecuted, but they became famous for their work and for breaking down the social divisions associated with the Church.

The Anglo-Catholic Movement indelibly changed the ethos of the Established Church with the foundation of religious orders, overseas missions, theological colleges and public schools, promoting new social doctrines often associated with socialist ideas.

Anglo-Catholicism traces the movement from the origins to the heyday in the 1920s and 1930s. It is the first study which analyses it from the sociological point of view. The book concentrates in the interwar period and the decline of the movement to the present time, showing now the ambiguities and tensions originated and the way they have been dealt with over the years.

This revised edition also contains a new chapter examining the impact of women's ordination to priesthood on the movement.

'By far the most searching, shrewd and substantial analysis of Anglo-Catholicism yet to appear.' – Theology

The Revd Dr William S.F. Pickering has been an Anglican priest since 1950, and for twenty years was a lecturer in Sociology at the University of Newcastle upon Tyne. He is currently the General Secretary of the British Centre for Durkheimian Studies, which he helped to found in 1991. It is based in the Institute of Social and Cultural Anthropology, Oxford University.

He has written and edited a number of books and articles on Durkheim and his followers, including *Durkheim on Religion*, *Durkheim's Sociology of Religion* and *Durkheim: Essays on Morals and Education*, all three of which have been reprinted by James Clarke and Co.

New Edition Published 2008
Paperback ISBN: 978 0 227 67988 3